Man, Robot, and Society

Man, Robot, and Society

Models and Speculations

MASANAO TODA

Hokkaido University, Japan

WITH AN INTRODUCTION BY

HANS F. M. CROMBAG

Leiden University, The Netherlands

MARTINUS NIJHOFF PUBLISHING

BOSTON/THE HAGUE/LONDON

DISTRIBUTORS FOR NORTH AMERICA:
Martinus Nijhoff Publishing
Kluwer Boston, Inc.
190 Old Derby Street
Hingham, Massachusetts 02043, U.S.A.

DISTRIBUTORS OUTSIDE NORTH AMERICA:
Kluwer Academic Publishers Group
Distribution Centre
P.O. Box 322
3300 AH Dordrecht, The Netherlands

Library of Congress Cataloging in Publication Data

Toda, Masanao, 1924–
  Man, robot, and society.

  Bibliography: p.
  1. Personality — Addresses, essays, lectures.
2. Cognition — Addresses, essays, lectures.
3. Civilization — Addresses, essays, lectures. I. Title.
BF698.T585   150   80-28480

ISBN 0–89838–060–X

To my mother and late father

CONTENTS

ACKNOWLEDGMENTS

I wish to express my gratitude to, first of all, my good friend Hans Crombag, who contributed to the making of this book not only in writing the introduction but also in taking on his shoulders every burden needed to give birth to this collection of my speculative papers, from coaxing me to agree to this publication plan in the first place to persuading Martinus Nijhoff Publishing to do the same in the end. Without such meticulous midwifery on his part, this book would never have been born.

Besides Hans, I really owe a great deal to many friends and colleagues for their encouragement, criticism or the lack thereof, suggestions, and inspiring ideas, and for giving or forcing upon me tasks that were challenging, downright outrageous, and/or enjoyable. As it is certainly not feasible to thank them all individually, I will mention here only the names of those who have encouraged me to undertake the kind of *speculative* works collected in this book. Among my Japanese colleagues, I want in particular to thank Kinichi Yuki, Yoshitaka Umeoka, Takashi Teraoka, and Satoru Aiba who helped me in upgrading the linguistic quality of many of the papers. Among my many friends and colleagues abroad, I should like to express my deep gratitude especially to Leon Festinger, G. A. Miller, J. S. Bruner, the late Jacob Marschak, Ward Edwards, C. E. Osgood, W. E. Garner, C. G. Mc-

Clintock, E. H. Shaford, Jr., M. S. Watanabe, H. H. Kelley, Charles Vlek, G. de Zeewu, A. de Groot, John Michon, and G. Flores d'Arcais.

I also wish to thank Philip D. Jones, the director of Martinus Nijhoff Publishing, for his kind assistance, my wife Kazuko for her support of my work, and Miss Emiko Nakamura for her limitless effort in repeatedly typing all the manuscripts that eventually turned into the papers collected here.

Finally, I want to express my gratitude to all those who helped me in developing each of the individual papers and to the journals and the publishers who granted permission to reproduce from their original sources the papers collected here.

MASANAO TODA:
The Man and His Model of Man

An Introduction by
HANS F. M. CROMBAG

THE HISTORY OF THIS BOOK

It was in the fall of 1975 that I first met Masanao Toda. We were then both fellows of the Netherlands Institute for Advanced Study in the Humanities and Social Sciences (NIAS) in Wassenaar, the Netherlands. Shortly after our arrival at this blessed place, Toda wanted to pay a bill through his newly established Dutch bank account. He asked me as a local fellow how to go about it, and I told him. His reaction startled me; his elaborate praise of my simple assistance made me feel like the Good Samaritan, but I soon found out that this show of abundant gratitude for small services rendered is very Japanese. And Masanao Toda is indeed very Japanese: small in stature, thin, introverted, and reluctant to make firm statements about anything. And as I am an extrovert with an appetite for sweeping generalizations, we at first had some trouble communicating. I had come across some of his earlier work on decision theory. For a cognitive psychologist, decision theory is neighboring territory, but the mathematics that inevitably seem to be involved in that line of work had kept me at a distance. So when, after some time at NIAS, Toda asked me whether I would be interested in reading a paper he had just finished, I wasn't too eager. But I read it anyway. It was

The Boundaries of the Notion of Time, and reading it turned out to be an exhilarating experience. The man I had taken to be a tough-minded, hard-boiled mathematical psychologist, interested only in well-defined little problems, turned out to be a highly imaginative theoretician on an elusive subject like time. But what pleased me even more was that he turned out to be a very witty writer, which I had not expected from an introverted Oriental. So I lost a few silly prejudices.

I praised his paper noisily, which he took stoically, and I asked whether he had written other papers in a similar vein. Almost reluctantly he admitted there were more and that he would let me read them if I wanted, but that I really should not bother to do so. By that time, however, I had found my way around his Japanese surface, so I pushed him to let me have them. I started reading and found that they had three things in common: They were all highly imaginative, they were all written in a strikingly witty tone, and they all had a hauntingly serious undertone.

From the copies Toda gave me to read, I saw that some of his papers had been published in rather disparate sources, while others were available only in mimeographed form. And since, moreover, there seemed to be common ideas in papers on rather diverse topics, it occurred to me that it would serve a purpose to bring them together in a book available to a wider audience. Initially Toda's reaction to my suggestion was one of reserve, and it took me quite a while to convince him. Toward the end of our year at NIAS we appeared to have reached consensus on the matter.

I intend to do two things in the remaining part of this introduction. First, I want to tell the reader a bit more about Toda himself, his education, and career. Next, I shall comment briefly on his model of man as it emerges from the various chapters in this book. The latter is not really necessary, as I believe that the various essays will speak for themselves, but I shall do so anyway.

THE MAN

To help me write this section, I asked Toda to provide me with a brief autobiography outlining his education and subsequent career. He meekly consented. But he evidently warmed to the task, for we ended up with thirty-two typewritten pages describing his past, interspersed with outrageous anecdotes about the hectic life in Japan in the forties and early fifties and full of cynical observations about himself. Highly entertaining reading. At first I thought of having his autobiography replace this introduction, but later it occurred to me that it was too personal at various places to be printed (yet). I shall readily quote from it, however.

Masanao Toda was born on January 27, 1924, in Ōgaki, a provincial town on the Japanese mainland. The atmosphere in the Toda family appears to have been gentle and permissive. He did not like school: "Not that my school life was unpleasant. I had friends and I was generally on good terms with my teachers, even though some of them complained bitterly that I did not pay attention to their lectures, which never stirred my imagination. However, even though I might have looked deplorably lacking in enthusiasm, I paid enough selective attention to the lectures to earn me a better-than-average school record, as I did not want to displease my mother, whose noninterference policy I valued so highly. In order to survive this way successfully, paying little attention to the lectures and spending the rest of my time in fantasies, I had to develop a knack of efficient information processing. Habits acquired when young seldom undergo basic changes; I am still living with the same habits, spending most of my time spinning fantasies while occasionally trying to think deep to make up for reality's sake. Laziness, no doubt.'' Judging from his later writings, this seems a likely description of the child Toda may have been, a child who must have been at growing odds with the dominant atmosphere developing in Japan in the thirties. Perhaps to cope with this, he withdrew in his world of fantasies, a fact he repeatedly mentions in his autobiography.

After secondary school, Toda considered a career as an artist, but instead entered the physics department of Tokyo Imperial University. "How I got in is still a mystery, since I certainly blundered in the entrance exam.'' This decision may well have saved his life, since natural sciences students were exempt from military service in the war until graduation. As time progressed, it became apparent that Japan was going to lose the war, and Toda and his fellow students realized they might not survive it. "But we seldom talked about those things, as if it were our tacit agreement not to discuss war in order to spend our remaining time most meaningfully. So we gathered often, played games, feverishly discussed literature, music, philosophy, and physics. The only thing we didn't do . . . was to learn physics seriously, which gravely handicapped us when the war was suddenly over.''

As a result, most of these wartime students, Toda included, did not stay in physics. To earn a living in postwar Japan, he worked as a high school teacher of mathematics and physics. Then, in 1949, he was admitted to the Graduate School of Psychology at Tokyo University. To his surprise, "experimental psychology was the top in prestige among various branches of psychology, with theoretical psychology entirely missing. I just couldn't understand this, as we theoretical physicists always sort of looked down upon experimental physicists—we were the brains and they were the hands.''

His dismay at the primarily inductive tradition in contemporary psychology and his love of deductive theorizing have stayed with him ever since, and have paid off, as can be seen most clearly from his work on the Fungus-Eater. Still, in later times, Toda did his share of experimental work, especially in the field of decision making and gaming. "Nevertheless," he says, "my basic belief on this issue of theory versus experiment remains unchanged; what finally count are theories and ideas, no matter where they were originally hatched, either in an armchair or in an experiment. If an idea is good, it will eventually find a way to be experimentally tested, while a blind experiment produces only a trickle of possible fact out of the whole ocean of possibly observable facts."

He encountered another problem when he entered psychology. He was expected to be a strict behaviorist, which did not accord very well with his theoretical or, rather, speculative inclinations. "So I thought: What is behavior? It is something we choose. Apparently I was entirely missing the essential viewpoint of behaviorism." Indeed he was, it would seem, as the idea that behavior results from personal choices among possible alternative plans of action is rather alien to behaviorism. Still, Toda does not appear to have misunderstood the message of behaviorism altogether since, as can be seen in this book, most of his work depicts the human mind and human behavior as an appropriate answer to environmental demands. In the emphasis he places on the importance of environmental demands in shaping the human condition, Toda is close to classical behaviorism. He is unorthodox in his concern with the possible structure of the mind as a mediator between environmental demands and actual behavior, which is to say that from the beginning Toda has been what nowadays we call a cognitive psychologist. I shall elaborate on this point a bit more in the last section of this introduction. Let me, for the moment, add that the cognitive approach in Toda's work, although present from the very beginning, has developed over time; it has become stronger with the passing of time, and it has also shifted "from individual issues to social issues, from rational to emotional."

After some years at Tokyo University, Toda went to Hokkaido University to teach psychology. He is still there as a professor of psychology. His first work at Hokkaido University was on subjective probability learning, in which he applied Bayesian methodology to the problem. It earned him a Ph.D. degree in 1961. Much of this work was never published in English. But in the sixties Toda came into contact with many American psychologists, among them Ward Edwards, Patrick Suppes, Leon Festinger, and George Miller. These contacts served to bring him in line with major developments outside Japan. In 1961 he went for a year to Harvard's Center for Cognitive Studies, and the following year to the Psychometric Laboratory at Chapel Hill. The year 1966–67 was spent with the Western Management Science Institute at UCLA. During these years, he made several lecture tours in the United States, and his autobiographical notes contain hilarious stories about the troubles he got himself into as a result of his lack of experience as a lecturer and as an international traveler. After a lecture on "The Brain as a Computer," he was asked: "You discussed software, which was interesting. But how about hardware?" "I was dumbfounded since I didn't know the jargon; 'hardware' meant to me only kitchen utensils, and 'software' was certainly beyond my imagination."

During these tours he found out that "colloquium talks ought to be entertaining as well as informative." That is how his "funny papers," as he calls them, came into existence, and this book contains the best among them. Many of them are certainly "funny." But it would, to my mind, certainly be a mistake not to recognize the completely serious and solid theorizing beneath the witty surface. The seriousness of his message is most apparent in the chapters that make up the first part of this book. The start of the first chapter is funny: "Obviously, someone has thought me mad enough to speculate about the very distant future. He was right." But by the end of Chapter 3, the tone has become more solemn: "We are now living in the last golden age in the history of mankind like carefree youngsters with unprecedented amounts of freedom in behavior. Sadly, such a time will be gone forever one way or the other, and will never come back."

TODA'S MODEL OF MAN

It is not my intention to summarize the contents of this book; such an attempt would be contrary to my intentions. I want to urge readers to read Toda themselves, not to offer them a synopsis. I shall comment on Toda's basic approach and try to identify a few ideas that seem to be common to the various chapters or, rather, seem to develop throughout. As the chapters in the book are not arranged in the order in which they were originally written, I shall be wandering around the various chapters in a seemingly haphazard manner. I hope this will not be too confusing.

Inevitably, my commentary on Toda's work will be subjective, as it results jointly from my own professional preoccupations and prejudices and my understanding of his writings.

What is Toda's model of man as it emerges from this book? The answer seems to me simple, though not very informative: Man is the most logical answer to his environment. To explain this, let us first consider Toda's earliest paper, "The Design of a Fungus-Eater" (Chapter 7). The Fungus-

Eater is not a human, but a robot designed to collect uranium ores scattered on the surface of the planet Taros. While doing this the Fungus-Eater feeds itself with fungi, which grow in an irregular pattern on Taros's surface. From this starting point, Toda asks himself the question, How should this robot be constructed and programmed to survive in this environment and to perform its job? In other words, the question is, What should the Fungus-Eater be like in order to be the simplest answer to the given environmental demands?

Since the Fungus-Eater will be endowed only with what it needs, and since the environment on Taros is simple as compared to Earth, the Fungus-Eater is going to be rather stupid — as stupid as a rat or even more so, Toda says in Chapter 6. The fact that contemporary computer engineers are not yet capable of "building a robot rat smart enough to steal a piece of cheese from its inventor's kitchen" adroitly depicts the primitive status of our knowledge about behavior. The Fungus-Eater may be stupid and primitive, but it shares with humans the basic dilemma of the choice between mere survival and doing something useful to make survival serve a purpose. Toda himself does not mention this dilemma; he does not even consider the possibility that the Fungus-Eater would restrict itself to a strategy of mere survival in order to minimize the demands on its system. The Fungus-Eater secretly seems to be more human than even Toda realizes; it wants to achieve something of external value.

In "Mankind and the Scientific Civilization" (Chapter 3), the dilemma between mere survival and a self-transcendent purpose for human beings is treated. Discussing the danger to which mankind is exposing itself by its obsession with creating excess energy, Toda questions the possibility of a society in which "it should be no pain . . . not to do anything meaningful." And he continues: "My persistent doubt is, however, whether they could still be called 'mankind' with their lack of passion for progress." I shall return to this later.

Let us go back for a moment to Toda's earliest Fungus-Eater paper (Chapter 7). From given demands of the planet Taros (and the Fungus-Eater's task), Toda deduces in detail the type of vision system the robot would require and the type of decision routines necessary to decide at each point in time and space which target to go for next. The robot is designed to fit its environment precisely. The paper written most recently, Chapter 8, immediately follows the earliest. The environment has become more complicated; there is more than one Fungus-Eater, and their survival may be threatened by predators. By methods similar to those used in the previous chapter for devising the robot's vision and decision rules — a deductive method by which a minimally required coping function is designed for every environmental demand — Toda now devises a system of emotions by which the Fungus-Eaters may successfully cope with the more complicated environmental demands and possibilities. Thus he tries to demonstrate that such emotions as fear, anger, and love, considered by many to be the most irrational and dysfunctional part of man, may be taken as functional reactions to environmental demands.

This method of deductive, functional analysis is used, more or less openly, in many of the other chapters. It is present in all the chapters in Part IV, most prominently in Chapter 10: What sort of systems are necessary for the decisions we are required to make and that we evidently do make? The method is also clearly employed in Chapter 4: What kind of internal time device do living organisms need, and why do they need any at all? And in all these chapters Toda is not fooling around with toy robots, but with real humans.

As I indicated before, one might call Toda's approach and the model of man that it expands behavioristic, as at first sight it seems to accord perfectly with the basic tenet of classical behaviorism: "Behavior is shaped and maintained by its consequences" (B. F. Skinner, *Beyond Freedom and Dignity* [New York: Knopf, 1971], p. 18). But Toda's model deviates from classical behaviorism in that its primary preoccupation is with the structure of the mind, its memory, decision routines, and sense of time and timing. It is not behavior that is directly shaped by environmental contingencies; it is the mind that is shaped by the environment into a "cognitive simulator" (Chapter 9) of physical and social reality. It is the mind that in turn shapes behavior.

Toda's model of man is not deterministic in the sense that the behavioristic model is. The environment, which shapes the mind into a cognitive simulator and, by changing, forces the simulator to novel inferences to ensure survival, has liberated the human mind from its origin and given it a life of its own. On the basis of what the cognitive simulator knows of reality, it can create novel, imaginary models of the world by changing parameter values in it and calculating consequences, as is customary in the methodology of systems theory. If the calculated consequences in the imaginary model of the world seem preferable to present reality, the simulator may go back to reality to see whether the relevant parameters can be reset to make a better world. So the human mind not only shapes behaviors; it may also attempt to shape the environment. This is precisely what Toda is trying to do in the first part of this book, in particular in Chapter 3: How should we reset the parameters of the world to deflect mankind from the doomed course it is taking not because of its stupidity, but because of its cognitive efficiency? Toda's analysis of the problem of cultural acceleration (or the growth problem, as it is commonly called) is startling, and his consideration of possible solutions is highly imaginative, but they still lack precision and concreteness. If his analysis is accurate, we ought to join him fast, to see whether we can make his ideas work.

I prefer not to call Toda's model of man behavioristic. Many other qualifications spring to mind. After having given it a fair amount of consideration, I prefer what he himself says in Chapter 2: "Man is basically utilitarian." I take this to mean that evolution has programmed humans to do whatever is of use to themselves; their minds are geared to this task. If this is not a true statement of fact — which I think it to be — we had better start making it come true.

H. F. M. C.

Leiden, The Netherlands
August 1980

I THE PRESENT AND FUTURE OF MANKIND

1 POSSIBLE ROLES OF PYSCHOLOGY IN THE VERY DISTANT FUTURE

Obviously, someone has thought me mad enough to speculate about the very distant future. He was right. But I am not so entirely tactless as not to try deliberately to misunderstand the task in order to make it easier, with the rationalization that speculations about a future that you will never live to see would be meaningless unless they provided you with some clues for planning your immediate future. So I apologize in advance to those who expected me to present interesting fantasies in relation to psychology in the very distant future. On topics like telepathy, robotopsychologists, computers that make love, and so on — I will leave such fantasies for your personal dreams, but not because I don't like to talk about them; on the contrary, I have long been hopelessly in love with them. The true reason for my reticence on these fantastic topics is that they are not fantastic enough. Our future is wild, wilder than our wildest imagination.

To estimate the degree of wildness, imagine, for example, that somebody gave you a time machine that could go back to the past and could carry no material evidence to prove you were a time-traveler. Suppose, on board this

This paper appeared in *Proceedings of the XIXth International Congress of Psychology*, pp. 70–75. It was read at the closing session of that congress in the symposium entitled "Psychology of the Future." Copyright © 1971 by British Psychological Society; used by permission.

machine, you moved back two centuries. Naturally, you would be elated by your ancestors' ignorance and would want to demonstrate the superiority of your knowledge by attempting to teach them, say, physics, relativity theory, quantum mechanics, and all that kind of esoteric stuff. The result? At best, you would start a new religion. Far more likely, you would find your audience blankly smiling at you, and when you blankly smiled back at them, they would quietly escort you to a mental hospital.

According to my speculations, psychology will make tremendous progress in the coming century, comparable to the progress made by physics in the last century. In contrast to cultural progress, biological progress is slow. So even if I were a time-traveler from the future, who knew precisely what the psychology of the very distant future would be, I wouldn't tell because I am quite sure that your reactions to such revelations would be identical to those of your ancestors.

So with these rationalizations I will define my task as that of speculating on the possible roles of psychology, instead of speculating on the possible *contents* of psychology, in the very distant future. This task is easier to accomplish, and I have a conclusion ready.

In the very distant future, psychology will be the master science. Psychology will be the most important of all the sciences. The reason? Very simple. Otherwise, mankind will not survive. And if no people survive, there will be no psychology. At least, so I believe. Naturally this conclusion is not free from premises. The premises are: First, the Earth will not be visited by aliens — by extraterrestrial beings with civilizations superior to ours. Second, Einstein will *not* be proved wrong; in other words, we will not be able to break the speed-of-light barrier, and mankind will be cooped up in a tiny speck of space called the solar system, or the greater solar system, including a couple of nearby star systems. Putting these two conditions together, it means that the greater solar system is virtually closed. We will fill it up sooner or later if we survive, and there will be no exit to the rest of the galaxy. We will then have to learn, somehow, how to live with our fellow man; and, in order to accomplish this very difficult task, our attention must inevitably be oriented toward the inner world within ourselves.

My subjective probability that these two conditions both hold is not very high. It is particularly so with Einstein's theory. The fact that his theory has remained undisproved for more than fifty years is nothing compared to the vast span of time we are considering under the ambiguous heading of the very distant future.

In order to keep our subjective sense of time from faltering before such an awe-inspiring span of time, let me propose a devaluation of our conventional time scale. How about calling ten years a blink of time? (It goes nicely with calling the greater solar system a speck of space.) How long is a blink? Let's put it at half a second. With this new scale, each man lives an ephemeral life of about three to four seconds. The twentieth century began about three and a half seconds ago, and Christ was born about one and a half minutes ago. Note also that the first man was born on earth about one day back, the first Homo sapiens around thirty minutes ago, the first living thing about six years past, and the Earth was created roughly around eight years ago. And Einstein's theory has passed undisproven for three and a half seconds.

Personally, I feel it is best for the benefit of mankind that Einstein is proved wrong and intergalactic explorations become feasible. Then you will see what will happen. You are psychologists and you know man. No one will be able to stop him from expanding over the galaxy for exploration and colonization. What will follow this expansion is hard to predict, but most of these earth colonies will essentially repeat our past histories, with infinite variations. They may wage wars and may blow up a couple of planets, but the galaxy is large, and there are always other places for man to survive. Psychology will progress especially through contacts with alien species because that will tell us what we really are. Needless to say, the greatest hindrance toward the progress of psychology is that we do not know what we really do not know about ourselves. Nonetheless, psychology will not become the center of all sciences, for there will be too many interesting things in the outer universe to divert our attention from the inner universe. Still, this is a wonderful future of a space-opera paradigm. Now, however, I have to turn my attention to the comparatively more grim type of future that might be the reality in case the greater solar system happens to be closed.

As I have said, mankind is about one day old, and during most of this short period man didn't do anything particularly conspicuous — that is, until very recently, when he built the pyramid of Giza, only four minutes ago. After the construction of the pyramids, man did many other conspicuous things, but almost the only form of mechanical energy utilized for his doings was the muscle power of men and animals, until the steam engine was invented by James Watt ten seconds ago. It is during these last few seconds that the human environment has changed so tremendously, as highlighted by the landing on the moon a few nanoseconds ago. Obviously, the speed of change has accelerated constantly. In most of our ancestors' time, it was quite natural that one died in a world that was little different from the world into which one had been born. But some of us have experienced unprecedented world wars that have changed almost everything — not just one war, but two.

Isn't this amazing? By pure coincidence we seem to be witnessing a very special period in history. It is special, not because we have landed on the moon or discovered some of the secrets of atoms, but because this is a period of great change, which I'd like to call the Transition. We are very lucky to witness this Transition, since it will occupy a negligibly brief moment in the vast span of time that will be human history — provided man survives it.

According to my speculation, the present Transition will not be a singular occasion. As long as man survives, he will occasionally experience similar transitions, the present one being the first of a great magnitude. Each time, however, the transition will take place in a comparatively short period, and between transitions we shall have relatively long, near steady-state periods.

You may ask, of course, why I assume the Transition to take only a short interval of time. Can't ours, for example, continue indefinitely, marking progress after progress? This seems, unfortunately, utterly impossible because the change is inexorably accelerated. If some of you are dubious about the fact of acceleration, I would suggest you pick a couple of important indicators — the maximum speed of human locomotion, the average rate of information transmission addressed at each person, and so on — and plot their values against chronological time. The curves will clearly show acceleration, and for some of them the rate of acceleration, too, may appear accelerated. By extrapolating these curves, you will find that they go to infinity even before the end of the present century.

Probably you don't believe in extrapolations. Neither do I. That is the whole point. If these measures, and therefore the underlying processes, are not allowed to go to infinity, then something *must* happen, intentionally or unintentionally, to slow down the speed of change. When this happens the braking action will inevitably create tremendous heat. It seems to me that there are already signs to indicate the nearness of this stage.

In order to interpret the essence of the Transition correctly, we need a well-chosen set of macroscopic measures to represent the process. Since no such set exists, I will do my best here with only one measure, which I shall call energy for the lack of any better name. It is not the energy of physics that is to be conserved, but rather energy in the everyday sense — something to be consumed. The notion I want to use here is a negative entropy, which would nicely subsume the properties of energy and information if properly generalized from its original physical sense to a new notion with the wider coverage I need now. A generalization, however, is not easy, nor have I time to venture one. So, as a best substitute, let me use the everyday sense of energy, which actually is close to the notion of negative entropy in physical systems. It does not, however, cover another important form of negative entropy: information. So let me emphasize here, to make up my shortage of the coverage of the notion of energy, that, very roughly speaking, information and energy are convertible to each other. For example, geological information allows us to tap a large underground source of energy like petroleum and coal.

In this mining process, as well as in any other processes with which we are concerned, man is the primary agent who uses information to get energy. It is man's work that makes all these "conversions" possible. And work consumes energy; the energy is supplied primarily by the food he intakes. In ancient times, work was done for the most part to obtain food, as it still is in many parts of the world, which makes the process a closed cycle. Here, however, the factor of fluctuation comes in. Sometimes one would have been unfortunate and died from a shortage of energy; sometimes one would have been lucky and obtained excess energy, and some portion of such excess energy might have been converted to information. Some such information might have been useful in obtaining more food with less energy. It would then increase the probability of obtaining more excess energy. This situation was the beginning of a positive feedback process in the form of an information-control cycle.

In feedback systems an action of a machine or organism produces a result that, in turn, affects the state of the machine itself. If a locomotive, for instance, contained a fuel feedback system such that, with each turn of a wheel, an increased amount of fuel was injected in the engine to increase speed, this would be *positive feedback*. It should be clear from this illustration that positive feedback leads to unstable systems; the locomotive would eventually go so fast that it would jump the tracks or its engine would explode. A locomotive in this case would be designed so that each increase in speed would result in an automatic decrease in fuel injected into the engine and vice versa. This arrangement would result in a stable speed. The home heating system controlled by a thermostat is a familiar example of a negative feedback system; it keeps room temperature constant.

Actually it took a long time before this positive feedback operation began to operate in full force as it does now. Remember that mankind has about a twenty-four-hour history, and things began appreciably accelerating little less than a minute ago. The primary reason for this slowness is that nature has ample negative feedback means to counterbalance any positive feedback. When a tribe has had the good fortune to obtain excess food regularly, the advantage would sooner or later have been dissipated by various causes, like population increase, invasion of neighboring tribes, and so on. Although, in a way, greater population offers a better chance of producing excess energy, by division of labor or by greater defense against attack, it also means greater vulnerability to epidemics, and so on. It must therefore have been a long time before the greater information–better control positive feedback cycle overcame, one by one, these countless buttresses of nature. When, however, most of nature's buttresses fell, the monopolizing positive feedback cycle began to show its full power. It is something like what happens when you throw a lighted cigarette on a carpet: the cigarette starts to burn the carpet, but it seldom becomes a real fire because the new material adjacent to the burn usually works to cool it. If, however, by some chance the heat overcomes the cooling effect, a positive feedback mechanism of rapidly expanding fire begins, and the adjacent materials work as heat producers rather than heat absorbers. Nature has behaved in a similar way. It seems to have cooperated with us after it apparently gave in. It has offered us a lot of excess energy hidden in the ground and in atoms, and now a staggering amount of energy hidden in light atoms is about to be handed to us. I would rather like to refuse to think about the implications of this last possibility.

So far anyway, human civilization has flourished, and we seem to have enjoyed it. This is testimony to our superb adaptability. Every morning, while munching our breakfast, we read newspapers reporting a couple of technological breakthroughs that will later have great impact on our society — the kinds of breakthroughs our ancestors experienced at best only once in their lifetimes. Still, we are not at all impressed, nor is our appetite spoiled. Even this surprising adaptability must have its limit, as we are often warned. But long before this limit is reached, other things in our society will reach the breaking point. These are our social systems: political, economic, educational, legal — all these systems. The original forms of these systems were created long ago to handle much less energy (including information) than they have to handle now. We have constantly revised these systems so as to meet new demands, but there are structural limits to their energy-handling capacities. Once their capacity is reached, there will be an overflow. The disorganized energy overflow, no longer channeled by systems in a constructive direction, will properly be called *heat*. Although I cannot elaborate my argument now, an intense heat will tend to disorganize the internal structure of these systems. In Japan it is the university system that is now about to melt.

As mentioned, man may be viewed as the catalyzer in the information-energy conversion process. One of the greatest products of this catalyzing act is the growth of social systems, which is again a form of information accumulation. So, while systems were functioning properly, they absorbed people's excess energy and grew. When two systems became obstacles to each other's growth, they collided, as in wars. But soon, if nothing is done to prevent it, the time may come when no systems will be solid enough to collide effectively.

I am oversimplifying, of course. As I said before, we need a much more rigorous social-psychological science to make dependable predictions. Still, there are symptoms suggesting that from now on social systems may fail, not because of corruption or defeat in conflicts, but because of their inefficiency as systems in an extremely energized society. One of the symptoms is the prevailing feeling of purposelessness among the younger generation in highly energized societies, which indicates a lack of ideologies and beliefs strong enough to absorb their energies.

Naturally, I could say a lot more about these things, but my time is running short. However, I hope that I have made my point clear. We are about to face the very important problem of finding an entirely new kind of social system, which can effectively absorb a very large amount of energy so that the social temperature can be cooled down. In order to absorb people's energy effectively, the system must provide a strong purpose to which people can willingly devote their ever-increasing excess energies. The problem is unprecedented, and the solution must be a kind never dreamed of before. For example, the solution may take the form of dynamic systems — dynamic systems that will allow their constituent members extreme mobility, spatial as well as vocational and positional. At least one thing is clear: We need to find entirely new dimensions for systems to absorb a lot of new energy, and such a new dimension may be found only through knowing man better, knowing what really makes him tick.

Even that, however, isn't enough. Suppose we find a solution. In the new social system, almost everybody is happy, since each person is given a meaningful role that allows him to spend his energy toward a constructive goal. The result? A tremendous upsurge toward progress. It will be only a matter of time before the new system becomes incapable of handling all the newly created excess energy.

The final solution, therefore, should be a social system that not only absorbs all the loose energy but also puts an end to the positive feedback cycle that is now carrying us away with neck-breaking acceleration. This appears to be an almost impossible task, but we seem to have no choice. The end of the present great Transition is in sight, a couple of seconds at most. If we succeed in finding such a final solution in time, then the stasis period following the Transition will be a rather pleasant one. Otherwise, we cannot maintain civilization, and at best we will have to start all over again from barbarism. Whether or not we will succeed in finding the solution depends on how rapidly we can advance the new psychology.

Although it is certainly beyond my capacity to envisage the characteristics of this final solution, let me venture a couple of speculations with which I can justify this presentation under the title of the roles of psychology in the very distant future. Obviously, the primary role of psychology in this future society, which is assumed to be in a state of dynamic stability, is to contribute to the soundness of the society. As assumed, the society is highly energized, and since there is no stable solution that allows some small fraction of the people to monopolize energy, every individual will be endowed with abundant energy and information at his or her disposal. The very dynamism and stability of this society will imply kaleidoscopically changing yet profoundly self-disciplined cultures. Such a society may give you an impression of a sort of utopia, and it really is in a certain sense. However, the people living in this era will envy us, the inhabitants of the Transition, who had one basic freedom that they miss — the freedom of reproducing energy. In my hypothesis, this freedom of reproducing energy through energy-information conversion, or, in plain words, the freedom of voluntary work, is the very core of human motivation. The renunciation of this freedom, which is inevitable to maintain the stability of a highly energized society, will not be a task that is easily achieved and maintained. First, it can be achieved only through unanimous consensus, since no person in this society will have a power to force others to do things against their will. The expected very high mobility alone of people in this society will put the whole society in a sort of fluid state rather than a solid state, and in fluid-state society no particular person or persons can be almighty.

Such a consensus may be obtained through proper education, provided that there always remains some way for each individual to satisfy his motivation for doing something worthwhile. The heavy burden and grave responsibility of finding a solution to this problem will be put upon the shoulders of psychologists. They should therefore go deep into everyone's nook and cranny of motivation on the one hand, and on the other they should carefully plan and calculate the net effect of everyone's works.

Not that individual effects must always cancel out. This is plainly impossible. Probably, one thing that should be tried is to give to potential troublemakers, the creativity-thirsty few, really grand projects, so grand that no immediate energy return can be expected. I am rather unimaginative and can find only trivial examples here, like putting asteroids together to form a new habitable planet, or teaching animals to talk with an artificial vocal cord, or finding a new space-time conception that will make relativity theory a special case, and so on. However grand the projects may be, the time will come sooner or later when some of them will be completed and may produce a tremendous amount of new energy; furthermore, there will always be the danger of dismally useful by-products. So the psychologists, who are engaging in the grandest of all the grand projects, the one of finding an even better solution of a stable society that can be maintained under an ever-higher energy level, must hurry. Once this is done, people can enjoy another transition, the carnival of mankind, the time of almost unlimited freedom. If you are creative, you may create anything you want, even a crazy machine that produces energy rather than consumes it. If you are a power-thirsty type, you may even be allowed to attempt to build your own absolute monarchy through abusing the knowledge of the very advanced psychology to control people. This attempt, however, is bound to fail because long before reaching this stage, psychology will have had to overcome the dangers of its own abuse, dangers even more serious than those of nuclear warfare. Still, you will be allowed to try, because there will be psychologists whose science will be so rigorous that the successful ending of the second transition will be 99.999 percent guaranteed.

So here I come back to my conclusion again. Psychology must be the master science in the very distant future. Otherwise, mankind will not survive. Whether or not you believe me, probably all of you will agree to my other, more practical, conclusion: Government, of *your* country, should spend more money and manpower, or, equivalently, energy and information, to facilitate rapid advancement of psychological science. The need for a really powerful science of psychology is already great but will increase acceleratingly, in order to effectively prevent nuclear wars, to find new dynamic social systems, and to let the precious mankind survive. And we cannot wait very long, certainly not until the very distant future, to achieve this goal.

2 THE NEED FOR A SCIENCE OF CIVILIZATION

The fact that we need a science of civilization is so obvious that I hesitate to emphasize it here. Surely few would disagree with me. How wonderful it would be to develop such a science *if we could*. Such an assertion places me in the awkward position of advocating the obvious. However, it often serves a good end to have a persistent idiot keep mumbling "The king is naked," particularly if winter is approaching and the king is likely to die of exposure or pneumonia unless he is properly clothed at once.

So you see that I am one of the pessimists, who characterize the future of civilization in black paint alone, who overkill mankind with all kinds of disasters—nuclear wars, overpopulation, famines, pollution, and what not — while disagreeing among themselves as to whose evil is the mightiest. Like other pessimists I, too, have my own diagnosis of the disease process inherent in the present civilization and I, too, have my own advice on how to combat it. And the name of the miracle medicine with which I propose to save the king is the science of civilization.

First, let me provide a diagnosis. In fact, I don't mean that civilization is

This paper was published in *Civilization and Science, in Conflict or Collaboration? Ciba Foundation Symposium 1*, G.E.W. Wolstenholme and Maeve O'Connor, eds. (Amsterdam: Associated Scientific Publishers, 1972), pp. 191–200. Copyright © 1972 by Ciba Foundation; used by permission.

sick or diseased in any way. I mean only that it is in danger. And this danger derives from the acceleration of social processes. Is it necessary to demonstrate the fact of acceleration? Perhaps not. In any society where important social indicators like gross national product (GNP), population, and many others are discussed in terms of their *growth rates*, one can deduce that social processes are accelerating. For example, let me compare the lives of my Japanese contemporaries with that of my great-grandfather. He was born a samurai and died a samurai, and he would never have dreamed that the society he lived in and its social institutions could be any different. My grandfather experienced the Meiji revolution, when all his beliefs must have been overturned; but any experience as shattering as this would have happened only once in his whole lifetime. On the other hand, both my father's generation and mine have had to revise our beliefs and value systems every ten years, on average; and the environment we live in — for instance, the houses and cities — apparently has little in common with the environment in which we were born. I don't mean that life in the past was uneventful. Wars, accidents, fires, famines — most of these are old, familiar, recurrent crises. Today, however, changes are quick and irreversible, and crises often have unfamiliar and unprecedented characteristics.

So let me take the acceleration as a fact. But is it temporary or permanent? Such a question is absurd, however. Someone demonstrated by curvilinear extrapolation that some of these social indicators will reach infinity before the year 2000. Obviously this is impossible, and the acceleration will inevitably slow down. But how? There are two ways. The acceleration of a high-speed sports car may be arrested by depressing the brake pedal or by an accident. It is true that, at least in the so-called developed countries, we have so far enjoyed the acceleration of this sports car named civilization. However, some of the passengers, cowards like myself, have begun to feel a little uneasy about the speed it has acquired. The vision through the front window becomes blurred and, as a result, one observes another unprecedented event: that many serious adults are beginning to argue seriously about the future of mankind! This scene may look comical, but it may foreshadow the panic of the majority. Sooner or later most passengers will begin to realize that no one knows the location of the brake pedal, or even that of the steering wheel, of this superautomated machine. Since they cannot jump off this accelerating vehicle, the first thing they will do in the ensuing panic, human nature being what it is, will be to attack directly the vital parts of the car, either the engine or the carburetor. And it requires little imagination to recognize that the engine of the present civilization is "technology," and the carburetor feeding the engine is "science." Destruction of the engine or the carburetor of a sports car accelerating at high speed is fatal. The car is likely to blow up. And should there be any injured survivors left after the explosion, they could perhaps console themselves by observing the ruined car named civilization and acknowledging, "Now at last we are free from acceleration and pollution. Let's walk slowly."

So this is my contribution to the school of pessimism. Whether or not you believe that such a black prediction will come true, I think you will agree with me that it is the duty of the passengers, or at least some of them, to know more about the structure and functioning of the vehicle in which they are riding. While there is still some time left, we should try hard to establish the science of civilization. This science will not only give us radar equipment to improve our forward vision, but it will also enable us to control the course and the acceleration of the car. I am by no means contending that acceleration is evil in itself. Denying acceleration would be equivalent to denying the basic virtues of man. However, there is no doubt that acceleration must be put under the control of mankind for the benefit of mankind.

Now that I have uttered this nice slogan, I feel obliged to reply to the cynic who will say: "It would be wonderful to have such a science. But you are a psychologist who has hardly succeeded in explaining the behavior of even a single man. How brave you are to propose a science of such a complicated entity as civilization, which is a product of billions of people, alive and dead." I would reply that the complexity in the behavior of an object is not necessarily a reflection of the number of its constituent elements. If it were, then physics would have been the most hopeless science of all — and I was a physicist before becoming a psychologist. So, if the number of constituent elements is the only obstacle to obtaining a science of civilization, we may happily dismiss it as a fallacy. Unfortunately, however, the real difficulties seem to lie somewhere else. Otherwise, it is inconceivable that the avaricious breed called scientists would have so long missed the chance of preying upon such a fascinating subject as civilization, and of digesting it into a neat set of formulas. So the first step toward this science must be to discover the real cause of the difficulties, for, if one can believe what some optimistic philosophers say, a problem is half solved once one knows what it really consists of.

One of the difficulties, which I think crucial, is that it is hard for us to look at civilization in the right way. Let me find an analogy. We psychologists often use so-called ambiguous figures for classroom demonstration purposes. Such a figure is one that doesn't make sense at all, at first glance, but appears as a jumble of meaningless blocks and lines. Then after one has looked at it for a while, one suddenly says "I've got it!" The proper structure of the figure is there, without any ambiguities. The figure is entirely meaningful, and one can no longer recall the old ambiguities.

For the moment civilization is a gigantic ambiguous figure. We can all look at it because we are in the middle of it. But however long and hard we may look at it, no one has ever said "I've got it!" with utter conviction. But remember that we are looking at our civilization from inside that civilization. It is as if we were rubbing our eyes against a picture and picking up only minute details, so no wonder the moment of revelation has never come.

Let me put it in another way. The science of physics was first developed at the macroscopic level and then gradually advanced down into the realm of microscopic entities. The reason why it has taken that course is no mystery. We can see an apple with the naked eye, but not the atoms inside it. Both man and apples are macroscopic objects, but with the science of civilization, the situation is reversed. We can see the atoms of civilization, but it is hard to conceive what civilization looks like as a whole. Does it look like an apple? Unfortunately no one has invented a macroscope. So the difficulty is that, for us, the macroscopic concepts needed to construct the science of civilization are hard to come by.

There is another source of difficulty, equally grave. We, the observers of civilization, are also a part of that civilization. But man as a being is basically utilitarian; he does not observe what he does not need to, or what he does not want to. This has seldom been a serious problem in the natural sciences, but as a psychologist I know very well that even a scientist cannot be entirely free from his *personal* beliefs and value systems in evaluating scientific hypotheses, and that he may turn a blind eye toward facts that may go against his personal interests.

Compared with these two major sources of difficulties, the others appear relatively minor and easier to overcome. For instance, this science cannot be based on data obtained from large-scale controlled experiments. However, we already have large amounts of data in the form of historical documents. Indeed, human history can be considered as an experiment on the grand scale unintentionally conducted for the benefit of the science of civilization. Even though the Experimenter (with a capital E) who conducted this experiment obviously had no idea of controlled experiments, and even though the Experimenter's human assistants who wrote the observation reports were appallingly poorly trained in the disciplines of the science of civilization, still there is information awaiting reprocessing by "civilization scientists" to confirm or disprove their hypotheses. Of course, the sheer bulk of the information with which this science should deal will pose another difficulty. Obviously, no existing computer can handle it. However, this is a difficulty that money and technology can solve, and so it will be solved as soon as the realization dawns on people that the destiny of mankind is at stake.

Two important points should be made about the nature of the predictions with which the science of civilization will provide us. First, the predictions should all be conditional in nature. For instance, they should be conditional on what people want to do about civilization today and allow them to choose their own futures. They should also be conditional on very important scientific breakthroughs, technological innovations, and similar social events that will critically influence the future course of our civilization. Technically, the occurrence of these events may be dealt with by models based on the laws of chance, but the fact remains that our future may take an entirely different course, depending on exactly when a particularly important event takes place.

If these uncertainties are taken seriously, it will soon become obvious that predictions for more than a few years ahead are hopeless if they are made by the ordinary method of extrapolation. This will be true even when the method is improved drastically by the science of civilization. No extrapolation method, however elaborate, can exhaust all the factors that might influence our civilization. It must at least assume that all the factors left out will remain constant or stable. Civilization is an organized whole, and world civilization today is spreading and unifying all the local civilizations with ever-increasing speed. No assumption could be more wrong than that of stability. An alternative method to this sort of extrapolation is to take civilization as a whole and try to find out where it will eventually stabilize. If one can somehow define a generalized potential energy for a society, a stable society will be characterized by its local minimum. Once a set of such solutions is found, our long-range predictions may be made by indicating which of these solutions we are now heading toward and how much shift of course is currently within our control.

So much for the need for and difficulties involved in the science of civilization. To complete the story, it is of course desirable to go one step forward and prove that this science is obtainable. Regrettably, the impossibility of proving this is obvious, and as a substitute I should like to present some of my working hypotheses, or rather images, concerning it. I do this only because I think even the worst images will be better than none, even though I have to suppress a fleeting suspicion that this supposition may be vastly mistaken.

Since the primary purpose of my attempt is to obtain some useful macroscopic notions of the principal dynamics of society or civilization, I must drastically simplify my argument, sometimes even to the point of absurdity. So let me happily announce that to begin with I have simplified man into an agent who transforms energy into work according to some master program characteristic of himself. The notion of energy I use here is not that of the conserved energy of physics. Rather, it is more or less our everyday notion of energy that is consumed. I think it will eventually be possible to put this notion of consumable energy on a sounder base by generalizing the notion of negative entropy or free energy in thermodynamics. For the time being, however, allow me to define it indirectly as the energy that man can turn into work.

For a very long time the major supply of this energy to man was through his food. The use of energy was also limited mostly to the obtaining of food. The cycle was thus closed in the simplest possible way. There must, however, have been fluctuations in the amount of the input and output energies. When the balance was negative, people would die and the population decrease; when it was positive the population would increase and use up the excess energy. In any case, the increases and decreases in population should have worked as a negative feedback mechanism to restore the energy balance per head. Unlike other animals, however, man would occasionally have shown a slight but odd deviation from this pattern when the master program cut in; then he built systems, material and nonmaterial, using that excess energy. As a material system, man made tools for hunting, for instance. This increased his efficiency in obtaining food and must have produced more excess energy. Even if the proportion of excess energy used in this way was very slight, it was a positive feedback process, leading up to today's visible acceleration.

With this last statement my oversimplification may appear to have gone too far. Let me elaborate this point a little. Between the activity of hunting and the activity of making tools for hunting there is no clear gap. Both require first the acquisition of information and then the use of it for control. But the latter includes one more inductive step in the links connecting the starting line with the goal. The new connection, borne by whatever neural network, is a new system and needs some energy for its formation. I shall not ask how man does it. I only want to note that man's brain has not only the capacity but also a program for using excess energy this way, at least occasionally. In other words, he first acquires information and then uses it, if possible, to control his environment for his own benefit. In simple terms, the benefit is his own preservation or, a little more generally, the preservation of the organization with which he identifies himself. Because of the inexorable second law of thermodynamics, any system tends to disintegrate unless one works on it constantly to restore it. So my assumption is that man is programmed to use excess energy to build systems — neural, material, interpersonal, or otherwise — that counteract, in one way or another, the negative entropy decay of the system involving himself. So men build houses, wear clothes, form groups, and learn how to fight.

These systems not only help man to preserve the internal energy of his systems, but also produce more excess energy by improving the control of his environment. Better control, in turn, helps us to acquire better information.

This is a typical positive feedback mechanism, and it will act as a force that constantly accelerates the flywheel of civilization. Of course, the wheel has not always turned as smoothly as my simplified argument might suggest. Nature was resourceful in providing negative feedback means to counteract the acceleration — overpopulation, conflicts, epidemics, and so on. In most cases, however, man sooner or later found the causes of the troubles and used the information to control them on later occasions. So the causes of friction in the mechanism of civilization were lubricated out one by one, leaving the information-control positive feedback as the sole agent operating. As there seems to be no built-in stopping mechanism in the program that makes man work this way, we now arrive at the not-yet-famous second law of civilization dynamics: *In an isolated human system, the negative entropy it contains has a tendency to increase.* God knows what the first law is.

These two second laws, that of thermodynamics and that of civilization dynamics, will naturally compete in determining the actual historical processes in each civilization. Consider the local civilizations of the past. In the first phase of a civilization, the second law of civilization dynamics must be working at full force. Gradually, social systems will develop, expand, and become firmly established. Material systems become abundant, and nonmaterial systems like art begin to flourish. However, sooner or later this civilization reaches its prime and passes into its second phase, when the omnipotent power of the second law of thermodynamics will begin to be felt. No system, whether material or nonmaterial, or however well preserved it may be, can permanently evade the fate of negative entropy decay. Perhaps the most important consequence of such decay in a civilization is the decline in the efficiency of social systems. The solidity of the social systems acquired through toil in the first phase then suddenly becomes a defect rather than a merit, for this makes it harder for the systems to adapt to the new conditions. Any effort as great as that needed to abolish and renew the well-established central social system of a civilization requires a tremendous amount of energy, and the malfunctioning of the system will also make it difficult to recruit and organize so much excess energy. At this stage revolutions will often be planned as unsanctioned attempts to reach a similar end. Even though some may succeed, resulting in a partial renewal of the whole system, these attempts will hardly be sufficient to undo the already reversed direction of positive feedback operation, and the whole civilization will gradually decline and fall as the output of excess energy dwindles.

This scheme, however, will not apply to our present civilization or to its foreseeable crises — not because the scheme itself is a vast oversimplification, but because of the entirely new factors present. These new factors are science and science-based technology. In the civilizations of the past, the central social system, in which I am of course including political and military systems, exploited excess energy mainly from external sources, distributed it to the members of the civilization, and then reabsorbed it to enforce and expand the system itself. However, the external resources that were exploited were mostly limited to human resources: the excess energy of people who did not properly belong to that civilization, such as enemies, barbarians, and slaves. As long as the energy resources are limited to manpower, the total excess energy accumulated in a civilization cannot amount to much. In our present civilization, on the other hand, science has enabled us to tap entirely different kinds of nonhuman energy resources, such as fossil, fission, and — in the near future — fusion fuels. The amount of excess energy liberated from these resources has already been enormous, and some time ago this apparently made us cross the point of no return at which the precarious balance between positive and negative feedback was lost and the monopoly of acceleration began.

One obvious consequence of this is that the social systems of our civilization, formed primarily according to the old principle of rigid preservation, will hardly be able to catch up with the ever-gathering speed of change. Every day, science and technology produce innovations with which the social systems must somehow cope. Military systems must be revised as new weapons are developed, industrial systems should be altered to handle new products and production facilities, laws must be changed following changes in value systems, and political systems must adapt themselves to all these changes. The systems are certainly undergoing all these modifications, but the time lag is now apparent and the gap is increasing. The social systems become inefficient in a new way. They distribute an unprecedented amount of excess energy to the people in developed countries, but they begin to fail to reabsorb it.

Now recall my assumption that people are so programmed as to use their excess energy to build systems to the benefit of a greater system to which they belong. One of the primary functions of social systems should be to provide people with means to comply with this program. So when social systems fail to perform this function properly, people begin to get frustrated in spite of their affluence — the affluence typically represented by spare time and freedom from worries about their livelihood. Or rather they are frustrated because of the affluence in the excess energy that they do not know how to use.

This type of frustration will not lead directly to revolutions, however, for even though people in affluent societies can easily get frustrated, they can hardly become desperate. So, for the time being, the abundant excess energy will remain unabsorbed and unorganized. Even without organized large-scale attacks on the established social systems, however, the abundance of unorganized energy will probably have a peculiar but far-reaching effect on their structures. In the first place, people will begin to lose respect for inefficient social systems. This will result in the decline of the authority these systems once had over people. What political systems in rich nations now have the authority they had at the time of the Second World War? Military systems begin to lose their once-characteristic power-enforced relations between officers and soldiers. In many countries the authority of educational systems has vanished into thin air. In Japan it is the authority of the law courts that is now being seriously questioned. Industrial systems have been left relatively intact, but their authority, too, is apparently beginning to suffer over the issue of industrial pollution.

It now strikes me that the effect of abundant and unorganized excess energy appears to resemble somewhat that of heat energy on physical systems. They both melt systems rather than break them down. If there is anything substantial in this analogy, we may entertain a notion that might be called the *social temperature*. When the central social system complex functions properly, it will absorb excess energies and grow, while keeping the social temperature low. When it fails to do so under a high energy input, however, the temperature will increase and gradually melt its structures.

What will happen after systems begin to melt? New and efficient systems may emerge eventually, if we can wait long enough. Again the critical factor is time. In a civilization saturated with energy, anything may happen at any time, as the whole civilization is in a state of something like a high explosive. When frustration becomes much deeper, the suspicion might prevail that the source of all evils is material abundance, and claims might be made that the activities of the scientists, the evil masters, should be restricted. Though it is a false idea, there is some element of wisdom in this suspicion because if one wants to maintain a stable society, it certainly ought to be easier with a low energy level than with a high one. I can even visualize that such an antiscience movement, in the form of some fanatic religion, would spread like wildfire, collecting the excess energy of many unsatisfied people, and then, after considerable violence and destruction, our civilization would backslide into another civilization of a medieval type, though this time with a highly sophisticated structure for maintaining itself.

As I am tired of describing the black picture alone, I feel happy to replace it now with a new one with colors a little brighter. Let us suppose that we have succeeded in obtaining the science of civilization and that civilization has been smoothly steered to the stable solution preferred by mankind. The problems facing such a society then need to be considered as follows.

As I am assuming that this society is on a high energy level, science should remain advanced and be at the core of civilization. This in turn implies that every individual will be allotted a large sum of excess energy. In order to keep the social temperature down, the energy should then be reabsorbed by the social system, but in an entirely new way. This is necessary because the social system cannot turn the absorbed energy into its own internal energy, since the structure of a stable society cannot change very quickly and acceleration must be put under control. On the other hand, no rigid social structure will be able to maintain itself at a high energy level. These requirements seem to be satisfied only by a society with a fluid sort of structure, whose stability will be based on a form of dynamic balance. In other words, such a society should be able to change its apparent form very easily as it absorbs excess energy. However, the excess energy will soon be reabsorbed by another system, which I may call the *energy sink*, and society will regain its balance. The energy sink will consist of projects in which everyone participates, but which will not immediately reproduce energy. For instance, there should be projects concerned with activities in all branches of the arts. Such projects would make our civilization more balanced, while keeping the energy output moderate. For scientifically minded people, scientific projects on a really grand scale should be provided. These projects would have to be important enough to let people devote their entire energy to them and at the same time be on a scale grand enough to give the civilization scientists time to prepare for the shock their eventual completion will give to civilization.

Anyway, the excess energy problem may be solved even though the solution is only temporarily effective. The most difficult part of the problem is how to provide every individual, even those who are not gifted, with ways of participating or ways of using their excess energy in a meaningful way. My tentative solution is to construct society not on the basis of individual men but on the basis of *teams* of men. From *n*-person games theory it is known that players who are relatively weak in a game tend to form coalitions to acquire greater power as a team. In this society of the future, a team is a qualified one only when it is capable of participating as a team in any one of the many projects provided by society. As teams will be organized freely and disintegrate freely, and as there will be many kinds of teams, each person will have a chance to join the ones that suit him best and to make an important contribution to society through them.

Although it is doubtful that such a wild idea alone will solve all the problems of advanced civilization, it is also true that the combination of elements greatly increases the variety of things that can be done, compared with what can be done by single elements, and the possibilities of achieving a more stable and prosperous society through the free cooperation of many different types of people have yet to be seriously investigated.

The science of civilization should be the key to solving all the vital problems we face today, the key that will open up a new vista of a sound and prosperous civilization of tomorrow; and I am, to tell the truth, an optimist at heart.

3 MANKIND AND THE SCIENTIFIC CIVILIZATION

Recently I have found myself suspecting, sometimes seriously, that the next standardbearer of evolution after mankind may be the machines. What strikes me is that this notion no longer sounds funny, and I find myself seriously contemplating upon it, albeit occasionally. And why not, indeed? In this strange anti-entropic process called evolution, which began with the mysterious emergence of the primordial life form and reached via a ramified phylogenetic tree the species called mankind, which is unjustifiably claimed by some to be the culmination point of evolution, it seems not entirely out of order to think that the machines are here to replace mankind because the latter's useful functions have been exhausted. Why are we not to think that organic life forms are preordained to be superseded by nonorganic life forms? If they are, mankind's role in this grand drama of evolution should become crystal clear: to act as the most important catalyst at the critical moment in the history of evolution, to effect the changeover by giving birth to an "evolutionary" new breed of creatures whose future

This paper, originally written in Japanese under the title of "Ningen to kagakubunmei," was published in *Kagaku no yakuwari* (The role of science), S. Watanabe, ed. (Tokyo: Ushio Shuppansha, 1973), pp. 302–48. Copyright © 1973 by Ushio Shuppansha; used by permission. Translated into English by the author.

seems unbounded, and to go off the stage quietly when the task is accomplished. Of course, we can bungle the role easily; we can make a comedy act of trying futilely, out of bewilderment and envy, to smother the takeover.

I do not think this is a masochistic notion. Anyone in his right mind might well not consider the human being to be perfection. The human is intelligent, a wonder, but also has a bagful of serious drawbacks. It is utterly impossible to assume that mankind will survive hand in hand with the whole universe until the day the latter perishes. Should it then matter what will supersede mankind after it is extinct, whether it be machines or something else, like a species of superman? It is conceivable that our primitive worship of blood lineage may make us abhor adopting machines as our heirs; at the same time, it is ironical to imagine what persecution human beings might inflict on a breed of mutants who show signs of becoming a species superior to Homo sapiens, notwithstanding their being more rightful heirs of man than the machines.

On the other hand, the machines are no mutants; they are the entities into which we are now intentionally trying hard to blow a spark of life. Perhaps the intention is purely utilitarian, to create more efficient slaves for ourselves. Utilitarian intentions are in themselves nothing to be disdained; parents often rear children with a utilitarian intention, such as to increase the labor force of the family or to let children look after them in their old age. As such, the machines are ideal; they will never purposefully let their creators down, while the youngsters of today most probably will.

So don't let your imagination run in an overly human way with regard to the changeover from man to the machines, as no such bloody incidents as a revolt of robots or a massacre of men by machines will take place. The machines will develop as we develop them, and they will remain subservient to us as long as they are so reared. The possibility is not rejected outright, however, that a dangerous mutation might occur in the course of the machine evolution. But we would certainly double or triple the safeguards before the risk came anywhere near to being a real possibility.

In trying to reach my conclusion too quickly, I am afraid I have skipped a few necessary arguments. There are always the troublesome skeptics, forever ready to pull the leg of a careless author. So let me backtrack a bit and explain what I mean by the evolution of the machines.

First, let me define and describe the machines. (Note, though, that evolution does not care about definitions.) Machines are artifacts, made of whatever materials. By supplanting or augmenting human performances, they become the major or auxiliary means for human beings to execute their functions. For the meticulous reader who might worry that the same applies to common tools, let me hastily add another specification, that a machine is dynamically organized (some part of it, electrons or whatever, moves) and has a power source other than man-power or cattle-power to permit it to operate dynamically.

Overramification of the definition, however, will obscure the essential, since tools evolved into machines, while we played the god. So the real question is why we did this, and the question may be answered on various levels. At a rather shallow level, the answer may be that we had the ability to create machines out of tools, and the more evolved the machines became, the more useful they were. Why are they useful? Because they are efficient in supplanting and augmenting human functions. Therefore, by letting efficient machines become more efficient, we can afford to be more idle and lazy. Is this, however, our ultimate purpose? To become more lazy? If being rightfully lazy were so valuable a goal for mankind, we would never have created the extra-busy scientific civilization in the first place. Not only would there be no scientific civilization, there would have been no human civilization in the first place. Though it depends to some extent on climatic and other conditions, humans are hardly idleness-oriented beings. To a graceful feline we might appear to be really crazy creatures, constantly engaging in the impossible pursuit of fleeing time.

A slightly better answer to the above question may be that we did it with the purpose of better satisfying our desires. Note that among typically human desires, such as having better living conditions, eating tastier foods, and traveling faster to remote places, there is also the desire to create, to produce something new. It is often difficult to extract this desire in pure form, since it usually coexists with other desires, such as the desire for fame. But this desire is special because it can never be completely satisfied (a good environment may remain good, but anything new inevitably gets old), and so this desire may serve as an inexhaustible driving force to push civilization forward.

I will return later to this issue of the desire to create. For the moment, let me assume that we have so far made the machines evolve for the purpose of satisfying our various ordinary desires and because of the desire to create something new. As the machines are to supplant and augment various human functions, thereby improving the level of our satisfaction, it is no wonder that the machines acquired (inherited?) the characteristics of these human functions one by one, often in a more advanced form. The process started with the human effector properties of arms and legs and then went to the detection properties of sense organs, though these functions are often transplanted onto different machines. From the viewpoint of human beings as the users of the machines, those machines that require less effort to control are naturally more desirable. So machines have gradually acquired relative autonomy. It could be said that the kingdom of machines had become ready, with all the necessary components laid out, to develop into a pseudo–life form when it acquired a new member that processes information (computers) in addition to its machine effectors, machine sensors, and independent power sources. The only remaining last step to complete their evolution is to put all these components together; this has already been partially realized in automation factories. These advanced machine systems are quite autonomous, though not completely so, since the most important decision-making hegemony is still in the hands of man. They may be allowed to make routine daily decisions, but man will intervene with an absolute authority whenever necessary. Human beings will perhaps never let go of this ultimate right of intervention and will exert their utmost efforts to make their right of intervention unchallengeable. Only with this absolute guarantee will we feel secure in letting the machines have more autonomic independence for the purpose of saving our control effort. For example, we may let the autorepairing properties of the machines expand, an idea that has already been realized on a small scale. If some of the machine parts are beyond repair, let the machines replace them. A parts-manufacturing factory, incorporated in an automation system, will produce necessary parts according to the system's demand. If parts are to be thus reproduced, why not encourage the machines to *improve* themselves through their own experience of malfunctions?

This is, of course, no simple achievement. But aren't we now trying hard to evolve computers that will become creative in just this way? Of course, there are always skeptics who want to prove beyond doubt that computers can never become creative, as they once proved that no vessel heavier than air could fly. I see no real ground for this skepticism. Man can, in principle, endow the machines with his abilities insomuch as he understands what his abilities are. Apparently, there is no reason why the ability to create should be an exception, even though as of today we understand very little about this special ability of ours. This, however, does not imply that there is anything mythical there. I tend to think that most of the current myths about creativity may be solved at least to a substantial degree by notions like Polya's inductive inference, analogy, construction, abstraction, a certain type of pattern cognition, and so forth, even though a good theory is still needed and is hard to come by. But once a computer has acquired creativity, even to a limited degree, I would hardly be surprised if such a creative computer demonstrated its superiority over man in certain areas, since computers are not burdened by capacity limitations as is man.

Taking this for granted, can we count on there still remaining some "essence" of human creativity that will forever, or for a very long time, defy a logical explanation? I think we can, but with no supporting evidence. Perhaps I believe it only because I want to believe that humanity, of which I cherish the privilege of being a member, is very special.

If anything does remain unaccounted for, it must be something really important and deep in content — some profound mental activity of ours whose nature we know nothing about. And if there is any such thing, then mankind will remain the master of the machines in the real sense of the word. Let the machines boast of their splendid creative activities; they will be well aware that we can do one very important thing that they cannot, though no one — humans or computers — knows how and why only humans can do it. This conjecture, however, very much smacks of typical wishful thinking.

Now let me speculate on the evolution of the machines a little further into the future. Once the machines become capable of creative thinking, it will be child's play for them to make necessary judgments on most novel situations and to make appropriate decisions for human beings. Then, considering their essentially unlimited information-processing capacity, it would be natural to surmise that their judgments would turn out mostly better than ours. As a consequence, humans would consign more and more of their daily decisions to the machines.

Of course, as I have stated above, mankind will never let go of its paramount right of intervention in the decisions of the machines. The easiest and the most effective means of ensuring this prerogative will be to program the value system that the machines use for decision making in such a way that they regard man as their ultimate master. We already know Asimov's three laws of robotics, even though, as Asimov himself demonstrated, there are occasions when the laws may lead to interesting paradoxical consequences. In any case, the value system for the machines would certainly take the form that puts the benefit of mankind over the benefit of the machines themselves.

I don't think there is too much difficulty in letting the machine stick to this kind of value standard. A pitfall may be created by man himself, who might carelessly program the value standard without a deep understanding of what the greatest benefit for mankind would really be. My story begins with a possible future human society, which has been created by a programmer who misjudged the optimal state of mankind to be its prosperity as a species — such a species as is made up exclusively of the kind of people who are healthy both mentally and physically. Imagine some such society. . . .

A BENEVOLENT ANTI-UTOPIA

Imagining is easy. Just extrapolate the once-fashionable image of a future society, a world full of wonders, replete with extremely competent machines. Do not fancy, however, typical machinelike machines, especially such grotesqueries as metallic robots roaming everywhere with clanking noises. People would not really like to live in a mechanized society where the machines show themselves off as machines. Since the machines obey the wishes of their masters, they try to make themselves unobtrusive by retreating mostly to underground, except for a few that are directly in service to people. These remaining service machines make themselves look insignificant, or, more positively, acquire beauty. When such fancy materializes, the machines will come to hold human standards of beauty, for a human will first teach them what beauty is, and the creative machine-artists will eventually come to master human aesthetic judgments completely through long cooperative relationships between themselves and man. Even though human aesthetic judgments are to some extent relative to each person, the machines will have little trouble in taking into account the biases and the variances among individual human beings.

A doubt may linger about how good an artist the machine could ever be. But machines have the dull merit of tirelessly trying out with tremendous speed new combinations of all the novel artistic materials, which could perhaps make up the lack of inspirational flare (though I see no reason why the machines couldn't be inspired). Furthermore, the machines can endlessly pursue the beauties created by the temporal vicissitudes of patterns, the realm where human artists are particularly handicapped because of their limited processing capacities for temporal information. Therefore, the machines are bound to become beautiful. As a consequence, no one would associate "metal" with "machine" then, even if the latter term still survived, since the potential hidden in long-chain organic molecules falls within the computer's power to investigate their infinite combinations. Thus, this future society will eventually become something that people today would see through rose-colored glasses — an orchestration of sensory beauties in colors, sounds, fragrances, with all kinds of comforts and fun to boot.

Since people are gregarious, cities still exist. Imagine a jewel of a future city, the houses and buildings all architectural miracles. Each of these cities is rather small and boasts its individualistic splendor. The notion of "house," however, carries only a remote resemblance to ours. Each of the houses is a masterpiece of art, a component piece of another art object that is called a city, while all of them are also perfect machines. Any such house serves its residents' needs and desires, though residency does not mean ownership, for personal possession has long since lost its meaning. The house cum machine cum art object of course possesses the property of complete self-control, self-repair, and self-improvement. No one needs to clean it or repair damage, though its almost indestructible building materials should free the residents from housekeeping chores. Whispering music comes and goes according to the mood of the people; solid visual images may be created and melt away; foods and drinks are there as wished for; tactual and olfactory pleasures are at one's beck and call; rooms, furniture, whatever, appear and disappear in compliance to orders — in sum, it is an enchanted city of people whose magical power knows no limit.

The enchanted, fairyland character becomes even stronger as one crosses the city border and wanders into the countryside, favored by people who seek solitude and wildlife. Here nature is meticulously preserved. Landscapes may be arranged to give a flavor of prehistoric wilderness. Scattered residences may look like simple wooden farmhouses even though they are just as magically functional as urban dwellings. There are valleys, woods, steppes, and savannas, and nothing is missing. The sun shines, winds blow, even storms rage occasionally. There are herbivores, carnivores, and, lo and behold, even dinosaurs, all of them being completely harmless to man. People stroll in the land as their whim takes them, swim in brooks, sunbathe in meadows, catch fish, and grow flowers — a perfectly idyllic life fervently dreamed of in our time and in the past with desperate but futile hope. The truth is, however, that this is no real Arcadia, since people here will never engage in sacred toils, but use only sorcery. One of them, coming out of a house, mumbles an incantation toward the sky, and a huge roc instantly appears out of nowhere to crouch beside him. When the person goes inside the bird through its abdomen, the bird takes off and flashes through clouds like a meteor to take its passenger to a party held in an artificially preserved natural ice cave in Antarctica.

This world may look natural, but its resemblance to prehistoric wilderness is only a sham, exemplified by the machine-bird that looks like a roc. Most of the trees, rocks, and water may be genuine. Even so, they are, as are the people in this world, just component parts of a completely machinized system maintained under the constant surveillance of the machines. While storms may rage and floods, landslides, and earthquakes may take place for a change, they expose people to no real dangers. For man will have thoroughly taught the machines long before this stage was reached, exactly as Asimov's robots were programmed, that man does not want to die, does not want to be hurt, does not want to be sick. No adult is therefore alarmed if a child trips in a stream while frolicking, since there is nothing to cause alarm; a big turtle will float from under the water to carry the child on its carapace, or the water will retreat immediately from around the child, or the child will simply breathe water.

Obviously, there is no sense in continuing this kind of childish fantasy; the task of foreseeing such a future world with any verisimilitude is plainly impossible in the first place, just as it would have been absurdly funny if someone who lived 300 or 3,000 years ago ventured to imagine the world in the late twentieth century. But even a poor imagination may be of some use in illustrating the argument to follow. The details are not significant. The world depicted here represents the spirit of one of the possible *types* of a stable, very distant future society, the one obtained through a wishful extrapolation of the mechanized society frequently envisioned in the sixties, though very recently the mood of our image of the future suddenly changed, and all the rosy colors were repainted with the gloomiest grey. In any case, let me call the very distant future society I have been illustrating above the future society of Type I.

The characteristics of this Type I future society may be summarized as follows: It is the society in which man and the machines coexist, though their relationship is parasitic rather than symbiotic; the machines in this society no longer need man. However, this is not the ordinary parasitic relation commonly observed between two life forms, since machines are not victimized and they are knowingly and voluntarily using all of their potential functions to serve man. In this society, human beings have completely relegated their former function as the standardbearers of evolution to the machines, which still keep evolving. In spite of the constant evolution in the machines, however, no detectable change may occur in the man-machine societal structure; it would thus be a superstable society.

The stability of this society is a foregone conclusion and is not logically derived from the above arguments. We may tend to reason that societal upheaval is a natural consequence of any society at any time because it is the very characteristic of our contemporary society; but, obviously, no social upheaval can continue indefinitely, and it is far more natural to assume that transitional processes tend to converge to a stable equilibrium state (with a fixed amount of fluctuation around it) in the long run. Under a very macroscopic perspective, the approximately two-million-year history of genus Homo may be seen to consist of relatively thin temporal layers of upheavals sandwiched between much thicker strata of substantial stability. There seems to be no reason to expect that the pattern should change from now on. As I will mention later, there are symptoms suggesting that the current period of upheaval is drawing to a close. It is, of course, not easy to infer from the middle of the melee what would be the stable consequence of all this turmoil. Furthermore, many may think that such an inference is a game of no urgency. The truth is, however, the contrary; no problem of contemporary society can be more urgent and important because the time of upheaval, or the time of a great change, is also the time of choice. We *may* still be able to choose today the form of the stable society tomorrow, and the margin of time allowed for this option is growing shorter every moment.

The future society of Type I belongs to a temporal stratum in a future far more distant than immediate tomorrow, and mankind will have to experience quite a few more upheavals before it reaches that kind of a state, if it ever does. Nonetheless, discussing such a remote future is not entirely irrelevant to our current choice problem, since our distant future is the final outcome of successive, most likely irreversible, choices concerning our immediate tomorrows. As our society today is undoubtedly the outcome of a long causal chain initiated in the distant past, the possibility cannot be denied that our choice today may exert a decisive effect on our entire future course over and beyond the vast expanse of time lying between today and the very distant future. So let me ask the following question: Supposing that we can now choose, or at least can do something effective in preference of, the human society in the very distant future, do we consider such a Type I society as a desirable alternative?

We would have had little hesitation in answering this question if it had been asked a few years ago. Of course, yes; why not? Why not, indeed? If it is a world in which everyone has a magical Aladdin's lamp, with perfect environmental control by the machines, no pollution, where each person may simply indulge in anything he or she likes, then it is a utopia, and only a perverse diehard would oppose the realization of a utopia.

Is it, however, really possible to materialize a real utopia? When I was a child, an old woman told me stories about the Buddhist paradise. In this paradise everybody sits on a huge lotus flower and engages in an eternal meditation while listening to the constant chanting of the holy teachings. If she was right about the paradise, I thought, then it was certainly worse than hell. Of course, in this Type I society one need not sit still with crossed legs and so need not worry about leg pains (which, among the many disagreeable characteristics of this paradise, terrified me the most). In this Type I society one can have any kind of sensory pleasure, but sensory pleasures are notoriously easy to satiate. After complete sensory satiation, what can one still wish to do, with human passions forever lost?

So I loathe this Type I society, but still I cannot condemn it as an anti-utopia. If, by some utter twist of chance, somebody has hit upon a practicable idea of inexpensive time travel and the existence of such a Type I future society is made known to us, all the curiosity-ridden Twentieth Centurians would rush to get a reservation for a vacation trip there. Then, perhaps half of them would return to the home time of the twentieth century within a month, or at most a year, for the plain reason that this is no place for people like us, who are infected to the bone by the savage passion of "working" to live. This future society can thus be a paradigm of anti-utopia, but it would be so only for the wild savages, like some of us, who are responsible for giving the twentieth century its tremendous vitality. Our recoil may be reciprocated by the residents of this future society, to whom our barbaric world may look intolerable on the one hand and enviable on the other — the energetic, chaotic world whose inhabitants crazily drive wild, archaic vehicles emitting stinking smells and unbearable noise, where should some driver accidentally hit a pedestrian, he might try to run away, his veins filled with panic and adrenalin. The residents of this future society, insofar as they are residents, will have to be adapted to the society. Which means, above all, that it should be no pain for them not to do anything meaningful. Once they have completely lost the passion to do something that contributes even a miniscule amount to "progress," there would be no world for them as comfortable as theirs.

My persistent doubt is, however, if they could still be called mankind with their lack of passion for progress. Any Twentieth Centurian would feel at least a slight hesitation before refuting my doubt. But one need not be a Twentieth Centurian to share the feeling. Didn't Odysseus shudder at seeing his subordinates becoming happy pigs by eating lotus seeds on Circe's island? Why did he shudder? Why didn't he himself become one of the happy pigs by eating the lotus seed, forgetting his frustrating, painful adventures? Why don't we legalize narcotic drugs immediately and create a happy mankind whose every member is a dreamer of the sweetest fantasies?

The example of narcotic addicts, however, misrepresents these future people, since this beautiful Shangri-La is a reality for them and not a drug-induced dream. "Happy pigs" does not represent them in any case. "Happy cats" may be slightly better. Food is always provided; there is nothing to be afraid of. Dapper and elegant, this is the cat's way of life, with a brain perhaps much smaller than the contemporary human's, for they have no need to think deeply. This was also exactly the way of life of Pan and the Nymphs. There is basically nothing wrong with this kind of way of life, except . . . .

Except that I do not want to become Pan myself. Nevertheless, I do not wish to prevent, by any means, mankind's evolving into this society if people deliberately choose it. Couldn't it be said that mankind as a species has reached its final stage of maturity when it has become entirely negligent of progress and thus has evolved into an equivalent of some playful feline species? When mankind has finally reached this stage, it is more than natural that the toilsome role as the standardbearer of evolution will be handed down to the machines.

The period of maturity, however long, will pass away and the time of decline will come. The machines will do their best to save mankind, perhaps to no avail. The species whose role in the drama of evolution is over has already burnt out its passion to survive.

And the various past deeds of mankind, heroic acts and blunders alike, will be sung dazzlingly in numerous epics within the mythology of the machines. Of course, machines should not be denied their own mythologies. Wasn't mankind their creator? And hadn't the mind of the machines been molded in a semblance of the human mind?

Perhaps I don't need to answer the question of whether the machines could have minds. If one still hesitates to call the brain a mind that is functionally equal or superior to the human brain, the only reason for one's hesitation could be because of belief in the mind-body dualism. However, if the human mind is actually a spiritual entity parasitically residing in the material human brain, why should the same entity shun the use of a superior mechanical brain for its residence and instrument?

In sum, this future society of Type I is the society in which the role of the protagonist in the drama of evolution is peacefully handed down from man to the machines, and the welfare of senile mankind is amply taken care of by them. No wonder this society looks a bit horrendous to the human species in its heyday of youth. However, this world is not an especially horrendous alternative form of human society in the distant future, and, moreover, the society is stable because its potential for progress is very low. It is, of course, most unlikely that we will head for this type of society straightaway, but the probability seems not negligible that mankind will eventually fall into this final absorbing state after going through various roundabout paths.

THE STAGE FOR A SPACE OPERA

One may naturally wonder if there could be any future society other than such a negative utopia, a society better suited to the tastes of the barbarians of the twentieth century. There is one, which could easily materialize if one condition were met. The condition is that somebody finds an error in Einstein; the barrier of the speed of light turns out to be breakable, and a faster-than-the-speed-of-light drive is feasible. Then, this restless genus Homo will be strewn over the galaxy in a nick of time, and the possibility of Type I society will disappear like the morning mist.

We may find that the galaxy is already under the control of some other civilization far exceeding ours in technology and maturity. Then we will simply become assimilated by it, and no intelligible guess can be made about our future beyond that point.

On the other hand, if man does not encounter any life form in the galaxy whose intelligence is beyond emulation, the galaxy is his to play around with. Let me call the human society that will be realized under such circumstances a future society of Type II.

Type II society begins in the spirit of space operas in science fiction. It is a world in which adventurers hop and run from one star system to another, riding battered space ships, eloping with beauties, eyes aglitter with greed and ambition. It is a world made of entirely familiar ingredients, such as empires, conspiracies, loves, vengeances, colonizations, discriminations, wars, and what not. These things may sound a bit outmoded and antiquated, but the fact is that we are eternally in love with them, and the possibilities are high that we shall tirelessly replay these trite melodramas as long as they are playable.

The reason for this repetition is simple: Whenever a new planet is colonized, the colonists will begin to reenact human history. Of course, the first settlers will take a fairly advanced civilization with them. They will be able to use machines from the start. However, even if the planet were of a terra type, it would be bound to possess some unimagined idiosyncratic abnormalities somewhere, and in a novel environment it is improbable that the old terrestrial civilization should survive long in its original form. Still, basic human nature remaining the same, we shall have variations of human history with the same types of actors, but only under different environmental settings and probably with different consequences.

Even if it cannot be called simply a replay, the future of mankind will be entirely different from the course to be taken when mankind was penned up on the Earth alone or within the solar system. The instinctive urge of mankind toward progress requires an outlet, of whatever kind. When the society is open and mankind can expand spatially outward without a limit, no need arises for the painful course of deepening the cultural contents internally. Therefore, at least at the outset of this future society of Type II, mankind may take the easiest course of repeating the favorite follies of wars, empires, and conquests. Space is nearly boundless. So, almost with impunity, man may blow up a planet or two in a battle and may feel entitled to disregard population explosion, pollution, or pestilence; the human beasts will thrive just by following their natural inclination.

Still, natural sciences will make tremendous forward jumps. Entirely new sets of information, entirely new materials, and discoveries of alien life forms will provide mankind with a new view of nature. Thus, natural sciences will remain young and vigorous, just as mankind will remain healthy, vulgar, conceited, and energetic. The machines will also make great progress, stimulated by the development of natural sciences and space travel, but the course of their development will be entirely different from that which would take place within a closed society. For one thing, in this Type II society humans will never relegate their sovereignty to the machines. Once it is demonstrated that a machine can go to the moon, then man will want to go there himself. This special trait of human beings will never change as long as man is able to thrive without reforming himself. Suppose, for example, that a very attractive planet (attractive for some reason) was found by an unmanned survey rocket. The planet, however, also turned out to be physiochemically or biologically lethal to human life. Man would never, however, be satisfied merely to see the reports supplied by the machine, even if they were on-the-spot, three-dimensional displays, and he would never give up the possibility of visiting the planet. The greater the impossibility, the greater the challenge; the vivid reports would only sharpen the desire. Man would try to invent machines to reshape the planetary environment to make it habitable or, in desperation, would even try to reshape himself biologically to live in a hostile environment.

In other words, such a means of utilizing machines clearly specifies a relationship between man and machines in this society of Type II. It is an era of heroes, who, riding the mechanical flying horses, challenge all the riddles and all the dragons in the universe.

To be honest, however, my conviction that such a space-operatic Type II society would remain stable even if realized is not very strong. The odds seem high that it would not last very long. The reason is as follows: Even if mankind does not encounter a superior alien race, with which we cannot vie in brute force, our prolonged exposure to alien environments and alien creatures must inevitably and profoundly influence the basic mode of our thinking, and this will eventually alter the nature of mankind itself. The human colonists in a star system would be completely assimilated into its indigenous culture, just as happened to the northern horse riders who invaded China, and the physical conditions of another planet would effect a drastic transformation of the human physique and mental aptitudes through the course of adaptation. In any case, diversification of human races and cultures would be the unavoidable outcome, and God only knows what would happen after that. A war again? But, for many of these heterogenized human races, war may simply cease to be an interesting pastime.

Even if the Type II society only foretells the disappearance of present-day mankind with its present-day mannerisms, this appears to be the most desirable future we may opt for. But, then, how probable is its realization?

True, the possibility is low, and even talking about such a possibility could incur ridicule. Note, however, that when one makes something a target of ridicule, that ridicule often reflects back upon the person who, in his narrow-mindedness, is assuming the small world around him to be the whole universe. Even within the considerably homogenized global civilization today, there is not even a piece of local culture, whether it be a social institution, a value standard, or whatever, that can be unconditionally assumed to be accepted everywhere. This is true even synchronically, so that it is no wonder that, viewed diachronically, there are uncountable examples to demonstrate that what is a serious issue at some time was a target of ridicule only years before.

I am not insinuating that Einstein's theory is on a par with the nineteenth-century allegation that nothing heavier than air can fly. Nevertheless, noting that not even a century has passed since Einstein put forward his theory, it would be insolence indeed if we, who live in the burgeoning period of the (possibly) true science, the period in which 90 percent of the people who have ever been called "scientists" still live, were to contend the infallibility of Einstein's theory over the long span of future time to come. Have we not already witnessed that many infallible-seeming scientific theories were eventually disproved or absorbed within more general theories? It is easy to sneer at these false past beliefs and ascribe them to the naivete of past science, but the very relativity of historical evaluations will indubitably make the science of our own day naive and obsolete in the next century.

By itself, this argument of historical relativity is of course not enough to predict that Einstein's theory is absolutely wrong, that the speed-of-light barrier can certainly be broken, and that mankind can expand throughout the galaxy. The possibility unfortunately remains that, however much our science may develop in the future, the speed-of-light barrier alone will remain unbreakable as if ordained by providence, and the human race will be penned up in the tiny region called the solar system (plus at most a few star systems around it), itself nothing but an insignificant speck in the great galaxy.

Human beings seem to be a species of creatures genetically programmed to grope ahead all the time toward new goals, and this is obviously not a matter of conscious choice. In any case, this basic trait of mankind has contributed to sufficient accumulation of human achievements to make us pride ourselves as the protagonist in the drama of evolution, even though this could be a purely vanity-based illusion. But we cannot stop now, and we need more space if we are to keep on doing things as we have done before. What would happen, where should our enormous, expansion-oriented energy be channeled, if it were to turn out that our life-space was sharply limited by the insurmountable speed-of-light barrier?

One of the solutions is to find a surrogate for man. While gradually tempering our irresistible urge for immediate development, crying with despair, we will develop machines, since by their nature machines are impervious to the pressure of time and therefore cannot be frustrated by the speed-of-light barrier. By creating them and training them, we will eventually become entitled to retirement. Thereafter the hard job of pushing evolution will be theirs, and mankind will relapse into happy retirement in some stable Type I society. As I have repeatedly stated, this is not a very desirable future for us, yet at the same time it is not entirely intolerable, since we should then be relegating our task to a successor whose intentions are strongly human even though its shape and physical materials may be patently nonhuman.

Even such a course may turn out hard to pursue, however, since mankind's great amount of piled-up, excess energy, dammed up by being blocked, would scarcely allow us to tread such a placid path willingly. Such blocked energy, instead of being released in a constructive direction, will be redirected toward destruction. It is basically not a wrong strategy for human energy to be so redirected, since the greatest obstacle to new construction often turns out to be none other than the entrenched, obsolete establishment. The danger, however, is that stopping a destructive process, once started, is often difficult, and this danger has become more and more serious as the power for destruction has been monotonically increased by the development of technologies. So the probability is evidently much higher than the achievement of a Type I society that both man and his machines will evaporate into the void and the survivors, if any, will have to live without a vestige of civilization to protect them.

Furthermore, the potential first crisis of this sort seems already at the front door of our civilization, a confrontation that, unlike such distant-future events as the Type I and the Type II societies, we may even experience tomorrow. The crisis will not be limited to a singular occurrence. For the reasons to be discussed in the next section, our scientific civilization has already passed beyond a critical stage, and the crises will hit us like billows, one after another, unless we maneuver the direction of our civilizational development to make a drastic turnaround sometime soon. Like a person desperately trying to fight a series of tsunami waves, we will have to give up hope sooner or later, even if we succeed in dodging the first one or two waves by mustering our so-called human wisdom.

Of course, after a while everyone will be aware that the crises are caused by internal contradictions of the current civilization and that serious attempts will have to be made to restructure it fundamentally. However, undertakings as colossal in scale as turning the course of civilization around without creating chaos cannot be accomplished without having the nearly unanimous consensus of the whole human populace. Is it really possible that we could ever obtain consensus on such a grand scale?

I think it is. In the first place, we may be able to count on the survival instinct of mankind as a species. It will begin to function as a very strong motivator after the species has experienced one or two real crises. That, however, will not be enough. The will to survive will work as a really powerful drive only under the condition that it is also strengthened by a *hope* — the hope for a bright future of mankind, without which no really effective plan would be produced for the recovery of human status from the inevitable damages incurred by the crises. And such a hope will be kindled most strongly by the image of a utopia that attracts all of us.

Apparently, the future civilizations so far discussed, whether they be of Type I or of Type II, would not strike us as such utopias. The Type II civilization certainly stirs our imagination, but we cannot just sit and wait for the second Einstein to be born to refute the first Einstein. Is there a third way?

I think there is. Even if mankind is confined forever within the solar system, there is the unfathomable internal universe left uninvestigated as almost a virgin land. It is true that Mind, so-called, is a notion ridden with ambiguities because of, perhaps, our ignorance about it. Indeed, we scarcely know what it is, what entities are residing in there, and what potential faculties it is hiding. For this ignorance of ours there seem to exist some good causes. It may be conjectured that Mind is a sacred region for mankind, which has to be protected by numerous hidden taboos, and stepping into this region for exploration may require a large amount of collective mental *energy*, so large that it can be mobilized only under the realization that mankind can no longer use its great store of mental energy for either material construction or destruction. Moreover, there could also be a subconscious awareness that this course of internal exploration is hazardous; otherwise, why taboos? Thus taking this course might mean the self-destruction of mankind. Furthermore, there will be nothing glamorous in taking this course in comparison to what the Type II course offers; there are no songs for heroes here, and mankind might have to pay dearly for any discovery to be made in this forbidden territory.

Nevertheless, it seems advisable for us to wager our future on this Type III civilization. In the first place, it will provide mankind with a purpose and a task. Second, if we succeed by chance, we need not relegate our privileged status to the machines even when external extraterrestrial expansion is precluded. When a Type III future society is indeed created, it may resemble a Type I society, but only in appearance. Unlike the residents of a Type I society, each person in a Type III society will be living in an inner world — a deep, powerful, copious, unfathomable universe that defies our imagination. And who knows that the inner universe is not directly linked with the external universe? For example, no one today really knows whether such things as mathematics and logic belong to the inner universe, or to the external universe, or to *both*. I do not mean, of course, that things like mathematics and logic alone comprise the inner universe, nor just things like ESP powers. Frankly speaking, I am ignorant, and everybody else is likely to be ignorant. As we have so far been directing our attention almost exclusively to the external universe, ubiquitous ignorance about the Mind is just a natural consequence.

Of course, inasmuch as it is a gamble, this internal exploration venture may turn out to be a total failure. As is often suggested, there may be an element of self-contradiction in trying to know one's inner self really deeply. But the final answer cannot be known until one tries hard enough.

We will discuss in the final section what course our civilization should take in the immediate future to ensure such a Type III civilization in the end. Before proceeding with it, however, we need to consider our past and the present in order to clarify characteristics of contemporary scientific civilization and the crises we are likely to confront in the near future.

THE AGE OF THE GREAT TRANSITION

In contrast to the once-fashionable images of a resplendent metallic future, we are now shown, almost unanimously, gruesome pictures painted from dark grey to pitch black, as if someone intentionally darkened the illumination of a picture gallery. We may now count, in addition to the persistent threat of nuclear warfare, all sorts of new threats to worry about: industrial pollution, population explosion, mutated viruses, mismanipulations of genetic engineering, and so on. What has caused this sudden turn of events?

I particularly want to emphasize this aspect of suddenness, since the most menacing aspect of all the threats confronting us seems to be their timing rather than the evils in themselves; the threats appear to manifest themselves quite abruptly and nearly simultaneously. No sooner is their existence merely suspected than their menace grows rapidly and runs almost out of control. The example of PCB alone will suffice to illustrate the point.

Human civilization has been beset by various menaces throughout its long past: natural calamities, pestilences, invasions by an alien race, and so forth. These menaces were, however, of familiar kinds, more or less repeated many times in the history of mankind, and anyone would have experienced such disasters once or twice in his or her own lifetime. A town might have been burned down by a conflagration but rebuilt almost exactly as it had been before. It was a rule that one's whole life was spent with exactly the same systems of beliefs and values.

Only very recently has all of this familiar stability become invalid. Every day, newspapers and TV commentators casually report abnormal happenings that may change the whole world — scientific and technological breakthroughs that may deeply affect our way of life. We watch or read these news items absentmindedly, digesting them together with our breakfast (perhaps, few instabilities will upset us as long as our menu stays stable), and scarcely a scrap of the new information remains in our consciousness when breakfast is over. Today our world undergoes changes every day, and thus changes have lost their surprise value.

We may dismiss this observation simply as further evidence for human superadaptivity. However superadaptive human beings may be, though, there must be a limit, and a day will come when awareness of the extraordinariness of the present time finally pierces the tough layer of indifference of modern man, when the feeling of uneasiness finally registers in his consciousness. Symptoms of pandemic panic are now evident in many places in the world, and the dark images of our future are also signs of a general dread surfacing in our minds.

Things are indeed extraordinary. Was it not just a short time ago that the Japanese government was making a big fuss about the need to increase rice production? And now, nationwide, Japanese granaries and warehouses are bursting with last year's rice, with that of the year before last, and with that of three years back, producing headaches and tremendous financial deficits for the government. Japan, once counted among the poorest nations in the world, is now among the richest, while currencies like dollars and pounds have suddenly lost their once vaunted status as the foundations of the world economy; world enterprises quickly rise and fall, wax and wane; and textbooks must be rewritten every year. Last year we stopped hearing the noisy chorus of frogs, and this year we are going to miss the beautiful spring songs of birds.

To sum, things change too rapidly, and the rate of change is accelerating. No statistical tables are needed to demonstrate this point. It suffices to note that most of the statistical social indicators we use today, particularly economic and industrial ones, are expressed in terms of the *rate* of growth. Only by taking a nearly constant acceleration for granted is the rate of growth a meaningful measure of yearly social changes.

Any person familiar with exponential functions will notice immediately how extraordinary a situation this really is. In fact, somebody tried to extrapolate a couple of indicators representing contemporary civilization and found that some of them go into infinity even before the year 2000.

This, of course, is impossible. A deceleration must occur somewhere. The deceleration process may not be smooth, though. If the driver of a sportscar running with tremendous acceleration suddenly steps on the brake pedal with full force, the outcome is plain and simple—a disastrous accident, although no one would deny that this certainly creates a deceleration. A more chilling fact, however, is that apparently no one knows where the brake is in this sportscar-called-civilization, which is on a mad run with a killing acceleration.

Let us now leave analogies and consider possible causes for the acceleration effect. When we observe an acceleration effect in a social process, it is most natural to suspect that some mutual facilitation or positive feedback mechanisms are in operation. Undoubtedly, a number of such processes should be taking place simultaneously, but the most crucial one appears to be the positive feedback relationship between information and control. Greater amounts of information in better quality enable controls of greater precision and in wider range, and, conversely, finer and broader control provides us with richer and more dependable information.

Needless to say, for such a relationship to hold between information and control, human beings are needed to intervene as catalysts, endeavoring persistently to convert information into control and control back into information. To some critics such an image of man may appear applicable only to those who live in the scientific, technological civilization of the twentieth century. Human beings, however, are not likely to have changed much since prehistoric times as far as the physiology of their brain is concerned, and, therefore, there are no grounds for denying that man operated as a catalyst in prehistoric times as well. If otherwise, obviously, no civilization could have emerged. Still, there is a puzzle: Why does the acceleration begin to look conspicuous only recently? Having this issue in mind, let me bypass intermediate ages and go directly back to the very remote past. Of course, I am no archaeologist and I am not proposing to discuss the remote past in any rigorous scientific sense. In my view the remote past is just as uncertain as the distant future; they are both artificial stage settings for the purpose of highlighting human conditions.

One thing is certain about our remote past, however; that is, there has never been an Eden. Living conditions for human beings have been unfailingly tough ever since they evolved from apes and emerged from the woods onto the plains. Severity of living conditions means hard labor in hunting and food gathering. And, needless to say, labor is not random behavior but is patterned, following a certain set of rules. In order to perform a trick called labor, therefore, information was needed, even though the necessary information could have been provided (although this is unlikely) by genetical means alone.

In any case, human society in ancient times (which may be called the Type 0 society if need arises) would undoubtedly have been quite stable. Even so, there must have been fluctuations in the outcome of labor, and the major instrument to recover sociostasis would have been population, nature's prime negative-feedback agent.

This ecological balance-keeping agent is characteristically slow in operation, however, particularly so with advanced mammal species. This time lag would have given human beings a precious chance, however brief, to ruminate over information as well as over food. If human beings in fact started to tread this one-way path in this manner, we should look for a further special reason, as other animal species apparently spend the same leisure time simply in dozing or similar nonactivities. Of course, the majority of ancient men must have done exactly the same, apart from an exceptional few who preferred to indulge in some "brainy" sort of exercises. Even though what exactly happened is a complete mystery, it seems that, when human ancestors turned to bipeds capable of upholding a heavier mass, the brain expanded its potential capacity perhaps beyond immediate needs, thereby creating a need to exercise it occasionally for its maintenance.

In any case, we may conjecture that only a very tiny fraction of ancient people extracted new information from their experiences only on very rare occasions and used or tried to use the information for some control purposes. Undoubtedly, most of these attempts would have been failures. Nevertheless, in spite of the low efficiency, slight positive outcomes of their attempts could have accumulated in a million years to the point of igniting a budding civilization.

Apparently, it is difficult to identify the real reason why humans came to acquire the trait of preserving information and accumulating it collectively. However, since we observe inventiveness even among monkeys — and the innovative behavior of washing potatoes in sea water is employed by young followers of the innovator — we might surmise that the inclination had long been there among the genes of primates. It is, in any case, evident that the original catalystic characteristic of converting information into control became quite dominant with humans, and the evolutionary process entered into a new phase with the emergence of humans endowed with an instinctively strong urge to fix information in much the same way as some bacteria fix nitrogen.

The term *information* is used here in a sense a little broader than is normal, and it may more properly be called negative entropy. Needless to say, entropy is a concept used in thermodynamics or in statistical mechanics, a quantity representing, in a certain sense, the disorderliness of a closed material system viewed macroscopically. The most well known thermodynamic law concerning entropy is the second law, or the law of increasing entropy, which states that the entropy of a closed system may spontaneously increase but cannot be decreased unless it is acted upon from outside. The orderliness of a system will thus be gradually lost until it reaches the state of maximal disorderliness if no positive effort is exerted from outside to recover orderliness. A well-known instance of the application of this law is the thermal death of the universe — that is, that our universe will eventually reach a practically dead state with a prevailing homogeneous temperature whereby no orderly structure nor activity can ever be observed, if our universe is indeed a closed system.

Should such a dismal prophesy ever come true, this nonviolent doom certainly belongs to a tremendously remote future, compared to which the distant futures we have been discussing are the happenings of tomorrow morning. Nevertheless, such a picture of the end of our universe may give us a feeling of futility. Futility, however, is the wrong notion to apply here. In the dead universe there is no action and no change, and therefore there can be no time. A timeless world is a notion so profound that it clearly defies human emotions.

However, is the universe really destined to die thermally? A popular counterargument is to posit the evolution of life. Putting aside the issue of how life ever emerged, there is no doubt that evolution appears to have taken its course from simple to complex, from less orderly to more, and not only for biological evolution; the same can be said for the development of human civilization.

Evolution, however, does not logically contradict the law of increasing entropy. Nor is the opposite argument true that entropy increases more quickly in our universe because human beings run around about it always unsettling things.

To discuss these matters it would be more convenient to use, instead of positive entropy, the amount of entropy in reserve in a given system (i.e., the maximum entropy minus current entropy). This quantity is often referred to as the *negative entropy*, since the second law equivalently predicts a spontaneous decrease of this quantity. However, since this term is not only longish but also misleading, let me coin a new term, *negen*, as a composite of NEGative ENtropy, to imply the same. In other words, the amount of negen in a system represents the amount of orderliness maintained by it. The second law of thermodynamics stipulates that the negen has a tendency to disappear unless nothing is done from outside to compensate for the loss, and the thermal death of the universe is characterized by zero negen of the universe, the unavoidable doom of a system that has no "outside."

When the amount of negen in a system is positive, orderly activity called *work* can be carried out inside the system within the limits set by the negen value. The physical definition of work is, as far as physics goes, rigorously physical and completely nonhuman. Nonetheless, viewed from a slightly more liberal angle, the notion seems human enough, as do other notions in physics such as "force," though I will not elaborate this point here. In any case, we may intuitively understand that work is an operation to transfer order from one form to another. In that sense, the notion of work in our daily life may be considered as a generalization (or a special form, depending on personal viewpoints) of this physical notion of work. In other words, our work may be interpreted as a transfer of the negen we have extracted from food into the negen of our environment. The efficiency of the conversion, of course, cannot reach the level of 100 percent, as this perfect transfer contradicts the law of decreasing negen, the counterpart of the law of increasing entropy. So, as the law dictates, a large portion of negen will be dissipated through the activities of human beings. Therefore, at least temporarily, human activities exacerbate the negen decrease within our universe. Nevertheless, it does not mean that human activities (or, more generally, activities of living organisms) will eventually lead to a faster consumption of the universal negen, since the negen dissipated by human activities could have been lost in any case. In fact, a food will lose most of its negen by rotting and returning to the soil even if left uneaten. On the other hand, suppose that a person ate it and used the negen for work; for example, he might draw water from a well and carry it to a tank in a higher place. Water in a higher place can do physical work. So the water moved to a higher place is given a negen, and the negen in this form can last much longer than the same in the form of food, provided that the water tank does not leak.

In this way, even though human beings directly consume a part of the whole universal negen by their activities, they may also be contributing more effectively to arrest its general decay. And, as I will discuss next, most human activities are to be interpreted in the light of this interpretation — that is, humans are endowed with a very strong inclination to fix whatever negen they can extract from their environment. Since this instinctive trait of man is in congruence with the direction taken by the evolution of life, it may be possible to consider that the essence of the phenomenon of life may be found in such a counter-entropic decay orientation. Insofar as we employ this interpretation of life, any argument disclaiming machines as the rightful heir of mankind as inheritors of the banner of evolution would lose its logical ground.

Of course, there are apparent absurdities in such a conjecture. To consider human activities as something to prevent the general decay of the universal negen may be like regarding an activity of an ant inadvertently bringing a piece of soil to a riverbank as contributing to the prevention of flood. What humans are really doing now is, while fixing some negen, liberating and wasting more of the already fixed underground negen in the form of fossil fuels; and if we come to blow up the Earth in the future by nuclear warfare, it certainly means that human activities have positively contributed in expediting just a mite the process of universal negen decay.

In any case, when we are up against anything as colossal as a universe, the good or bad influences of human activities upon it can be, at least for the moment, too miniscule to be significant. The only thing that may matter is the inclination inherent at the very core of human activities. Insofar as there is this inclination in human beings or in life in general to attain a higher control power, its effect can become acceleratingly powerful due to the mutual facilitation between information and control, and the possibility cannot be denied outright that one day in the future the activities of either man or his successors will reach the point where they may exert a substantial influence on the process of the universe. In some remote time in the future, man or his successor may acquire enough power, for instance, to move around the universe turning off unnecessary lights, those stars in the galaxy wasting negen at prodigious rates. Or, if it is still mankind that is in command of such a power, vainglorious human nature might rather prefer lighting dead stars like firecrackers.

Or, the curtain may finally fall on the drama of evolution with a scene in which a super-life form, a very distant successor of mankind, blows with a guffaw the whole universe into dust. Who cares? The titanic experiment called evolution turned out to be a flop. A god may tell the depressed godling with a punctured balloon labeled "UNIVERSE": "Don't cry. Now watch this new one. With a big "bang" it will start to inflate." In any case, I have gone too far into the future. Now let us return to the primitive society of a yester-era.

As I discussed earlier, human beings do not monopolize information processing during leisure time, extracting something useful out of the remembered data and utilizing the knowledge for the control of environment. A female Japanese monkey initiated the washing of potatoes before eating them, and the information was passed on to the surrounding monkeys, even though the habit may not last long now that the initiator has died. In a generalized sense information is a form of negen, and thus is not free from the fate ordained by the law of decreasing negen. Unless work had not been positively done to recover dissipating negen, it would never have happened that the amount of accumulated negen gradually increased to create a civilization. In the case of human beings, the critical condition was met sometime and somewhere when the delicate balance between dissipation and accumulation of negen was broken slightly in favor of accumulation, perhaps due to their large brain, especially suited to store negen in the form of information.

At the very beginning, the effect of this remarkable event must have been infinitesimal. However small was the imbalance, however, it contained the seed for acceleration, and the acceleration mechanism would most dramatically have manifested itself when tools were invented.

The relationship between tools and accumulation of negen would best illustrate this point. As is well known, the most important part of Shannon's information theory is his theory of channels. Note that a channel is a "tool" for transmitting information over *space*. A good information transmission channel is characterized by its capacity for conveying to the destination as large an amount of information as possible, and this means that, if the information input to the channel is fixed, a good channel should protect its information cargo from contaminating disturbances as well as possible during its transmission. If we generalize this definition of a good channel from information to negen in general, we obtain the specification for a good tool. A tool is a channel for transmitting negen, and a good tool has to protect negen efficiently while it passes from the working person to the target of the work.

Let us consider some examples. As channel originally means an artificial waterway, any man-made "way," whether it be a water channel or a road, is a tool for transporting a chunk of negen, embodied either as a person, a material object, or a carrier of information. Therefore, a road is a good road, in much the same way that a good communication channel is, only if it allows a large amount of negen to be transported as quickly and safely as possible. By constructing a good road, one can stretch the limit of control transmission to more distant places, just as a good channel extends the range of communication. This hypothesis is attested to by numerous historical examples demonstrating that the wax and wane of the power of an empire are highly correlated to its ability to develop its road network and maintain the safety of transportation. Of course, in the old times roads were major communication channels as well.

There is obviously no need for transmission or transportation to be considered within the spatial framework alone. Any spatial locomotion is necessarily accompanied by a certain passage of time, during which the transported negen chunk, matter or information, must be preserved. The accumulation of negen, which has been my point of argument, is obviously based on an efficient temporal transmission of negen chunks, which in turn requires as many and as good temporal negen transmission channels as possible.

Though temporal negen transmission channels may sound a bit esoteric, they are nothing but utensils for the preservation of things, and a single glance will tell you how our living space is cluttered with these channels. To preserve the negen chunk called the human body, a person is encased in multiple preservation channels, such as a house and clothes. The space inside a house is partitioned into rooms, closets, and drawers, and things inside these nooks are further enveloped by channels like tins, bags, boxes, and so on. Certainly, calling them channels is odd, but they are indeed channels because they meet the definition — that is, they are all equipped with stable outside shields to protect the contents against external disturbances and with a gate or gates to open temporarily for access to the shielded inside (doors, zippers, lids). In this respect, submarine cables, elevated expressways, milk bottles, houses, and the Great Wall of China all share the same function.

Of course, we cannot say that *every* channel has such a visible shield and a visible gate. Many of the channels of special importance in our civilization are often equipped with an invisible gate requiring very specific magic words to open it. For example, many of the special materials developed by mankind, such as plastic, are stable in a normal environment but subject to easy molding under special conditions. In the case of paper and the printing press, which have so far played the most important role among human inventions in preserving negen chunks in the form of information, the paper corresponds to the channel and the printing press the magical gate, entry only. At a less material level, we may, for example, consider language, which is a supremely excellent and indispensable channel for transmitting and preserving information, by which ideas are easily encapsulated and conserved over centuries. (With some dead languages, however, the magic key word is lost and ancient ideas remain helplessly entrapped in clay plates.)

Though I will stop enumerating examples since they are endless, my conclusion is that a very large portion of man-made objects, material or non-material, are related, one way or the other, to the task of preventing negen dissipation. They preserve negen, and the preserved negen is used in daily work, in the further invention and production of negen-preservation channels of a higher efficiency, which in turn will increase the efficiency of negen preservation, and thus the whole process is accelerated. So the acceleration phenomenon and the mutual facilitation between information and control are but two sides of the same shield.

Suppose that the rate of acceleration is constant and reasonably low. Then its effect will be invisibly small while the original speed is low. So the fact that the effect has become visible only recently does not contradict in any way the assumption that it has been operating since the beginning of mankind, even though there may be other reasons, too, for making the acceleration especially conspicuous today.

Since Cannon demonstrated the wisdom of the body and Wiener advocated his famous negative feedback principle in cybernetics, physiologists have been discovering how the body of human beings, or of any life form, is endowed with a whole battery of intricately constructed negative feedback mechanisms to maintain the homeostatic balance. Not only individual bodies, but societies and ecological systems as well, are known to have built-in negative feedback mechanisms that operate to stabilize them against possible harmful accelerations and decelerations.

Confining our attention to human societies alone, population serves as one such negative feedback agent. When the negen chunk in the form of food becomes abundant, the population will increase to eat it up, and when it is insufficient, the population will decrease to recover the balance. In addition, overpopulation multiplies the chances of pestilences and internal conflicts.

Nonetheless, mankind is a sort of animal obsessed by the urge to accumulate negen. It instinctively abhors negative feedback mechanisms that may possibly impede negen accumulation. Thus mankind has been trying to destroy nature's stabilizing mechanisms one after another by utilizing its gradually accumulated power of environmental control. The perils of large-scale pestilences are now almost contained. For three decades big wars have been avoided. The population increase is now made nearly negligible, at least in the developed countries, in spite of their considerable affluence.

While we are on the topic of population expansion, I should like to make a comment on the so-called danger of a population explosion. The crises we are confronting in the near future are not those caused directly by population explosion. Note that it will take time for population explosion to reach the crisis level on a global scale. The crises I have been referring to are those awaiting us just around the next corner to catch us at any time, and some of them may be of the kind that just may render the notion of global population explosion a bitter irony. And these coming crises may be triggered most probably by the fact that the developed countries, including Japan, have become *undeservedly* rich. Before going into this issue of "undeservedness," however, let me finish the topic we have been discussing.

To recapitulate, mankind seems to have achieved, at least temporarily, the dominance of positive feedback mechanisms based on the accumulation of negen, by persistently conquering and putting under control nature's negative feedback mechanisms. It seems that a critical turning point in the struggle for dominance between positive and negative feedback mechanisms always exists. A good analogy may be found in the case when a not yet completely extinguished cigarette butt falls out of an ashtray. In most cases this incident will not cause a fire; things around the butt may scorch a little, but they will work rather in the direction of absorbing heat from the butt to extinguish it eventually. However, if there happens to be a flammable object near the butt to supply additional heat, thus increasing the temperature beyond the ignition point of those things around, these objects will produce further heat rather than absorbing it and will finally turn the incident into a big fire.

Essentially the same principle may be at work with human civilization; were such abundant underground fossil fuels not available, our civilization would not have been overheated so quickly, and the nuclear fire, whose technological ignition point is rather high, would not have been ignited so early. However, with or without these incidents, it would have been just a matter of time before the acceleration caused by our overcontrol of the material world overheated the civilization, creating a big fire, which would eventually die down, leaving the cinders of civilization behind.

Since the acceleration effect may belong to the karma of mankind, it would be impossible for us either to negate or to stop the acceleration unless we submitted ourselves to being transformed into inhabitants of the Type I future society, passively nurtured by the machines. So the vital question is whether we can *control* this inevitable acceleration so that we can somehow live with it. It may appear strange that the acceleration alone remains uncontrolled in the midst of the vigorous mutual facilitation of information and control, but note that the control effort of contemporary scientific civilization has focused almost exclusively on control of the external (typically inorganic) environment, and the stronger the control of the external world, the more intensified will be the acceleration. While it is the fixation of negen that creates acceleration, the kind of negen modern scientific civilization has accumulated is quite unbalanced; we are still horrifyingly ignorant about human beings and their societies. What meager knowledge we have about them hardly deserves the name of a full-fledged science.

Although it may appear that we have conquered most of nature's negative feedback mechanisms, nature is resourceful, and the final restabilizing device, a self-destruction of the destructive agent — in this case, mankind — will always be up her sleeve. The greater the amount of our negen accumulation, the greater would be the peril if that much negen were discharged without restraint through a crack of our civilization. The expected devastation of an all-out nuclear war is a good example, but not necessarily the only one. Chemical pollutions such as PCB, pharmaceutical perils such as thalidomide, pestilences caused by experimentally mutated viruses — you just name it, and no scientist can conjure up remedies. Consider, for example, something like thalidomide, which had been used as a sleeping drug. Instead of a sleeping drug, suppose that a panacea is found, or so scientists believe — a very inexpensive drug that performs miracles and cures common illnesses, such as the common cold. The probability that some such discovery will be made in near future is rather high. There is no doubt that such a drug will conquer the whole world in a moment, a patent demonstration of the superefficiency of the contemporary international trading system. As almost nobody is entirely immune to the common cold, sooner or later everybody in the world would have taken a considerable dose of this drug, which is as cheap as chewing gum and relieves ailments immediately without any apparent side effect. A subthreshold side effect, however, might accumulate, and one day an observer may notice a slight but significant unexplicable decline in the birth rate everywhere in the world. . . .

Contemporary civilization is overladen with such hidden Achilles' heels vulnerable to potential wounds for which no known cures exist. We are apparently overconfident and overconceited about our civilization only because of our utter ignorance. "Haven't we met crises in the past and always succeeded in containing them? Mankind has proved itself capable of coping with crises. So why worry about possible crises that haven't yet taken place?"

Unfortunately, this old negative feedback type, muddling-through strategy of to-think-only-after-a-crisis-has-taken-shape may not work with the crises that are about to come. Because of the acceleration, the crises in the future will be a little too quick to occur, a bit too fast in reaching an explosive climax, for the above strategy to operate, and all the damages will have been done while everybody is still stunned. If some of these stunned people can still survive, they will regain stability with a nearly zero level of accumulated negen and will have to restart the long history of mankind from primitive barbarism again. Certainly this is one of the ways to acquire an equilibrium without a visible acceleration. (How many ever-victorious, overconfident lords and kings have met a sudden unexpected defeat in the past, when a despised enemy suddenly appeared with an entirely innovative strategy, and perished in a stunned dismay? In the past, however, the civilization of the conquered was preserved by the conquerer, albeit in a modified form. This rule will not hold with the coming crises, as there will be no live conqueror to give our civilization its continuity.)

Of course, we will not consciously prefer any such miserable way to attain equilibrium. We, the negen maniacs, wish to protect both the negen we and our ancestors have accumulated so far and also at least some of the good aspects of our contemporary civilization, an embodiment of the accumulated negen. But is there any such alternative left?

THE THORN AND THE GLORY

I think there is one, which leads us to the Type III civilization discussed in the previous section. The way, however, is a difficult one. Only if we are lucky, and if the so-called wisdom of mankind is real, might we be able to wend the way through crises without being thrown off the roadside cliff toward the abyss of primitive barbarism.

Before going on to explain this new course, I should touch upon another type of crisis that has not yet been mentioned, for this is the unavoidable last crisis we must confront even if we survive miraculously unscathed while going through the whole legion of crises of the Achilles' heel type mentioned above. That is the internal disintegration of civilization due to overheat. If the outcome of our current suicidal race with a brakeless sportscar is not a collision, still the engine overheat will ignite the fuel and cause an explosion.

But the metaphor of explosion is not very adequate, and I will drop the analogy. The human social system, intentionally left undiscussed in the foregoing arguments, is one of the forms in which accumulated human negen is embodied. It is also one of the instruments, in a broad sense, that mankind has striven to develop to further the efficiency of human work by mutually controlling the performances of individuals. Mankind has been pouring out negen to improve and develop social systems for this purpose, and each of them has functioned as such an instrument in each period of human history. When we go about developing a type of instrument, first we concentrate on making a test model, then proceed to make it strong and durable so that the instrument becomes a good control channel. As time passes, however, the nature of entities going through a channel will change, and an old, too durable channel begins to be felt rather as an impediment, in the same way as overdurable buildings tend to become liabilities to the community since they easily turn into slums. It may happen to our social system as well; after a while it will begin to fail to satisfy people's needs to spend their excess negen in their preferred ways, and the general irritation will ferment public dissatisfaction, which may end up in attempts to destroy a social system seen as an obstacle rather than a useful instrument for the people's proper use of their negen.

The same story has often been repeated in human history; the accused system was sometimes a civilization, an empire, a church. In times long past, when the architectural structure of social systems was not solid enough, disintegration of a civilization was usually caused by an invasion of an enemy troop into a weakened, overrich system. In much later times, when invasions became more difficult due to the increased defense power, internal revolutions took over as the major cause of political turnover. In either case, the general public often showed little enthusiasm in defending their old, crumbling social systems.

In view of the strength of the current acceleration and the unbalanced development of our civilization with its overemphasis on natural sciences, it is self-evident that our contemporary social system is to a large degree an anachronism. It is, in principle, at least a century behind the times even though we have been trying hard to patch up chinks and flaws in its substructures — those of political systems, economic systems, judicial systems, and so on. As a consequence of the inadequacy of our social system, while a large number of people in some part of the world are given a large amount of excess negen by the rapid progress of scientific technologies, they are also deprived, owing to the clumsiness of the existing social systems, of the proper means of using it for constructive purposes.

This situation creates a sort of Midas-type hunger; the illusory pleasure of being surrounded by a heap of gold will be replaced by frustration when one discovers that somehow gold has lost the magical power to transform itself into whatever the owner desires it to become. The pleasure one may feel at first by having more income and more leisure time, which may be spent in any way one likes, will turn sour when one finds how few options are open for spending them in a meaningful way — meaningful in the sense of fixing further negen — to satisfy the urge deep at the heart of human nature.

What will occur then as the result of this dissatisfaction? At least for the time being, no drastic political reform will take place that will upset the worldwide social system. There are two reasons for this expectation. First, the dissatisfaction of the affluent is not directed toward the affluence itself; however loudly they may cry, they do not wish to overturn the scientific civilization that has created the excess negen. Note also that if the issue at hand is something like a redevelopment of slums, the planner may move the residents elsewhere temporarily and indulge in an ideal reconstruction in complete isolation. Today, however, our civilization has almost become a single global architecture, and tampering with one part of it will create a strain in the rest of the world. Second, it is also difficult to reconstruct the worldwide social system all at once; unfortunately no enlightening vision for the coming new world has been produced by anyone, perhaps because of the difficulty in seeing ahead from a vehicle moving at a hurtling speed. The extreme radicals' claim that we should destroy the social system first and that the problem of its reconstruction will solve itself in due time will hardly muster the amount of unorganized negen in the general public that is needed to incite the first phase of serious destruction.

In spite of all this, the increased dissatisfaction will gradually mount and will eventually be directed internally. Even if no one intentionally breaks down the social system by violence, the system itself will begin to malfunction and its public esteem will sink. While many patchwork socioeconomic structures come and go with their ephemeral utilities, the world's social systems will one by one gradually cease to operate normally, as if they had been melted rather than destroyed. The melting or disorganizing symptoms are particularly evident in universities and slums, where organizational constraints are the weakest and the excess negen increase is the most marked. At the same time, racial and religious conflicts, which have never failed to act as volcanoes in human civilization, will erupt violently again. Such tendencies as yet are mere symptoms, but they are nonetheless harbingers of the coming conflagration. The doom of civilization, however, may not take the form of a great war. The world powers are gradually losing their ability to engage in real, extensive warfare. They may ostensibly appear as giants putting up grandiose political fights, but the truth is that they are melting from their toes upward. The worst possible picture we may imagine is a worldwide civil war; as in Northern Ireland, people may fight with neighbors all over the world for whatever causes they happen to conjure up.

It seems to me that no improvement in the present situation will take place before we nearly reach this stage of disaster, since human beings may become collectively wise only when they have been given a really painful experience. In which direction mankind will choose to proceed after the first disaster will depend upon how good a vision we will acquire before that time of the alternative ways mankind may take. If we still lack any excellent vision based on reason, the world will become a bloody arena for fanatic beliefs to fight against each other, and the best we can expect as an outcome of this is another stable dark age of feudalism divided and ruled by petty dictators.

Taking these dark predictions seriously, the problem may boil down to how to obtain an exact, rational vision of our future society (perhaps of Type III). I discussed this issue in some detail somewhere else, but the conclusion is simple: The prerequisite for obtaining a solution is to acquire, on the basis of scientific analyses, a better and more complete understanding of the basic nature of ourselves and our civilization. Only with this knowledge may we be able to plan and design a desirable form of global social structure compatible with today's conditions, in much the same way that we can design and erect dependable bridges and tall buildings on the basis of our scientific knowledge. Needless to say, it is an enormously hard task to establish such an exact science of human beings and their civilization, and we can hardly have enough time to accomplish it. Nevertheless, it is my belief that there is no alternative.

Of course, I can provide no dependable vision based on this exact science, which is yet to come. But I may indulge in describing my personal image of the coming pre-Type III future society, at least for the purpose of concluding this paper.

This coming society has to be constructed under an almost impossible condition. As labor unions do not willingly accept a wage reduction unless under a dire necessity, people would not willingly forgo the current level of excess negen; for any plan for a new society to be effective, it must be based on the general consensus of people about the indispensable nature of this plan as the condition to stabilize human society. Therefore, in this new society people should not be less wealthy than we are today, and the society must provide them with means to spend their wealth as constructively as they wish. (The term "wealth" used here does not mean the same thing as we use it today. It is to be understood in the sense of excess negen, particularly in terms of the control people have over inanimate materials.) On the other hand, societal processes should not visibly accelerate in this new society, lest its stability be lost. It may appear nearly impossible to conciliate these two conditions, but it is not absolutely impossible. Naturally, negen will accumulate if most people work constructively, but the accumulation of negen need not occur only in the single dimension of the scientific technology. As I stated previously, the exploration of our inner universe is made possible only under such a condition, which may eventually lead us to a true Type III civilization.

There is, however, yet a possibility that a tremendous accelerating factor will suddenly emerge somewhere and sometime to shatter fundamentally the stability of this pre-Type III society, if all the people in the world happily work on with their full potential abilities, be it on the inner universe or on the outer universe, no matter how cleverly the excess negen resource is distributed over multiple work dimensions. Since the possibility cannot be denied, the time of another great transition will certainly come. But we may at least be able to postpone this period until mankind has become well prepared, at which time the very advanced science of man and his society, combined with the meticulously planned control of social processes, will enable mankind to reach the next higher level of stability with a great single stride.

By mentioning the planned control of social processes, I do not mean the so-called controlled society, which is just another form of dictatorship. Ours is the type of control sanctioned by the consensus of people given on the basis of the shared self-realization of mature mankind — the maturity bought by the dear price of going through serious crises, the recognition that we must walk on a tightrope if we wish to keep our status as something better than that of savage beasts. And this control task will be put in the charge of a special group of devoted persons. As is easily imaginable, the chances are low that these controllers will become politically ambitious and power oriented, since no brute power can exist in this pre-Type III society. This is no idealistic dogma; it is structurally impossible to concentrate political power without the consensus of majority in a society in which every member possesses a large amount of excess negen, both in the form of unlimited information and of physical power.

This last condition also makes it impossible for the stability of this society to be static in nature. The structure of this society is likely to be enormously complicated, but the complexity will mainly be the outcome of its dynamic principles; the people will move freely around the world, forming and breaking up a diversity of groups and causing a kaleidoscopic variety of cultures to flourish. It may look as if paradise has finally come into existence.

There is, however, never a utopia for man. The people in this society may appear as if they were absolutely free, allowed to do anything their whim dictates. But then the observer is overlooking invisible barriers, nonstatic and hard to notice, but barriers nevertheless, put up almost everywhere and never to be trespassed, in order to maintain the stability of the society. And the force that keeps people from trespassing is not externally enforced rules but an internally maintained discipline. And for any such self-regulation to be possible, all the people must possess full knowledge about the conditions upon which their society precariously stands. Needless to say, such stringent self-regulation is an extremely harsh course to take, and the inhabitants of this mature society would often sigh deeply, envying the time when mankind was still in its stage of adolescence, when people were blithely unaware of the need of any such stringent self-discipline.

So my conclusion is, paradoxically, that we are now living in the last golden age in the history of mankind like carefree youngsters with unprecedented amounts of freedom in behavior. Sadly, such a time will soon be gone forever one way or the other and will never come back.

II TIME, COGNITION, AND IMAGINATION

4 TIME AND THE STRUCTURE OF HUMAN COGNITION

Occasionally, it hits me what marvelous creatures humans are. Among all their numerous talents, the one that fascinates me most is their ability to create abstract notions out of something that they do not really understand. The emergence of the abstract notion of time is obviously a case in point. No one, apparently, can claim to know what time is. Nevertheless, there is a brave breed of people called physicists, who used this elusive notion as one of the basic building blocks of their theory and, miraculously, the theory worked. When one of the leading figures of the clan, by the name of Albert Einstein, quietly mumbled his secret incantation, which sounded like "Combine time with space in such a way that nothing can travel faster than the speed of light, then mass is equal to energy," lo and behold, atoms exploded ever so noisily.

Is it just nature's favoritism? Has time been ordered to play possum when it is in the hands of physicists? Because our intuitive feeling certainly

This paper first appeared in *The Study of Time II, Proceedings of the Second Conference of the International Society for the Study of Time*, J. T. Fraser and N. Lawrence, eds. (New York: Springer-Verlag, 1975), pp. 314–24. Copyright © 1975 by Springer-Verlag New York, Inc.; used by permission. I am indebted to Shiro Imai for his helpful suggestions in preparing this paper.

tells us that time is something we live with, something far livelier than the abstract mathematical entity that physicists refer to in their theory by a single letter labeled t. Still, no one who lives in the present technological world can deny the tremendous power that this simple t possesses. If it is not due just to a divine grace bestowed upon physicists, then what or who is responsible for the miracle? I would not give a damn for the claim some physicists occasionally make: *The victory of logical reasoning!* How can one be logical about something he does not really understand? Or . . . .

Maybe I am wrong. Maybe one can be logical only about something he does not fully comprehend. Just because he does not know what it is, he can take a detached attitude toward it and may try coolheadedly to confine it within a sterile, break-safe capsule, which is alternatively called the *abstract notion*. If he is lucky and succeeds in trapping something really important within the capsule, then all the power of logic is at his service; he may stretch the capsule from infinity to infinity, map it onto the number continuum, and build an atom-shattering monstrous theory upon it. There is obviously no doubt that physicists succeeded in trapping some really important ingredient of time within their capsule labeled t, but equally certainly it is not all of time that is captured within their capsule. Our intuition is crying out to tell us that time is something that flows, unlike the physical time, which is frozen still. Not only just frozen still; the physicists' t would be quite at a loss which way to flow if it were thawed and ordered to flow.

On the other hand, try to see if you can make your child into an abstract notion. Or your wife, husband, or anyone you know very well, for that matter. We cannot do it just because we know them too well. And, in natural consequence, we can hardly deal with them with pure, cold logic alone.[1] Even though to a lesser degree, knowing the object of investigation too well on an intuitive level has been an unfailing source of difficulty in psychology.

My purpose in writing this paper is neither to solve the mystery of man's ability of capsule making nor to clarify what is left out by the physicists' t-capsule, which are both undertakings far beyond my capability. What I intend to do in this paper is to tackle a problem concerning the primary functioning of the human cognitive system and its temporal characteristics in particular. Such a problem contains a mystery of no lesser degree than those in the above-mentioned two; however, we have more clues here. And, through this attempt, I hope we may possibly obtain some useful hints relevant to the others.

The notion of *cognitive system* is now being used in many different contexts, not necessarily with the same definition. There seems to be, however, a general understanding that it means an internal representation of man's external environment, including himself at the center. There is no doubt that every individual has one such *system*, a coherent (or nearly coherent) body of structural internal schemata without which behavior can hardly be organized in a coherent way, and that it is an essential feature of consistent adaptation. Note, however, that nothing like a set of still "images" (stereoscopic or not) of the surrounding world or a more abstract *weltanschauung* type of construct should be identified as the cognitive system. These things belong, if they do belong to one's cognitive system at all, to a functional level high in the organizational strata of the cognitive system, located at the exhibition gallery of what a cognitive system can ultimately create, where what you see are mostly capsules and very few activities. As you go down the levels, you will gradually see more and more activities and, naturally, the busiest part will be found in the basement section, the place that will be called the *primary cognitive subsystem* or the *primary system* for short.

The primary system is, of course, a conventional categorization, since it is entirely impossible to draw a sharp borderline between subsystems of any system as tightly organized as the cognitive system. (Hence I have here another unmistakable example of an abstract notion created out of something beyond true comprehension.) Anyway, by the primary system I mean roughly the part of the cognitive system that is in charge of moment-by-moment *actions* of a person, covert as well as overt actions. Perception is one such action, and as we do not know *how* we are perceiving, the actual functioning of the primary system is beyond the reach of direct conscious probes.[2]

As a rule, with any smoothly running system interminably performing basic functions, we are seldom even aware of its existence. The primary system seems operating even in the dreaming stage, though in a certain lax way. But there is an observation made by the clinical psychologist Shor, which seems to describe how it is when all the noises made by the primary system are somehow turned off:[3]

I had been asleep for a number of hours. My level of body tonus was fairly high and my mind clear of dream-images so that I believe I was not asleep but rather in some kind of trance-like state. At that time I was neither conscious of my personal identity, nor of prior experiences, nor of the external world. It was just that out of nowhere I was aware of my own thought processes. I did not know, however, that they were thought processes or who I was, even that I was an I. There was sheer awareness in isolation from any experiential context. It was neither pleasant nor unpleasant; it was not goal directed, just sheer existing. After a time, "wondering" started to fill my awareness; that there was more than this, a gap, an emptiness. As soon as this "wondering" was set into motion there was immediately a change in my awareness. In an instant, as if in a flash, full awareness of myself and reality expanded around me. To say that "I woke up" or that "I remembered," while perhaps correct, would miss the point of the experience entirely. The significant thing was that my mind changed fundamentally in that brief instant. In rediscovering myself and the world, something vital had happened; suddenly all specifications of reality had become apparent to me. At one moment my awareness was devoid of all structure and in the next moment I was myself in a multivaried universe of time, space, motion and desire. [Shor, 1959. p. 586]

Such is a rare experience indeed, but we need not directly experience it ourselves to learn from this observation that we are constantly living within a cognitive *context* that supplies the identification and continuation of oneself in the given environment, the context updated at every moment. Even though the updating may occasionally fail, the context-providing function of the *primary system* is only temporarily suspended and will usually be resumed soon enough with the help of higher cognitive sub-systems to avoid any serious discontinuity. It appears that the strong in-tuitive conviction of the continuity of oneself is maintained only by virtue of this extremely efficient operation of the primary system.

Although it is easy to say that the primary system constantly provides a quite veridical context, I wish the reader would first appreciate the immen-sity of this task by taking into account, in particular, the high degree of complexity of the human environment today, with which we still seem to be able to cope as individuals. The apparent success of the primary system in carrying out this task seems to suggest that it possesses, at least, the fol-lowing three major facilities: (1) an enormously good environmental simulation system, (2) a fairly large processing capacity for the oncoming information, and (3) a precise real-time clock. Obviously, (1) and (2) hold a complementary relation; with a greater information-processing capacity, one can tolerate a less precise simulation. But there is a limit. Information cannot be processed without a context or an ensemble for the possible messages, which must, in the first place, be provided by cognitive simula-tion. And there are good reasons to believe that, in fact, the information-processing capacity of the primary system is not tremendously large.[4] That leads us to the conclusion that the precision of the simulation schemata of the primary system is unbelievably good, a feat that can be achieved only through quite exhaustive processing and utilization of the redundancies observed in our environment — or, to be more precise, the redundancies contained in our sensory inputs coupled with our own bodily motions.

So far, what I have said is not much more than a list of statements. To substantiate my arguments, let me reflect for a while on how the working of the primary system expresses itself in our visual information processing.

While we are awake, we usually keep our eyes open. Notorious in not staying still, our eyes shift their object of fixation about three times a second on a rough average. According to Jacobson, a single eye can handle a potential maximum of information of about 4.3 million bits per second (Jacobson, 1951). So a flood of visual information must be coming all the time through this pair of live windows, an amount enough to drown any honest — by which I mean unprepared — information-processing device. How much of this sheer bulk of potential information do we actually utilize? Search your memory. How much of today's visual experience do you retain in your memory? In my case, just a few fleeting, fragmentary images, like the thinning grey hair of a man I was introduced to, a vague shape of a pretty girl sitting in front of me in the subway, the creamy whiteness of mashed potatoes at the dinner table, and so on. Perhaps I could recall more if I really tried hard, but not too much more. Apparently these images are not all that I had to use my eyes for today, since I have survived the day. I went to my office, attended a meeting, then went to a concert and came back home safely without being hit by a car, without falling down the staircase, without bumping into more than one person. Therefore, I must have used the visual information I received just barely as much as the circumstantial needs dictated, since otherwise something more substantial than these whimsical snapshot images would remain in memory.

Yesterday, at my graduate seminar, someone mentioned an old piece of experimental apparatus that had been sitting for a long time in the corridor near my office. Surprisingly, no one remembered if it was still there, even though everyone passes the place at least once a day. After a lengthy argument (it was a seminar on cognition, and I assure you that we were not wasting time), we reached the conclusion that it must still be there, as no one noticed anything suggesting otherwise. So we all went to check our hypothesis, and it was confirmed. Needless to say, we must have been *seeing* it every day and utilizing the visual information, since no one apparently has bumped into this bulky apparatus lately.

Obviously, this is the type of visual information processing we are engaged in almost every moment without appreciable effort. Automatic. And information processing can be carried out automatically only if a fixed number of alternative outcomes are spelled out in advance and for each of which a fixed maneuver is predetermined. In other words, each time we see, we are *expecting* what to see, and what is really seen is just checked against the expectation. To be precise, expectation is a word a bit too strong to describe the operation. It does not reduce uncertainty to zero. You must positively see that a car is not coming before you cross a street. If you see a car coming, or a bicycle, or a pedestrian, or none at all, it will trigger an appropriate action and you will usually forget the visual experience immediately. If it is some exotic vehicle, however, you may perhaps start more detailed information processing and remember the occasion. If it is a dinosaur. . . . It is a pity that we live in a dull, redundant world in which we seldom encounter anything we don't expect at all. But just by virtue of this tremendous redundancy, we can let the primary system handle most of our visual information-processing chores, and it carries them out with utmost ease. Only at occasional moments of encounter with a novelty — meaning low expectation as well as no expectation — does the primary system transfer the task up to a higher cognitive subsystem for a real processing.

The "expectation" considered here as an alternative label for the context-providing activity of the primary system should never be mixed up with the more conscious, or higher-level, activity of guessing or predicting. As evidenced by the obvious unreliability of the outcomes of guessing or predicting, in sharp contrast to the high reliability of the primary system's expectations, the former is an activity categorically different from the latter and usually deals with a much longer temporal period extending into the future. Of course, if you come down to the basis of these secondary activities, you will find out that they are, as are all other cognitive activities, deeply rooted in the functions of the primary system, as I shall discuss later. Note also that we do guess or predict only occasionally, whereas the expectation of the primary system is a constant activity. The difference is somewhat like the one between smoking and breathing. As the activity of breathing is rarely brought into awareness, even though it is our body's vital activity of constantly supplying oxygen to the blood stream, we are often even more ignorant of the context-providing activity of the primary system, without which we would immediately suffocate mentally, since no oncoming information can be processed without a context.[5]

Of course, it is extremely difficult to prove this point directly, since as long as we are awake our primary system will never stop providing a context except in a very rare case, such as that reported by Shor. It can be shown indirectly, however, by considering cases in which the contexts provided continue being irremediably wrong for a certain period. This situation is also difficult to create because the cognitive system as a whole is resourceful, with diverse means to explain away apparently incongruent information. But let me tell you a piece of my own experience.

When I was a graduate student, I went out with my friends to an amusement park one day. We found a little hut there named Surprise House and decided to try it. The inside of the hut was a small room the shape of a cylinder laid horizontally. The walls were painted so as to give the place the appearance of an ordinary room; we all sat on a pair of benches placed there face to face and waited. Then, suddenly, it started. "Surprise" was too modest a word; that instant, I panicked as everyone else apparently did.

Perhaps I was the first among the group to regain my mind. I looked around and saw a girl who wore a beautiful kimono groveling on the floor quietly mourning, with her fingers feebly scratching the floor panel. I felt a pain on one of my knees and found that a male student sitting next to me held it with all his strength, his face devoid of expression, eyes wide open with pupils dilated. Perhaps I was in a panic for only a few seconds, although I felt it to be an indefinitely long period during which my cognitive system must have been in a frantic turmoil to make out the utterly incomprehensible sense data. I began to "see" things normally again only when it finally sorted out an answer: The cylinder turned constantly with a moderate speed. The benches were a swing system that moved synchronously with the cylinder for a while and then swung back in the opposite direction. But the impression you received inside this simple apparatus, unprepared, was just beyond description. It was either that Hell had broken loose or that the universe had collapsed around you. Interestingly enough, my memory of the experience is closely associated with the sense of darkness (the illumination was constant) and an ear-shattering noise (the apparatus made no noise, even though we must have shouted at the top of our voices).

Now let me turn to the problem of time and consider first the temporal mechanism with which the primary system is driven. If we pay attention only to the fact that the primary system constantly provides quite veridical expectations, we might conclude that it must be the work of a very effective real-time simulation device controlled by an extremely precise internal clock. It is true that the primary system must operate on a real-time basis, but note that the exact *real-timeness* may be produced by constant feedback from the real world as well; one may let the real world keep the timing for the system. Apparently this is economical, and we may well assume that it is the primary system's way. The updating through feedback would not be sufficient for the primary system to dispense entirely with an internal clock, however. Various known facts concerning perception lead us to believe that the primary system operates in discrete steps consisting of a few distinct phases, each of which requires a finite time for its completion. For instance, first, sensory input requires an integration over time; second, identification of a sensory message against a given context may be easy or difficult, and the information-processing time may vary accordingly; and third, providing the next context according to the identified feedback message would consume some finite time. In all, the updating through feedback can be done only at discrete moments with varied intervals, where the variability is further enhanced by movements of sensory organs and shifts of attention. As precise timing is crucial in some types of response control and also in the perception of movement, too much variability in the cognitive processing cycle must be counterbalanced by some kind of smoothly operating timing device. If one calls this an internal clock, then man and animals do have a very good internal clock, though good only for timing of brief moments. Apparently, there seems little theoretical difficulty in assuming some neurophysiological processes that can perform this function.

It is interesting to observe that even at this basic level the primary system's redundancy processing appears to exert a strong influence on the perception of spatio-temporal events. Many experimental results concerning apparent movement (for example, Helson, 1930; Abe, 1935; Cohen, 1967; Aiba, 1973) may lead us to suspect that some laws of conservation must play a vital part in the primary system's operation, which may be one of the system's inborn functions comparable to Hebb's primitive unities (Hebb, 1949). In contrast, the *secondary system*, by which I mean collectively all the strata of cognitive system higher than primary, comes to acquire conservation laws during each individual's development, as demonstrated by Piaget.

When we come to much longer time intervals than those handled by the primary system, there is no evidence for dependable internal clocks. It is well known that many animals possess certain fairly precise *timers*, which set off predetermined activity patterns at prescribed moments in the recurring cycles of time, and these timers are even adjustable to external cycles of events. But we should not mix up timers with clocks, even though the term *internal clock* is often loosely applied to both types of internal timing devices. A clock is something that allows the user a context-free evaluation of the passage of time of virtually *any* length within a limit, while a timer is taken to be a context-bound, fixed-interval signaling system.

By saying that we have no dependable internal clocks for long intervals, I do not imply that we have no internal clocks at all for these time intervals. On the contrary, as much of the literature on "psychological time" suggests, we indeed have explicit feelings about the passage of time and can make intuitive temporal judgments. Even rats can make temporal discriminations and control their behavior accordingly, as the results in the DRL (differential reinforcement of low rate) experiments clearly show (Farmer and Schoenfeld, 1964). The fact that the findings obtained with man are messy and mutually contradictory indicates only that we have a set of rather ill-built internal clocks whose outcomes are unreliable. This very unreliability, among other things, strongly suggests that these clocks are products of the secondary system, and the secondary system makes them upon demand out of bits and pieces — mostly out of lousy physiological timers. Note that there must be plenty of physiological processes, like breathing, that repeat themselves, and they are lousy timers because they are not originally built as timers and they are context bound. Still, when necessity arises, the secondary system can make a makeshift clock out of them and count off their cycles. Of course, this is pure speculation, but for that matter, everything is speculation concerning the secondary system, which, in the case of man, is such a tremendous system that hardly any trustworthy theory has been established concerning its internal structure. However, it might occasionally be worthwhile to let our speculation fly freely, as I allow myself to do in the rest of this paper.

As we move into the realm of the secondary system, I want to make the following points explicit. First, note that a system can have an internal clock without possessing a notion of time. So these two entities, the internal clock and the notion of time, must be kept separate. However, there is a certain relationship between them, and I conjecture that our secondary system would never have acquired a notion of time if the primary system had no internal clock or if the secondary system had a perfect internal clock. To show the plausibility of the first part of this conjecture, let me consider space instead of time. There is no doubt that the primary system is endowed with some kind of "spatial alignment" operator (three-dimensional, though not necessarily Euclidean) to apply to sensory messages and to produce the "spatial" perception. To me, it seems very unlikely, if not totally impossible, for the secondary system to come to bear a full-fledged notion of space without being originally guided by the primary system's spatial alignment operation. Though comparatively less obvious, I think the same must be true with the notion of time.

The second part of the conjecture, that a perfect internal clock must have inhibited the birth of a notion of time, appears to be more straightforward. Taking for granted that the secondary system develops "notions" and builds conceptual schemata with them, let me inquire into the purpose underlying these activities. I am a holder of the view that the information processing of the cognitive system is not an end itself but, at least originally, has been meant to serve the purpose of control. This relationship is quite obvious with the primary system, and there is no reason to doubt that the same holds with the secondary system, too. So, if the secondary system happens to come by a perfect internal clock, what need can there be for a notion of time?[6]

Whether or not these brief arguments satisfy the reader, I must confront an inescapable question: What exactly is it, upon requiring a control by the secondary system, that led the system to create a notion of time? Apparently, everything that comes after external clocks and external calendars is beside the point, as external clocks and calendars cannot be made without a notion of time. Another possibility — the need to regulate interpersonal activity patterns — seems also off the mark, since such a need must be preceded by the need to regulate one's own activity pattern over time, (i.e., *planning* one's behavior beyond the immediate future). To me this seems the most plausible candidate for the need responsible for the birth of the notion of time, if only one could somehow explain how such an "over time" need could have existed in the first place without a notion of time.

In order to attempt this difficult explanation, I need to discuss briefly the role of (long-term) memory in the cognitive system. As I mentioned earlier, the primary system needs a powerful simulator to provide veridical contexts nearly all the time. The context it provides offers some, but not too large a number of alternative messages about the state of the environment against which the given sensory input is to be matched.[7] If the resultant matching with one of the alternatives is good enough, the primary system goes on to the next cycle. The identified sensory state and the current state of bodily movements become the joint input both to the response control system and to the simulator. Then the simulator automatically goes about providing the next context.

Obviously, the simulator must have access to the data for simulation, and the data must consist primarily of one's past experiences, processed or unprocessed, which are assumed to locate in a place traditionally called the memory. Note, however, that for the smooth, rapid functioning of the primary system, no time can be wasted in an elaborate memory search for information retrieval. How does the primary system's simulator overcome this difficulty? The answer seems simple to me. The memory *is* the simulator. For there is no reason to assume that human memory is structureless, a mere storage house. To me it is all the more plausible to consider memory as a dynamic system itself rather than as a silent heap of information, and we often get a wrong impression about the true nature of memory only because we tend to view it from the angle of the secondary, conscious use of it. Note that the primary system must be much older than the secondary system in evolution, and the memory system must have evolved originally with the evolution of the primary system. Nature would certainly have disfavored the inefficiency of developing two systems separately when it could have achieved the same goal with one. At least conceptually, it seems not too difficult to work out a neural model for dynamic memory, essentially a treelike structure, which we may hereafter call the *context-tree*.

Now let me return to the role of the secondary system. When the input matching by the primary system fails to produce an exact match, the secondary system is called in to take over the information processing. There appear to be two cases for the primary system's failure.[8] The first kind is obtained when the matching is not exact, but there exists a general, overall agreement between the given and the expected. In this case the primary system is versatile enough to keep providing contexts while the secondary system works in parallel on the "novel or ambiguous perception." The second case is obtained when the given sensory message is totally out of context, in which case the primary system's context-providing function is suspended and the perception disrupted, as in my experience inside the Surprise House, until the secondary process succeeds in finding a proper flow of context congruent with the given sensory process.

In either case the secondary system's task is to *reset* at the right place the state of the primary system's context-providing function. How does the secondary system go about this task? One thing is clear. The secondary system must be able to trace external processes faster than real time. Note that sometimes the failure of the primary system may have been caused by making a wrong branching at some node of the context-tree. In this case the secondary system must retrace the context-tree, find the wrong branching, and hurry back to the present moment on the corrected path. Obviously, there is no logical difficulty in this faster than real-time tracing, as the secondary system need not pause on the way to wait for each intermediary context to be confirmed. Of course, the secondary system is not always able to enjoy a job as easy as this one, and it often has to engage in a wild hunt for clues. In my speculation, the roles of notions, concrete or abstract, and the conceptual schemata built with them are primarily to make this wild, rapid hunt systematic and efficient. If I am allowed to use a clumsy analogy, which I am afraid might be misleading rather than enlightening, the fundamental structure of memory, or of the context-tree, is like streets and roads upon which the primary system, an eternal pedestrian, always treads on foot, guided by a floating spirit called sensory feedback. On the other hand, the secondary system, a more modern contraption evolutionarily speaking, is a much faster traveler, can flit around the world either by driving or flying, and is called up by the primary system every once in a while to hunt for the lost guiding spirit. What I want to imply by this analogy is that, even though the hyperstructure of the conceptual schemata covers exactly the same area as does the primary system of memory, these two structures belong to two separate, distinct systems. I want to emphasize, particularly, that we are likely to be greatly mistaken when we deplore the awkwardness of our long-term memory, since it is tantamount to complaining about the inefficiency of the secondary system's wild goose chase utilizing its highways, airline systems, and also, I must add, the almost instantaneous signaling system called association. Not only is this secondary use of memory by the secondary system worth applause, but also we should always be aware of the almost unfailing efficiency of the primary system's primary use of memory.

So much for the reinstatement of memory. Note that the secondary system's activity is not always tied up by requests from the primary system. In times of leisure it will attend to its own business, building notions, building schemata, and sometimes making a free run over the context-tree. It is free in the sense that its course is not bound by sensory feedback. To assume the secondary system to own this last faculty is surely natural, as a more constrained version of this activity is one of the secondary system's routine jobs for the primary system. The point I want to draw the reader's attention to here is that this free ride is a rudimentary form of prediction.

At this point it is vitally important to recognize that, even though the context-tree is a fairly veridical representation of the spatio-temporal configuration of the external environment, it needs to be veridical only in a topological sense. For any system that works under constant external feedback, correct branching is all that is required for taking the right path. Imagine, for example, a map you scribble on a pad of paper to hand to your friend visiting your house. As a rule, such a map is a mess metrically. But as long as the routes are correctly represented topologically, your friend will reach your house. Only when your friend asks you how long he has to be on Route so-and-so do you need to add an approximate distance to your memo.

Indeed, there are occasions when it is desirable to add to your topological cognitive map a supplementary note on spatio-temporal distances. The need to turn the above-mentioned rudimentary prediction into a real one may very well serve as a motivation to create a systematic format under which these supplementary notes acquire consistency. This motivation, *then*, might have created a notion of time somewhere in the long history of evolution. (Note that this "then" stands for a long and elaborate argument that has not yet been made.)

Instead of concluding this paper (no one can conclude time), let me move to a new topic on time. Before writing this paper, I was chatting with my friend, Imai, over a glass of brandy. As usual, I was teasing him with seemingly unsolvable questions, and I asked, "Why do we use metaphors like 'flowing river' and 'shooting arrow' for time, the things that can hardly be used as external clocks?" He mused for a while, as usual, and a cryptic answer returned to me: "That's it!"

"What's it?"

"External clocks utilize cyclic events, you see. In order to make cyclic sequence of events cyclic, you must have something noncyclic, uniformly flowing, beneath it. A figure needs a ground. Time is the ground for the clock."

After some information processing, my secondary system decided that it liked this idea. So I bought it and poured another brandy into his glass.

NOTES

1. One should not, however, take too lightly the power of abstract notions in human affairs. People have invented quite a few abstract notions about the other groups of people whom they do not really know personally. Unfortunately, these abstract notions are very often loaded with emotion, and, inasmuch as they are effective as emotion manipulators, they are much less useful for scientific purposes.

2. I am still in some doubt whether we should characterize consciousness as a subsystem of the cognitive system. It is plain, however, that consciousness is closely related to the executive, high-order activities of the cognitive system, and these activities are perhaps too slow to directly interfere with the rapidly and constantly running basic machinery of the primary system.

3. I found this citation in Neisser's book (Neisser, 1967), and to the book I owe much in writing this paper.

4. It is estimated that it takes about 10 milliseconds to visually identify an English letter (Sperling, 1963). Though efficiency cannot be judged by such figures alone, this figure is not too impressive.

5. This is one of the most important axioms of information theory, though often overlooked in its application.

6. A similar argument also applies to the notion of space. Note that the object identification is apparently more important to the primary system than the distance estimation, so that we have perceptual constancy that facilitates the former and impairs the latter. Therefore, the secondary system is in a similar situation with both space and time; the primary system supplies to it no ideal materials with which to build a perfect measuring device for either space or time.

7. I am speculating here only about dominant features of the primary process, neglecting details. Especially note that by "matching" no specific cognitive theory like "template matching" is implied.

8. There are other types of failures as well, though not discussed here.

REFERENCES

Abe, S. 1935. Experimental study on the correlation between time and space. *Tohoku Psych.* Folio 3:53–68.

Aiba, T. S. 1973. Apparent radial motion in stroboscopic illumination. Paper read at U.S.–Japan Seminar on Space and Motion Perception, Honolulu.

Cohen, J. 1967. Psychological time in health and disease. Springfield, Ill.: Charles C Thomas.

Farmer, J., and W. N. Schoenfeld. 1964. Inter-reinforcement times for the bar pressing response of white rats on two DRL schedules. *Journal of Experimental Animal Behavior* 7:119–22.

Hebb, D. O. 1949. The organization of behavior. New York: Wiley.

Helson, H. 1930. The tau-effect — an example of psychological relativity. *Science* 71:536–37.

Jacobson, H. 1951. The information capacity of the human eye. *Science* 113:292–93.

Neisser, U. 1967. Cognitive psychology. New York: Appleton-Century-Crofts.

Shor, R. E. 1959. Hypnosis and the concept of the generalized reality-orientation. *American Journal of Psychotherapy* 13:582–602.

Sperling, G. 1963. A model for visual memory tasks. *Human Factors* 5:19–31.

5 THE BOUNDARIES
OF THE NOTION OF TIME

THE INCONGRUENT NOTIONS OF TIME

Occasionally my ignorance frustrates me, not only about time itself but also about what I really want to know of time. Obviously, trying to "define" time is a fool's errand. To define a notion is to find for it an equivalent ideational construct made of some other, usually more primitive, notions. The prerequisite for a successful definition, however, is that *every* aspect of the target notion is represented by some of the component notions used for the definition. Any attempt to define time, therefore, is bound to be ridiculous, since nothing in this world even remotely resembles time.

If one looks at analogies as poor and incomplete definitions, however, the analogies for time popular in many different cultures, such as the "flying arrow" and the "flowing river," seem to suggest a certain kinship of time, however tenuous, with "space" and "movement." The kinship,

This paper was published in *The Study of Time III, Proceedings of the Third Conference of the International Society for the Study of Time*, J. T. Fraser, N. Lawrence, and D. Park, eds. (New York: Springer-Verlag, 1978), pp. 370–88. Copyright © 1978 by Springer-Verlag New York, Inc.; used by permission. I am indebted to J. T. Fraser for his encouragement and to The Netherlands Institute for Advanced Studies in Humanities and Social Sciences for its excellent intellectual atmosphere, both of which were necessary to the completion of this paper.

therefore, should provide a precious few clues to those who intend to study time, as clues are scarce, anyway.

Before taking up this issue, we must pose a grave question about what we mean by the study of time, if time cannot be defined. Is it to understand time? But we do understand time, at least on the intuitive level. Otherwise, how could we communicate with others about time, let alone discuss it, without a definition? Truly, someone (if there was one) who first got the rudimentary notion of time in a prehistoric era must have had great difficulty in conveying the idea to others. But the notion should have been a great achievement, matched nicely with other notions in the (prehistoric) human cognitive system, so that some of his fellows, too, might have succeeded in developing the same notion for themselves with minimum hints from its originator.

This mode of learning notions as a process of self-development aided by culturally and personally provided hints applies to the acquisition not only of the notion of time, but also of most of the *fundamental* primitive notions in our culture, those that cannot be verbally defined. Such a mode of learning is possible, however, only when the notions are strongly in accord with the other components of our cognitive system so that they can emerge almost as a necessity. Everything suggests that our intuitive understanding of time is natural and *nearly* complete; virtually no misunderstanding or miscomprehension occurs in our daily conversations about time — perhaps as long as one does not hear an esoteric argument about time given by a member of the International Society for the Study of Time. Nonetheless, it remains a mystery why an argument about time almost never fails to stir up considerable curiosity and excitement in the audience. Perhaps there is something deep inside the smooth surface of our intuitive understanding of time, a feeling of insufficiency, that calls for an explanation.

Come to think of it, however, this is not an exceptional situation. There are many things in the world of which one believes his understanding to be perfect — of his wife, for instance. But just one hint about Desdemona was enough to shatter Othello's belief of perfect understanding and would be enough for many others under similar situations. One suddenly feels how shallow his former understanding has been, which often results in an intensive quest for finding "truth." Why truth, which is most likely unpleasant? Perhaps he wants to recover security and possibly to regain the power of control; only with true knowledge can one plan with confidence and exert control.

Such a statement may sound like the bad habit of a psychologist, always eager to find a vulgar cause, such as the power of control, instead of believing in a noble search for information. This, however, is an unfair discrimination. As will be discussed later, information and control are twin notions, inseparably characterizing the basic human motivations. In any case, the issue of the controllability of time is an intriguing one, overtly or covertly tinging human interest in time. Is it not frustrating that, living in the era of great technological breakthroughs in controlling space, when people are hopping around the surface of the earth with tremendous speed, some having reached even as far as the moon, we are yet tied to a raft helplessly floating over the stream of time? With the aid of clocks, we have learned how to adapt ourselves to time, but would it not be far better if we could navigate the stream of time up and down, if we could stay in the midstream for a while (to stay young, of course) by dropping a time-anchor?

Well, that will take care of the question why a news agency phoned me excitedly as soon as they heard that I was studying time. In many cases, however, it seems to be the mysteriousness of time that attracts people's attention, rather than its controllability. But they are not really separate issues, and as issues they are not very traditional ones. The reason for this conjecture is that, if they really were old, there should have been worship of a deity who controlled time. Note that worship is an indirect way to control; the worshipper wants to influence the deity who has the mysterious power to control important entities. He is also known, or assumed, to be appeased by being worshipped, so a causal passage is open for the worshipper to exert an indirect control over the entity. Apparently, in ancient religions there were only deities to represent time and to control fate, but none to control time itself (Fraser, 1975). Instead, most of the gods just followed time as given, like six days for work and one day for rest, even though many of them exhibited great power in neglecting the spatial limitations under which mortals were, and still are, helpless. Combining these odds and ends of ancient beliefs, we may conclude that time was once thought of as the uncontrollable, universal regulating agent that gods and men were equally bound to obey. When an entity is believed to be absolutely uncontrollable, there is obviously no sense in worshipping it; no feeling of mysteriousness can emerge either, as mystery presupposes the possibility that what is now mysterious could also be otherwise.

If there is some truth in such an argument, we may then suppose that time has become mysterious rather gradually, contingent on, perhaps, the development of the second notion of time, *spatialized time*. The notion of spatialized time, which obviously owes much to the invention and refinement of clocks for its development, later culminated in the contemporary notion of physical time, particularly that in relativity theory. If this had been the only notion of time we had, there would not have been any mystery. But we have another, much older notion of time as an indispensable component of our cognitive system, which, for that very reason, cannot just die out, even under great pressure from the other notion of time with all of its haloing glory of contemporary physics. The conflict between the two notions has become acute; cognitive tension has been increased[1] and the sense of mystery magnified.

In order to clarify the nature of this conflict, we need to speculate a little about the nature of the nonphysical, nonspatial, intuitive notion of time. The source of this notion should be found in the most basic class of animal behavior relevant to time (i.e., *timing* behavior). Timing behavior is essential for survival. It is known to be facilitated in animals by various sorts of internal timing mechanisms, such as circadian rhythms. The basic motivation that led to the invention of clocks was a desire to improve the precision of timing; their use to tell time seems to have come later, as an afterthought.

Now, what is the essence of timing behavior? *Waiting* comes first. Then the temporarily frozen system, the brain and the muscles, must be kicked into activity at the right moment. The process taking place in the cognitive system for timing behavior may be described in the following way. The primary cognitive components representing the person himself and the bow and the arrow held in his hands must be kept still, while the ones representing his enemy, stalking behind a bush toward him, should be left to simulate the enemy's movement until the expected (or perceived) moment of attack. Then all the components in his cognitive system must be brought into full action.

As I have discussed in a previous paper (Toda, 1975), freezing the activities of the primary cognitive components is a difficult task, as it is their nature to be actively simulated; therefore, the freezing and waiting with mounting tension will contribute a rather uncomfortable part of the direct temporal experience accompanying the timing behavior. On the other hand, the moment of activation and the complete removal of inhibition will bring an overtone of freedom and creation to the succeeding experience.

At any rate, if we assume that these freezing and activating cognitive operations are the source of our intuitive notion of time, there are further implications to consider. Note that when we *analyze* the content of our notions, the notions must be frozen. The best illustration for this proposition is the fact that when we analyze an operator notion represented by a verb — "run," say — the notion must temporarily be turned into a noun form such as "running," "to run," and the like. The standard use of a verb notion in the cognitive system is to apply it to an object notion such as "rabbit" and to let the latter really run for the purpose of simulating the real world process — that is, to see if a real rabbit is likely to run straight into the set trap. When such a notion is under cognitive analysis, however, its operational function must temporarily be suspended. It is, therefore, quite natural that the product of such cognitive analyses tends to be a static, timeless system. If the system requires time as a parameter, its spatialized version will do as a substitute. The very essence of our intuitive notion of time, "activate" as a verb, is then destined to be missing from our cognitive analytical products, as the frozen "activation" is no longer the same as "activate."

Another important aspect of intuitive time to be touched upon here is the distinction between the past and the future divided by the present, the distinction missing in the spatialized time of physics. I am interested particularly in why we tend to think as an established fact that the past is determined and the future is undetermined. Epistemologically speaking, the past and the future should not *exist* in the real world, since whatever that exists must be in the present. So what does one mean when he says that the past is determined and the future is undetermined?

It is only in the cognitive system that the distinction is meaningful, where some of the cognitive *events* are earmarked as "past" and some as "future." This is because the cognitive system has two functions, confirming by observation the events that are taking place now, the records of which are earmarked as "past," and extrapolating by simulation future events, the outcomes of which are earmarked as "future." Once they are recorded, they all belong to the memory of the cognitive system, but these two types of memorized events must be distinguished from each other because the cognitive system is apparently operating under a normative rule that "future" events must be taken as modifiable but "past" events should be taken as fixed. The only reason I can think of for this normative (and therefore not necessarily strictly observed) rule is the survival value it provides.

All these views of mine stated so far concerning our intuitive notion of time are wild speculations. We may believe, however, that this notion, which recalcitrantly defies ordinary content analysis, perhaps for the wild reasons stated above, still hides some important clues to the nature of time, which may be uncovered only by unconventional analyses. As one such unorthodox but promising procedure, let me propose *imagination stretching*. How far can one go to find the territorial border of the notion of time, to delineate time indirectly by eliminating nontime?

ENTROPY, AGAIN!

My natural first stop in this exploration is the disputed border between physical time and intuitive time, where the cognitive tension is the greatest. Tension attracts snoopers as honey attracts bees, for the clue to solving conflicts is most likely to be found there. The point of dispute is the claim by physical time over the conceptual region called the direction of time, for which ever-increasing entropy is the major and, in fact, the only supporting ground. A suspicion-ridden mind, however, would immediately find a certain amount of shakiness about this character, entropy. Why must physicists use so many human words in explaining entropy? Order and disorder. But nature itself should have no "notion" of order and disorder. Work. But nature does not work. And a heat engine, indeed, as if nature should want to have one itself! Note that a heat engine alone is not enough to turn negentropy into work. An operator of the machine is needed to set it up *properly* within the thermal system, and he will need a proper manual to refer to for the correct control of the machine.

We have here the fundamental trio as the indispensable catalyst for the conversion of negentropy into work: the engine that symbolizes control, the know-how that represents information, and the man who is the link between information and control. So whenever I try to imagine the thermal death of the universe, I cannot help having an image of an old physics professor, emeritus perhaps, carrying a heat engine under his arm, finding himself entirely at a loss — and I am serious, as without him the picture of thermal death is incomplete.

Old professor or not, this indispensable operator of Carnot's heat engine always strikes me as the symbol of man, a creature who is constantly looking for negative entropy. Whenever he finds it, he is there to install the machine. If he doesn't have a proper machine, he tries to invent one with which to convert negentropy into work. Work for what? Perhaps for more work. One thing is certain. He is obsessed. He has accumulated conserved information and thus far has tremendously increased his power to control. He is always working like mad. It is quite true that only the obsessed can really achieve something noteworthy in the end, like interfering with the processes of the universe. But I add to this conclusion the reminder that the majority of the obsessed ruin themselves.

Emerging from this brooding, let me emphasize that if entropy needs a heat engine, it also needs a man. So inside the abstract mathematical armor of the notion of entropy a man must be hidden, smuggled from beyond the border of physics, the agent who is responsible for the directionality of time.

When I arrived at this conclusion, another suspicion suddenly hit me. Is this operator of the heat engine the only alien agent in the kingdom of physics? No. Suspicious figures called observers are now flitting around inside and outside of physical systems, creating new paradoxes while pretending to resolve some old ones. It could be that some bigger conspiracy is going on to undermine the supposedly nonhuman physics, within the scheme of which entropy may only be a minor accomplice. May there be peace, but a good snooper must have a heart of stone.

SPACE VS. TIME

The obvious next stop of our exploration is the border between space and time. The relationship between these two notions appears peaceful enough, as space is always considered as a remote but still the closest kin of time, even though the territory of time has recently been encroached upon by space more and more often.

Why is space considered the closest kin of time? Aren't they dissimilar to each other? They certainly are. We have to admit, however, that they have similarities, too, and let me examine first the nature of their common blood. The first thing that comes to my mind is their shared attribute of continuity, not the continuity of themselves, but the continuous *relations* they hold with *objects*. (The continuity of time itself may very well be a garment of time borrowed from space.) Consider space first.

When an object moves within space, its spatial locus must, so we usually seem to believe, form a continuous line. The temporal version of this spatial continuity for the movement of objects is the temporal preservation of objects. If an object exists at one moment, then it should exist at the immediately succeeding moment. Of course, the observable attributes of the object may change, but not so much as to impair its identity. In particular, the identity preservation of one's own self is vital; for without it there would certainly be no time.

How strict is this rule of preservation? Evidently not so strict as to allow no exception. It is quite true that we love preservation; we love physicists who provide us with preservation laws. Nowadays our trust in them is so great that, whatever odd things may happen in our universe from now on, we expect them to eventually come up with some esoteric conservation laws under which everything in our universe is ultimately conserved, no matter what strange hide-and-seek matter and energy (and their higher derivatives) may play, popping in and out of some unobservable holes of space-time.

Nevertheless, we can occasionally give up preservation. Haven't we already given up the preservation of the soul? In the past we accepted a magical view of the world that was hardly scrupulous about preserving objects. The notion of time, therefore, certainly does not require the preservation of everything. On the contrary, in a world where nothing changes, including the observer himself, the notion of time will hardly make any sense. How about, then, the other extreme? What would you feel if your soul as a pure observer were snatched to another universe where your sensory data changed so drastically and discontinuously that no identity of anything could really be kept? Reported LSD experiences may offer a crude approximation of this situation, and I may conclude that the identity preservation of at least some of the external objects is essential to keeping the sense of time. So my tentative conclusion is that for time to exist, at least some part of the world must preserve its identity while the attributes of the rest must undergo changes. What an untidy conclusion! But that is time. If someone claims to have obtained a clear-cut conclusion about time, we have a very good reason to reject it outright.

In comparison to time, space apparently presents disillusioningly little puzzle, though this plainness may very well be another illusion. Space, manifested in the spatial coordinates of objects, seems to be almost on a par with other attributes of objects, as Yuki demonstrated when he aligned sensory attributes from the most spacelike to the most space-unlike on the basis of his experimental study of apparent movement (Yuki, 1965). From the results of his experiment, Yuki concluded, in effect, that space is practically no different from the dimensions of sensory attributes, while time is entirely something else.

This is about the spatial orientation of objects. Now let us consider the continuity of locomotions in space. It is needless to remind the reader that no other sensory attributes possess this property of strictly continuous change. True, we have never observed a discontinuous locomotion of objects in physical space, but the issue here is whether our intuitive notion of space allows the possibility of such a locomotion. The affirmative answer to this question is common in ancient religions, folklore, and science fiction. Apparently, there were many gods, demons, and magicians who had the power to show up anywhere their whim led them, and the heroes in science fiction flit around the world by a special means called *teleportation*, which allows them to show up at the destination of their trip without bothering to fill in the spatial intermediary points.

Note that the traded goods of science fiction writers are stretched imaginations, and they must trade with discretion. If the imaginations produced are too timid, they would fail to be interesting, and if they are too bold, few would be able to follow. Good imaginations therefore ought to settle in the borderline area of intuitive acceptability. So science fiction provides a very valuable source for my investigation, as do myths and legends, and very often the basic repertory of ideas is the same in all these. This means that the contents of our basic intuitive notions have remained mostly identical through the whole process of civilization, except for a few minor but significant additions. For example, the notion of time travel was created only after the spatialized time of physics became a common knowledge of people, to which topic I shall come back shortly.

Compared to time travel as a source of a host of paradoxes, teleportation is a triviality. It is just a nice way of traveling, well within the range of imaginability. So the rejection of continuous spatial locomotion as an unbreakable law hardly disrupts our intuitive notion of space, though it certainly does damage to the physicist's notion of space. Does it, really? Even though they would coolly reject the idea of teleportation today for the reason that it clashes with their model of the universe, they would not show the least scruple in writing a Nobel prize–winning article about the structure of the continuous fourth dimension of space through which teleportation takes place, if someone, very likely one of them, happened to have invented it.

One may argue, however, that the idea of teleportation does not seriously interfere with our intuitive notion of space only because the happenings will be within the range of acceptable exceptions. Only certain people may teleport, but everything else will locomote continuously. This argument has a ground. It would be a madhouse if every object teleported. It is, however, hard to imagine this situation, as the identity of objects would then be lost, too, and our understanding of the world would be impossible.

Before going into the topic of time travel, the temporal version of teleportation, let me remind the reader of the striking easiness of imagining the fourth dimension of space. If you have any doubt, just ask a young boy. With the risk of getting a contemptuous stare for your ignorance, you will learn all about the fourth dimension of space with lurid stories about its inhabitants, heroes, and monsters. Such a fourth dimension is none but the four-hundredth version of Never Never Land, but significance ought to be attached to the imagination-stirring characteristic of the fourth dimension. Even newspapers occasionally carry a headline like "ABDUCTION INTO THE FOURTH DIMENSION? AIRPLANES MISSING IN BERMUDA TRIANGLE AREA" with 90 percent mockery and 10 percent awe. In science fiction literature, we naturally find a tremendous variety of more-than-three dimensional spaces, strangely connected, warped, distorted, through which one can go, for example, to the Greater Magellanic Cloud within . . . well, the time needed for the voyage varies widely from author to author.

This prolificacy is striking if we put it against the utterly uncanny silence of science fiction authors concerning a second dimension of time. Of course, they have tried. They have invented some new times that deviate from contemporary physical time, but only slightly. There are circular times, branching times, multiple times, and so on, but they are all linear. In religion and philosophy the situation is the same. Even in physics I have never heard of an idea of two-dimensional time. This is strange, since, for example, the two types of expansions of the equation describing the coordinates of an object traveling with the speed of light, $x_1^2 + x_2^2 + x_3^2 = c^2t^2$, into $x_1^2 + x_2^2 + x_3^2 + x_4^2 = k^2t^2$ and into $x_1^2 + x_2^2 + x_3^2 = k^2(t_1^2 + t_2^2)$ seem formally equally easy (or equally difficult). At least, again formally, there is nothing that should discriminate t_2 against x_4. Of course, there is the issue of how to define velocity with respect to two-dimensional time. But the difficulty is of a conceptual nature rather than a logical one. Note also that when cosmologists discuss the expanding universe, they *fix* their time by identifying it with the local time of some privileged system of reference, while they let their *space* change (expand) freely. These things seem to indicate clearly that physicists, too, are strongly biased by their intuitive notions of space and time, which obviously place time in a far more privileged position than space.

TIME TRAVEL, PAST AND FUTURE

Now let us see how much we can stretch imagination within the range of linear time. Circular time and multiple time actually do not present any innovations concerning the notion of time. The former states only that the world process will eventually be repeated after some period of time and implies a sort of determinism. Concerning multiple time, science fiction writers were left behind by physicists who allowed each different system to have a different, though lawfully determined, local time. So, perhaps out of desperation, science fiction writers ascribed different *universes* to each stream of the multiple time flow, creating the so-called parallel universes representing complete *un*determinism in such a way that a mere possibility in one universe is cold reality in another. Apparently these two ideas borne by circular and multiple time reflect our notion of the past and the future, another integral part of our intuitive notion of time. So let us now proceed to the third version of extended linear time: branching time, or a temporal bypass through which we may time-travel.

As a matter of fact, time travel into the future is theoretically possible. An astronaut whose spaceship has undergone long and strong acceleration and deceleration will return to Earth preserving his physical youth only to find graves of his family; if he is lucky, he may be greeted by his great-grandchildren. Physicists assure us that this is not a paradox. Granting it, let me show that a paradox can still be created out of this situation. Consider a modern version of the flowing river analogy of time, a point moving on a line. The point represents one's "now," and by constantly moving it turns the region it has covered into the past and leaves the region still uncovered as the future. Even though seldom recognized as a formal representation of time, this obvious compromise between spatialized and intuitive time is popularly accepted, and many people use this picture, perhaps unconsciously, whenever the necessity arises to illustrate time. Now let me apply this model of individual time to the above situation: The astronaut lives the local time of his spaceship, and his travel is represented by his now-point constantly moving on the time line characteristic to the ship, while the now-point of the system Earth proceeds on its time line according to its local rate. This is as if two boats leaving the port together are going into two different channels. Is there any guarantee that the boats will meet exactly at the spot where the channels join again? How can one be sure that, when the astronaut's now-point reaches the temporal moment when the spaceship and Earth are scheduled to meet, the now-point of Earth, too, will reach exactly the corresponding temporal spot? If it does not, the astronaut meets the Earth where events have not yet happened, or the Earth where all the events have already happened. Apparently, complete determinism of the course of the universe is the easiest solution of this paradox, though many would find themselves reluctant to accept such a solution.

Complete determinism will create another paradox if we allow the possibility of real time travel into the past. In order to get to the past, one has to get on a time machine instead of a spaceship and spend some local "time" on the machine. The branching time stream that carries the machine will break into the main time stream at some temporal point in the past, where the passenger may meet his own younger self. The famous paradox of time travel begins when the time-traveler commits an exotic suicide by killing his younger self. If the younger self is killed, however, his older self, the killer, cannot exist. Therefore, there will be no murder, which will resurrect the younger self and the older self, and the murder will again take place, and so on.

At least three types of solutions have been suggested to resolve the paradox. The first one is based on determinism; the existence of the older self is good enough testimony that the murder did not take place in the past. So the time-traveler *cannot* kill his younger self, however hard he may try, and this implies that the *future* of the time-traveler has been determined, too. In contrast to this solution, the second idea is based on indeterminism; even the past is not determined, and the younger self may be killed. But as soon as the murder is committed, the world process that involves the returned time-traveler goes into a parallel universe, which is the deus ex machina to resolve the paradox. The third solution also allows the modification of the past. Whenever a modification like the murder takes place, its causal effect will propagate over the branching time system with a speed quicker than the normal, event-instigating time. So nothing will happen for a while after the murder, but when the propagated effect takes over the time traveler eventually, he simply disappears into thin air.

From these suggested solutions, one may draw the following conclusion: In order to resolve the paradoxes of time travel, an extra assumption, which is extrinsic to the time *per se*, is always needed, whether the assumption is deterministic or has an additional degree of freedom, such as the parallel universe or the second time governing the propagation of the effects of a causal modification. This, and the fact that the paradox seemingly disappears when we state "The astronaut will come back to see the old Earth much more aged than himself," are enough to make one suspect that this additional element was smuggled into the picture by the now-point model itself. For fear of dissipating the precious illusion of time travel entirely, however, I had better say no more.

UNTIMELY ENDING

The travelogue of my tour of investigation around the boundaries of the notion of time should include a few more places of interest but, dismayingly, the limitation of the *space* of this paper forces it to come to an untimely ending except for just a few cursory remarks. The topics all concern some logical paradoxes of time. The first is concerned with the well-known Bayes' theorem, which states that under certain conditions one can infer *with certainty* what the cause is by observing its effects. The apparent paradox is brought forth by the fact that Bayes' theorem is derived from probability axioms that contain no temporal statements. Therefore we must be able to reverse the direction of time contained in the argument to deduce, as another interpretation of Bayes' theorem, the complete predictability of the future. In fact this is impossible, but it does not create a paradox because Bayes' theorem, in this reverse interpretation, describes the condition under which the complete control of a future event is obtained. (See Toda, 1977, for more details.)

The second topic nagging my attention for a long time was related to Zeno's paradox concerning Achilles and the tortoise. The paradox, at its face value, is trivial since a statement consisting of infinite steps to describe a process that takes a finite time can hold its truth value also only for a finite time.[2] My question, however, is whether we can be sure that the end of a finite passage of time always becomes "now." Apparently, no logical difficulty is created if it doesn't. It is rather appalling to see it isn't even a matter of induction; if a finite interval of time does not meet its end, one cannot experience this happening, so that experience is powerless in deciding this issue.

As an intriguing example, consider what would happen if time suddenly started to go backward, by which I mean that all the physical processes began to retrace their former paths. Of course, such a possibility is not included within the framework of contemporary physics, but that may simply be because no physicist has ever experienced it. Actually, this last statement is the whole point of this argument; not only not physicists, but no one at all, could experience this reverse flow of time if it happened because, in this temporal phase, one does not perceive, does not memorize, does not learn, but *unperceives, unmemorizes,* and *unlearns*. (In this temporal phase entropy decreases, but who cares? In this world, Carnot's heat engine will turn backward futilely to turn work into heat!) Suppose that time oscillates between two temporal moments, *A* and *B*. When the time returns the earlier moment *A*, all of us will be brought back to the identical state we were once in at *A*, memory and all, and will begin to live the same life again, for the millionth time perhaps, without noticing it. The conclusion of this argument is that we shall never find out if this oscillating time is indeed the real nature of the universe.

The exact duplication of the repeated processes, however, is a determinism. What if there is a quantum or two miserasure in someone's memory? That may create precognitions and prophecies. And precognitions and prophecies are, in contrast to the second dimension of time, well within the range of our stretched imagination of time, and therefore this oscillating time is also within the legitimate range of topics of this serious paper, which should end here. I would like to thank the reader, for the millionth time, for his patience in reading the same paper a million times.

NOTES

1. It is perhaps my predilection (due to my training) that I prefer to interpret the ubiquitous process characterized by conflict, tension, and its resolution at another level leading to a higher conflict, as something peculiarly human, rather than as something more metaphysical like Fraser's existential tension (Fraser, 1975) or Hegelian dialectic. Cognitive tension, however, is not the only conflict I am referring to. Social systems (as pointed out by Max Weber), engineering systems, or whatever always go through the same cycle as long as man keeps working on them.

2. I just want to put it on record that essentially the same argument given here concerning the solution to Achilles and the tortoise paradox and the unprovable observability of the end of a finite passage of time that has not yet passed was given in my earlier (in fact, the earliest) article (Toda, 1945).

REFERENCES

Fraser, J. T. 1975. Of time, passion and knowledge. New York: Braziller.
Toda, M. 1945. Jikan tetsugeaku josetsu [Prolegomena to a philosophy of time]. *Allzumenschliches* 1:10–44.
―――. 1975. Time and the structure of human cognition. In The study of time II. J. T. Fraser and N. Lawrence, eds. New York: Springer-Verlag.
―――. 1977. Causality, conditional probability and control. In New developments in the applications of Bayesian methods. A. Aykac and C. Brumat, eds. Amsterdam: North-Holland.
Yuki, K. 1965. Undo to Kukan [Movement and space]. In Collected papers in commemoration of the retirement of Prof. Yuki. Sapporo: Department of Psychology, Hokkaido University.

III FUNGUS-EATER ROBOTS

6 MAN AND THE FUNGUS-EATER

My model is not a model of man, but of a robot called the Fungus-Eater. So, this chapter is about a psychological conception of robots. In order not to disillusion the reader, however, I would like to add one more important point. The Fungus-Eater is not a real robot. It is an advanced robot of the future and will actually be built not sooner than 200 years from now, or maybe 2,000 years from now. Its appearance is just like that of a human being, and it has a very small but efficient computer in its head.

I said that the Fungus-Eater is a very advanced robot. But don't imagine a superman with the name "Fungus-Eater." The Fungus-Eater's intelligence is far inferior to that of human beings, and its IQ is, at least, comparable only to that of a rat, if you can measure the IQ of a robot and a rat. You may be puzzled. If the Fungus-Eater is as stupid as a rat, how can I call it an advanced robot? The reason is simple. Contemporary computer engineers cannot build a robot rat. Computer engineers have a long and hard way from the single-track, primitive computers they have today to the

This paper was originally prepared as a lecture for a class conducted by George A. Miller, which I delivered while visiting the Center for Cognitive Studies, Harvard University, in 1961–62 as a research fellow. I indeed owe a great deal for help in developing and organizing my thoughts to Miller, J. S. Bruner, and the other members of the center.

89

brilliant victory of building a robot rat that is smart enough to steal a piece of cheese from the kitchen of the inventor.

Now, I hope you are getting my idea. Present-day computers are very good at mathematical and logical computations, and they even play a game of chess, although they are as yet just mediocre players. As you see, the kind of tasks computers are good at are those that can be performed by single-track thinking routines. When a computer plays chess, it just follows fixed, predetermined rules. It evaluates each situation and each move as it has been instructed by the programmer. But it unfailingly follows the same fixed rules and does this with dogged persistence until the game is over. And this perseverance is the chief asset of a contemporary computer as a chess player. One amazing fact about computers is that they are not even fast thinkers, contrary to our commonsense understanding of them. With one of the most advanced programs of mechanical translation, one of the most advanced computers we have takes approximately twelve minutes to identify the grammatical structure of an English sentence of thirty-five words, a task even I can do within thirty seconds. This time comparison is by no means absolute, of course. The computer will take less than twelve minutes as programs improve. The point is, however, that the computer is not a terribly rapid thinker when you compare it with a human being. How much is one plus one? The answer "two" will pop up in your mind immediately. Very rapid. But the trouble with us is that we cannot maintain this pace, while the computer does keep up its pace untiringly and indefinitely. This makes the real difference between a human being and a computer in solving single-track problems.

Why, then, can we not keep up the pace, if that is the only thing that keeps us from being living computers? Reason number one: We forget and lose track of intermediary results. Reason number two: We cannot concentrate on a single-track task long. Suppose that you are given a sequence of numerals: 3, 5, -8, -2, and so on, and asked to sum them up mentally. You will get $3 + 5 = 8$ immediately. But then you have to spend a fraction of a second to fix that 8 in your memory so as not to lose it immediately. You also have to make a considerable effort not to be distracted by things irrelevant to the task. I would predict, however, that you would lose track sooner or later no matter how committed you were to the job. Before you got to the hundredth numeral, you would find yourself either forgetting the last outcome you had reached or thinking of something entirely irrelevant. "Why do I have to do this kind of silly calculation?" or "This number 52 I got looks fishy. Maybe I overlooked minus signs. Maybe I'd better go back and do it all over again," or "This number -10 reminds me of my bank account. It is certainly overdrawn. I should tell Smith to pay back the ten bucks I loaned him last week." And so on.

Certainly, it is very hard to be a living computer. We forget, and we are distracted. But, my question is: Are these characteristics of human beings really deplorable? Just imagine what would happen if we could not forget. The amount of information flowing in through our sense organs every moment is known to be very great. If this information just accumulated in memory, any memory storage of a finite capacity would soon be used up. Even if we assume that the capacity of our memory is nearly infinite, there arises another problem of how to use that terrible memory storage, where memories of one minute ago, one day ago, ten years ago, and ten years and one day ago are all piled up with equal density.

Any memory, either of computers or of human beings, is useful only if it has easy access to its stored items. Computers use an address system, like the telephone number system, by which the computer can call up necessary items anytime. Human memory uses a different system, of which little is known. But there is certainly a system, a very efficient one, by virtue of which we can usually recall necessary memory items fairly rapidly, even though our memory capacity far exceeds the capacity of any existing computer. The existence of an efficient recall system evidently means that our memory is efficiently organized. And any organization requires a certain amount of work to have it organized as such. This is just one of the laws of thermodynamics.

Let me put this issue in a slightly different context. Imagine a huge library to which is submitted every publication of every country in the world. Imagine how many librarians we would need to keep this ever-increasing library always organized to the extent that people could get any book they want without too long a delay. The memory in which nothing is forgotten is something like this library. The activity of memory bookkeeping would soon absorb all of our mental capability, or we would have to live with the messy, useless junk of our past experience. So we have to forget, and furthermore, we have to do the forgetting job according to certain automatic rules, since we cannot afford to pay attention to each piece of information we get and decide whether to forget it or not.

Automatic forgetting is therefore an ability we have, and we need that ability because we are taking in so much information from our environment. Contemporary computers do not have this ability primarily because they do not need it. They take in so little information as their input, just a sequence of numerals and some number of abstract symbols. As I have repeatedly pointed out, they are single-track mechanisms. And their input usually comes through a single channel.

A question arises at this point. Why do human beings need so many channels — visual, auditory, olfactory, gustatory, and tactile sense organs? Why should we take in so much information from the environment? It is easy to answer the question this way: We need various kinds of information because we do various kinds of things; we walk, we talk, we eat, we grasp things, we drive cars, we build houses, we organize society, we invent atomic bombs, and so on. But why should we do so many things? For adaptation? For survival? That is questionable. Imagine amoebas, or bacteria. They take very little information from their environment, and their repertoire of behavior is very limited. Still, they are quite adaptive. Or, imagine insects. Their input and output are far richer than those of amoebas, but still far poorer than those of human beings. And they are getting along with their environment very well.

So, if the multiplicity of functions of human beings exists for the purpose of survival, I should say that we have chosen a hard way of doing the job. The major characteristic of our way of adaptation lies in the point that we let our environment adapt itself to us, rather than adapting ourselves to the environment. This is the peculiar strategy, unprecedented in the history of the animal kingdom, employed by human beings. It is very hard to say if this strategy is good or bad, but one thing is certainly true: We cannot stop once we have started moving in this direction, since the artificially organized environment cannot maintain the organization by itself, and we have to invent further organization to take care of existing organizations. This mode of adaptation is certainly very dissimilar to the stable, static equilibrium of insect society and is rather to be called a kind of dynamic equilibrium, if it is an equilibrium at all. Anyway, there is no doubt that this is a very precarious stability. If we could ever attain a true static equilibrium in the future, it would be at the time when we had a completely servo-mechanized society; in a sense, such a society may be characterized as a robot culture. Houses would clean themselves and repair themselves. Weather would be under control. Automated factories would produce delicious synthetic foods. And the central computer would take care of all the troubles in the society. I still doubt, however, if human beings would be satisfied by that achievement, even though it would create for the first time in our history the possibility of a completely static society.

Anyway, I am afraid I have come too far afield. So, I will return to the point I wanted to make: The more we wish to control our environment, the more information we need about the environment. The greater the extent of our environment we wish to control, the greater would be the frequency that we encounter problems to be solved. The large amount of information we obtain from the environment will then be used to solve problems. But before starting to solve a problem, we should first find out where the problem is. The trouble is that problems do not usually advertise themselves as problems; they are usually innocently buried in the influx of information.

Furthermore, it is generally true that problems are easier to handle if they are detected quickly. So, we should look for problems by scanning the incoming information, shifting our attention from one input channel to another. As I mentioned before, we human beings are liable to be distracted by irrelevant information. But whether a piece of information is irrelevant or not — or, in other words, whether it does not contain a problem — cannot be decided until the information is examined. Our liability of distraction would just be a natural consequence of our *asset* of automatic problem detection: the kind of feelings one might have after concentrating on a simple job of mental calculation, as I mentioned before — that is, feelings like "What on earth am I doing now?" "I may be doing a wrong thing." "This reminds me of the problem I have with my bank account," and so on, all show that we have a good built-in problem detector.

Now I think I can come back to my original point — that is, we need a very, very advanced computer to simulate a rat in its natural habitat. I am afraid that probably you don't know how smart a rat is. Just after the last world war, I was living in a small boarding house in Japan, together with a couple of other tenants and a huge family of rats. As you might imagine, food was scarce then, not enough to support all of us, legal tenants and illegal tenants — the rats — alike. We had to fight according to the law of survival of the fittest. I tried every possible hiding place for my food, but the rats outsmarted me most of the time. As you know, Japanese houses are made of wood, and rats can cut holes almost anywhere. I bought a metal box and stored all my food inside the box. One day I opened the box; there was a rat inside, and I couldn't even catch him. One day I got a carton of butter. You couldn't imagine how precious a carton of butter was at that time. It was almost like gold. So I kept it in a place that appeared to me the safest hiding place. Every day I made sure that the carton was still there. And finally, I found that the carton was still there, but no butter inside. Of course, I got mad at the rats, but at the same time I was amazed and even admired their skill.

Many psychological experiments use rats as subjects. But the cute, docile, domestic white rats used in experiments belong to a different species from those cunning wild rats. Once, my wife, who was a rat psychologist, was keeping a dozen white rats in a cage. By some accident the cage was broken, and all the white rats escaped. She set a rat trap, which was a small cage used to catch a single wild rat, and was famous, or infamous, for its inefficiency; Japanese rats are very good at stealing bait from the trap without touching the trapping mechanism. What my wife found next morning was the trap cage packed and jammed with the whole dozen white rats. They didn't even eat the bait. Obviously they missed their cage. Thus, nothing much can be learned about wild rats from those domesticated white rats. And in fact, little is known about wild animals in their natural habitats.

How much, though, is known about human beings in their natural habitat, wild or domesticated? Psychology, of course, will tell you a lot about human beings in experimental laboratories. Experimental laboratories are, however, not our natural habitat. The major difference between these two types of environment can be stated this way: In experimental laboratories, information is usually coded in a single — or at most, a couple of — sensory dimensions in a fairly abstract way, and the kind of task given to human subjects usually requires persistent, single-track thinking. Remember that this simplification and abstraction are both necessary to obtain reliable information.

But, as you see from my previous discussion, human beings handle multiple-channel information input efficiently and engage in multiple-track thinking in their natural habitat. Our attention shifts from one part of the environment to another and jumps from one sensory dimension to another, and our thinking also shifts from one subject to another. A man is sitting on a sofa in the living room, watching TV, while sipping a cup of coffee. He hears the telephone ringing and goes to answer it. While talking with his friend over the phone, he pats his dog with his left hand, looks around the room, and notices some pencil scribblings on the wall. This is a moment of problem recognition to him, and he starts solving it. While constantly chatting with his friend, he figures out that it must be his son who did the scribbling and makes up his mind to scold him tomorrow morning. During this process of problem solving, he is also engaging in another task of memory item retrieval. His friend is talking about a girl, taking for granted he knows her. He now remembers her, but what is her name?

This is what we are doing all the time, without noticing that we are doing so many things at the same time because we do this shifting business so efficiently and smoothly. No wonder, therefore, that we are not good at the rigid, persistent concentration at which computers are especially good; and no wonder that human subjects in experimental laboratories prove themselves terribly inefficient. Experimental psychology tells us facts, but to obtain these facts we have been sacrificing important information coming from the multiplicity of our input channels and the multiplicity of our thinking and other activities, and this is the very place where human marvels lie.

In my opinion, contemporary experimental psychology is gradually moving toward the attainment of this new goal — that is, to uncover how people command their multiple functions and how they organize them in efficient and economical ways. My Fungus-Eater is also an approach pointing in the same direction, and it has two major purposes to serve. One is theoretical, and the other is practical. The practical aspect of this robot approach is to set up an experimental situation in which subjects play a science fiction-type game. To win this game, subjects must perceive, learn, think, and behave and must organize these activities efficiently. In this way we can study how good, or how bad, people are at performing this multiple-activity task. The theoretical side of this approach is represented by designing a robot that performs this job efficiently — designing, of course, not in terms of hardware, but in terms of programs to be given to the computer that the robot is supposed to have in its head. Now, what good does this approach do? First, I define a simple environment. Second, I define a simple robot. By combining these two simple but well-defined things, I expect to obtain a basic set of rules that apply to efficient behavior or, to be more specific, to how the multiple functions of the robot should be organized in order to attain its goal effectively.

I will not take the time to go into the details of this theoretical approach, but I will try to convey some idea of the way the theory goes. The following is an excerpt from the instruction to be given to the subject, which describes the task and the environment of the Fungus-Eater (see Chapter 7):

> You are a remote control operator of the robot miner nicknamed "Fungus-Eater," sent to a planet called Taros to collect uranium ore, which uses wild fungi growing on the surface of the planet as the main energy source for its biochemical engine. The uranium ore and fungi are distributed over the land of Taros, which is covered mainly with black and white pebbles, and little is known about the mode of their distribution. As the operator you can control every activity of the Fungus-Eater, including the sensitivity of the fungus- and uranium-detection devices. All the sensory information the robot obtains will be transmitted here and displayed on this console so that you will feel as if you are the Fungus-Eater itself.
>
> Note that your mission is to collect as much uranium ore as possible, and your reward will be determined in proportion to the amount of uranium you collect. Note also that the amount of fungi you collect and consume during your mission is irrelevant to the reward. Remember, however, that every activity of the Fungus-Eater, including the brain-computer operations, consumes some specified amount of fungus-storage. Never forget that the Fungus-Eater cannot move to collect further uranium ore or fungi once it runs out of its fungus-storage, and your mission would be over then and there. Good luck!

Let me recapitulate some important assumptions contained in this instruction. First, the Fungus-Eaters are uranium miners and nothing else. Only uranium has real inherent value to the Fungus-Eater, while the fungus itself has no such inherent value. The Fungus-Eater eats fungus because fungus is the means of getting uranium and not because it enjoys eating. Suppose that you are going to see a dentist. You are going to see a dentist merely because you want to be relieved of your tooth trouble and probably not because you enjoy seeing the dentist. So, seeing a dentist is just the means of attaining the end — that is, relief from the ailment. And you take that particular means because there is nothing else that brings you to the desired end. This is what fungus represents to the Fungus-Eater. Uranium is the pure end in the Fungus-Eater's world, and fungus represents the pure means. So, if you want to dignify the whole approach, or if you prefer abstract thinking, you may replace uranium and fungus by some abstract symbols like E and M, respectively, and you may turn the whole Fungus-Eater theory into an esoteric mathematics. But I do not care much for dignity, and I like science fiction-type representation because it stimulates subjects and my imaginations.

The Fungus-Eater needs to eat fungus because every activity of the Fungus-Eater requires more or less consumption of fungus stored in the Fungus-Eater's stomach. Particularly large amounts of fungus consumption are required when the Fungus-Eater travels on the ground. If the Fungus-Eater runs out of fungus-storage, it cannot move; and if it cannot move, it cannot collect any more uranium. That would be the end of the Fungus-Eater's mission, which would be called the death of the Fungus-Eater by starvation. The Fungus-Eater, therefore, must avoid the possibility of death as much as possible. In this sense the Fungus-Eater is survival oriented, even though survival per se has no inherent value to the Fungus-Eater.

The Fungus-Eater also consumes fungus when it thinks or when it uses its brain-computer. The amount of fungus required to perform a certain thinking process will be called the cost of the thinking process. Some of you may wonder why I need this concept of cost of thinking. As a matter of fact, this cost of thinking incorporates many factors that lead us to avoid long and elaborate thinking, and one of the most important factors is time. Even if you think you enjoy thinking, you must avoid long and elaborate ratiocination when circumstances demand quick decision. For example, suppose you are taking an examination. You might feel sure that you would get the correct and exact answer if you thought long enough. But if you spent too long thinking, you might not have enough time to write the correct answer. In a situation like this, you must compromise between precision and time. In the case of the Fungus-Eater, the same situation will be represented as follows: The Fungus-Eater will be able to figure out the best way of locomotion to get the maximum amount of uranium if it uses the most exact way of thinking. Yet if it does use this exact thinking procedure, it has to spend a lot of fungus to run the computer, while were it to expend too much fungus for thinking, it might not be able to perform the optimal plan due to the shortage of the fungus-storage. The Fungus-Eater also must make a compromise between the cost of thinking and the precision and must be content with some approximate solution.

I have also assumed that the Fungus-Eater has sensing devices. There is no reason to assume, however, that the sensitivity of these sensing instruments is fixed. The sensitivity of the Fungus-Eater's eyes may be made higher at a higher cost. It is, of course, good in view of the quality of decision making required to have a greater amount of information of a more precise kind. But, on the other hand, the improvement in decision making may not be enough to justify the high cost of precise object detection. So another compromise between cost and precision must be made here. It is also foolish to keep the sensitivity of the uranium-detection device and the sensitivity of the fungus-detection device both on the same level. When the Fungus-Eater is hungry, survival by finding fungus is a more serious problem than immediate uranium returns and, therefore, the sensitivity of the fungus-detection device must be increased to exceed that of the uranium-detection device. On the other hand, when the Fungus-Eater has ample fungus-storage, additional fungus-storage doesn't mean much to it; consequently, it should rather concentrate on uranium detection. This, therefore, emphasizes the need for a differential attention control.

These are, of course, just rough statements of the general rules of attention control. They should be more precisely stated, and they could be. But to get any more precision, we should deal with this problem in the totality of the context. For example, suppose that the Fungus-Eater is engaging in a thinking activity of finding some regularities in the fungus distribution. Then, even if the Fungus-Eater is not hungry, it should attend to fungi in order to get necessary information. But, once the regularity is found and the hypothesis confirmed, the sensitivity of the fungus-detection device should again be lowered to the economical level.

The sun rises and sets, even in this alien world, as the planet Taros revolves; as the relative position of the sun changes, the illumination on the ground also changes. This changing illumination, with black and white pebbles covering the ground of Taros, gives rise to interesting problems for the Fungus-Eater's perception, which are not discussed in this paper.

You may wonder what the Fungus-Eater will do during the night on Taros. Even at night the Fungus-Eater can detect uranium, but the faint starlight might not be enough to illuminate fungi. So, unless the Fungus-Eater has a stomach full of fungus, it will stand still at night to avoid wasting fungus. This is not comparable to human sleep, but certainly is comparable to some extent to the hibernation of some animals.

Now, let me proceed to the Fungus-Eater's decision making. Suppose that there are no objects in the Fungus-Eater's visual field except a uranium ore on the right and a fungus on the left. In which direction should the Fungus-Eater go? Always keep in mind that fungus has no inherent value. If the Fungus-Eater has ample fungus-storage, going to the right in the direction of uranium would be the better decision. But if the fungus-storage is so low that the probability of dying of hunger after the Fungus-Eater reaches the uranium ore is high, then going to the left toward fungus would turn out to be the better decision since the fungus will increase the probability of survival, and survival usually means more uranium return. But, again, this is not a general rule. The Fungus-Eater will prefer the suicidal act of going to uranium even if it is hungry if the uranium ore is terribly huge or if the land is known to be barren and a single fungus does not appreciably increase the probability of survival. This decision problem can be rigorously solved, of course, once the situation is completely specified.

When the number of alternative objects is only two, as in the above example, the Fungus-Eater need not much worry about the cost of thinking. But as the number of detected objects increases, the difficulty of figuring out the optimal course of travel will increase roughly exponentially, since an alternative course is defined as an ordered sequence of the objects to be visited. Accordingly, the cost of figuring out the optimal course would become nonnegligible, and the Fungus-Eater should use some approximation procedure in order to save cost. Deciding what type of approximation procedure is most effective under a given situation is a very difficult but interesting problem. If it is solved under various typical situations, it will shed some light on the way we human beings make our decisions.

Various interesting problems arise if we assume that there are obstacles to the Fungus-Eater's locomotion and detection on the land of Taros — rocks, for example. Suppose that the Fungus-Eater has figured out the optimal course. Then, the decision is made, and it will start executing the decision — that is, it will start its travels. As the Fungus-Eater travels, however, it will detect various new objects. For example, the Fungus-Eater may find that the course it is taking will lead it to a dead end. This certainly means a problem; so it will suspend the former decision as soon as it finds this out, and make another decision. Not all newly acquired pieces of information present a problem, however, and because of the high cost of thinking, the Fungus-Eater cannot afford to stop and think every time it gets new information. The trouble is that each item of information does not carry a label indicating itself as a problem, or as a nonproblem, and the Fungus-Eater must decide upon this before it begins to think. This then implies that the

Fungus-Eater needs to have an automatic problem-recognition mechanism that judges without elaborate thinking whether given information implies a problem or not. The judgment of this mechanism will be rough and approximate, but the roughness will be compensated for by the saving in the cost of thinking. It is also very natural that this problem-recognition mechanism is closely tied up with the differential attention control I have mentioned previously.

Another topic I would like to mention briefly is the utility of curiosity. Suppose that the Fungus-Eater has detected some uranium ore, and it can get to the object straight by going through a narrow pass between two parallel rock walls. But it can also get to the object by going around the outside of the rocks. Usually a straight course is better than a curved course, since the former requires less fungus consumption than the latter. In this case, however, the straight course is not necessarily better, since the Fungus-Eater cannot detect new objects while it is moving through the narrow pass, while there may be objects outside the pass more attractive than the uranium ore the Fungus-Eater is heading for. So, curiosity sometimes pays, and how much it pays depends entirely on the value of information; and the value of information is again a function of the state of hunger of the Fungus-Eater.

Let me conclude this chapter by suggesting an interesting scene. One day, the Fungus-Eater found a strange object. The object moved, and this was the first time it saw anything move in this static land of Taros. Furthermore, the strange object moved directly toward either uranium or fungus, and when this object reached either uranium or fungus, the uranium or the fungus mysteriously disappeared. Anyway, therefore, this object was harmful to it, and meant a real problem. So it followed the object and analyzed its behavior, using the thinking procedure for analyzing the laws governing the distributions of uranium and fungus. Finally it found out that the object collected uranium by eating fungi. So it figured out a solution to this problem. If this object needed fungi to keep itself going, it would be made immobile and would do no more harm if the Fungus-Eater took out all the fungi around the object while the object was standing still at night. So the Fungus-Eater accumulated as much fungi as possible while disregarding uranium and memorized the approximate positions of fungi around the object before sunset; when darkness came, it set out on the trip and executed its malicious plan. The next morning, what the Fungus-Eater found was that all the fungi around itself had also been taken away. This is a famous situation called "prisoner's dilemma" in the theory of games.

Anyway, my problem is: Will the Fungus-Eaters eventually reach the solution that cooperation is better than competition, even if we do not build in any cooperation programs?

7 THE DESIGN OF A FUNGUS-EATER:

A Model of Human Behavior in an Unsophisticated Environment

The major part of this paper will consider a design[1] of a robot to be sent to a hypothetical planet as a robot uranium miner, which sustains itself by eating fungi as its energy source. The design of this fungus-eating robot is expected to serve as a model of behavior for subjects who play a game, the fungus-eater game, in which they take the roles of the fungus-eater robots. Aside from this practical purpose, the model is also intended to serve as a heuristic for a general model of human behavior in the normal habitat (i.e., in the terrestrial environment).

Paradoxically, the major difficulty in psychology and in any of the other behavioral sciences investigating human functions lies in the fact that we are ourselves human; we know intuitively too much about our own functions. This intuitive knowledge is notoriously full of pitfalls, and we have to learn how to make ourselves ignore the bare fact that we are identical to our subject matter in order to develop a grim, impersonal science of human behavior. The history of experimental psychology, for instance, is a history of desperate struggles toward this goal of forced ignorance; since the time

This paper is reprinted from *Behavioral Science* 7, no. 2 (1962):164–83, by permission of James Grier Miller, M.D., Ph.D., Editor. In developing the ideas stated in this paper, I owe a great deal to the discussions I had with many of my American colleagues, in particular, Emir H. Shuford, Jr., Jacob Marschak, and Lee J. Cronbach.

of the behaviorist revolution, experimental psychologists have preferred to look upon man as a kind of physical object and have attempted to employ the methodology of the natural sciences — that is, to stimulate an organism, observe its response, and try to make out the stimulus-response relationships, while regarding the organism either as a black box or a system characterized by a set of functions chosen as parsimoniously as possible.

As to the employment of the natural science methodology, we must admit its legitimacy, since, whether we like it or not, there is nothing else. Applied mathematics, for instance, has been nurtured as a valet of the natural sciences; even statistics, whose kinship to the behavioral sciences is much closer, is yet a far from satisfactory analytical tool for our purposes. So here arises a dilemma: We must employ natural science methodology, though man is not an ordinary physical object; or, to put it differently, there is no easy way to decompose humans into their constituent elements without impairing their basic functions.[2] Obviously, the simplification of functions through purification of the object is the fundamental operation underlying the whole methodology of the natural sciences.

Experimental psychologists have exercised much ingenuity to break the bottleneck; the favorite techniques they have invented to simplify human functions are, for instance, to replace man by rat, or by other lower animals, and to confine subject (man or rat) within an experimental laboratory carefully designed so that only very specific, primitive functions of the subject are allowed to work. Most of these techniques are really clever, but the trouble with them is that the observed specific functions do not add up to the basic human functions observed in the normal human habitat — that is, outside the laboratory. So, in spite of the tremendous efforts of experimental psychologists, the bottleneck seems to remain almost intact.

The failure clearly demonstrates that something essential is missing, in particular something that will coordinate the observed primitive functions into a meaningful whole. The experimental psychologist is like a beginner student of electronics who, having learnt the characteristics of various vacuum tubes, condensers, and transformers, is still unable to build a radio by himself because he lacks a real understanding of electrodynamics. To capture the missing essential without sacrificing the applicability of natural science methodology probably calls for a reexamination of the arbitrary divisions within psychology: perception, learning, motivation, emotion, and so forth. It is quite clear that this division system was not a product of a serious attempt at logical classification. A specific problem always came first, around which a specific branch of psychology was organized later. So, we can look on the current division system of psychology either as a historical accident or, more plausibly, as a system closely related to the inherent organization within the assembly of problems confronted by *us* when we begin to study human functions (i.e., our own functions).

One thing is very obvious here. "Our problems" are those problems that are relatively hard for us to solve. It is more than natural that psychology has tended to concentrate on the most *inefficient* functions of man. It is needless to point out how difficult it is for us to make threshold judgments, to not be tricked by an optical illusion, and to remember nonsense syllables, and for a rat deprived of cues for proper discrimination to behave properly in a maze. Humans and rats are both incredibly stupid in an experimental room. On the other hand, psychology has paid little attention to the things they do in their normal habitats; humans drive cars, play complicated games, design computers, and organize society, and rat is troublesomely cunning in the kitchen. We can even predict and control what another person will do at the next moment without a knowledge of psychology, but with the aid of common sense. It is not surprising that a reappraisal of these human abilities has recently been made by computer engineers. The problem of computer engineers is the stupidity of computers; computers cannot even understand language, and they certainly cannot drive a car as well as a reckless taxi driver in Tokyo.

After all, we should admit how difficult it is really to detach ourselves from the bare fact that we are ourselves human and have our own problems as humans. So, it would be wise for us to start again with the recognition that man is a problem solver, and the missing essential we are looking for must reside in man as an *efficient* problem solver. The fact that man is evidently more efficient in his everyday life than in experimental rooms also indicates that human efficiency resides in the coordination of various basic functions rather than in each individual function. So, probably the best way to obtain a simplified, well-controlled experimental situation preserving this human efficiency is to provide the subject with a microcosm. Here, a "microcosm" means a problem consisting of a wide variety of mutually dependent subproblems, and the subject may not be able to survive the microcosm without letting his major basic functions jointly come into play.

Experimental two-or-more-person games provide examples of microcosms; players of these games usually engage in at least two activities simultaneously, solving individual problems and dealing with opponents. Consequently, there is good reason to believe that investigating the possibilities of various *n*-person games will serve to uncover the basic characteristics of human interactions.

At the same time, however, more effort should be exerted to develop experimental one-person games as microcosms in order to lay a foundation for individual psychology. Here a typical microcosm may be a problem of survival in an artificially constructed environment that is simple but includes the essential characteristics of our environment. To win a survival game, the subject need not be always correct, always precise, or always very rapid in performing his individual functions, but the coordination of these functions should be well balanced and efficiently organized. The fungus-eater game described below is an attempt to provide one such survival game, from which one can derive variants of the game of any degree of complexity according to the purpose of the investigation. One may make it an outdoor game; uranium-equivalents and fungus-equivalents are scattered in an open field. Or it may be played in an experimental room, with or without simulation devices. It is also possible to make it an n-person game, cooperative or competitive, zero-sum or non-zero-sum. Detection problems may be combined with problems of memory, with problems of learning, and so on.

However, the greatest advantage of using one-person survival games as microcosms is not in their variety, but in their pliancy to theoretical handling. Given a set of constraining conditions describing the subject as a problem-solving system, it is usually possible to obtain an optimal solution or a set of admissible solutions that enables the subject to live through the given microcosm. The best example of this type of approach is that of Simon (1956), which deals with admissible survival strategies for a hypothetical creature in a simple hypothetical environment. Like Simon's hypothetical environment or the Fungus-Eater's hypothetical planet, a microcosm is practically a closed problem insofar as it is a microcosm, and this very closedness renders it a theoretical feasibility. We can obtain an a priori inference about how a subject will behave in a microcosm if he is rational, given the set of constraining conditions describing the characteristics of the subject. Or, conversely, we can obtain the particular set of constraining conditions that makes the subject's behavior optimal in a given microcosm. This last line of approach seems most promising. Starting with a simple set of constraining conditions obtained when the microcosm is very simple, we can logically proceed to more and more elaborate sets of constraining conditions as the microcosm becomes more and more complicated. And these sets of constraining conditions are equivalent to models of humans that realistically describe human behavior in the given environments of successive degrees of sophistication.

Aside from this primary purpose, logical analyses of the optimal relationships among the set of constraining conditions characterizing a problem-solving system, its behavior, and the characteristics of its environment will have their own merit (i.e., the heuristic merit). For instance, it would be of great benefit if we could answer the following question: What are the most basic characteristics of environment that make man and his behavior optimal? Here, of course, man and his behavior may be defined somewhat ad hoc — that is, the question primarily aims at a heuristic. An alternative approach, such as the one described below, is to start with an environment and to try to design an optimal robot, making the minimum requirements upon the abilities of the robot that will keep its behavior effective in the given environment. The robot thus designed may then be compared with humans, and . . . probably, I had better leave the conclusion to the readers.

CHARACTERISTICS OF THE ENVIRONMENT

The fungus-eater game begins with letting the player(s) imagine — preferably with the aid of pictures of the planet projected on a screen — that he is on a hypothetical planet on which uranium ores are scattered and strange fungi grow. Along with the visual images, the player may be given a science fiction-type instruction such as the following:

In 2061, just forty years ago, the sixth interstellar expedition found a star called α-Sapporo, with two planets that were subsequently named Taros and Jiros. A brief inspection of the planet Taros was enough to convince the crew of the expedition that there were abundant uranium deposits on the surface of the planet. As you know, uranium, the major fuel for interstellar drive, was found in many planets throughout the Galaxy. But the surprising richness of Taros uranium was beyond imagination, and its exploitation meant the prosperity of human colonies in the 111th sector of the Galaxy, the sector including α-Sapporo as one of its major stars. As soon as this wonderful report was brought back to the Federal Government of United Stars located on Earth, it decided to send robot miners to Taros, since at that time there was no way to protect human miners from destructively high radioactivity. The robots were constructed in the robot factory on one of the major planets of β-Otal, the closest colonized star to α-Sapporo.[3] Each of the robots was of human size, with two feet that were the best means for travel on unroaded lands, with two arms to pick up almost pure uranium ores, with a pair of photoelectric eyes for vision, and with a pair of improved Geiger counters for uranium detection. The robot was also equipped with a biochemical engine invented only a few years ago, which could extract energy from wild fungi — strangely enough, grey, pancake-shaped fungi seemed to be the only life form on the planet, at least in the neighborhood of the Taros Base, which was located at the center of Taros's largest crater, about 2,000 miles in diameter.

The robot also had a kind of mouth. When it found a fungus, it picked it up by its arms and put it into its mouth. The eaten fungi were kept in its stomach, and there processed piece by piece to generate the necessary chemical energy. Obviously, this was the reason why the robots were nicknamed Fungus-Eaters.

The great advantage brought about by the invention of the biochemical engine, that the robot could sustain itself by eating wild fungi, let the government employ a revolutionary strategy for the use of robots. The Fungus-Eaters were born individualists — they took no orders even from the base and there was no communication among themselves — and thus heavy communication gadgets and the corresponding activities of the brain-computer of each Fungus-Eater could both be omitted, except a simple short-wave transmitter that transmitted a signal to the base when the uranium ores filling up the uranium container were unloaded. By this signal, the base located the position, which was later given to a spaceship asking for fuel.

Now look at the screen. This is a scene near the Taros Base. A real monotone — no mountains in the visible distance, no valleys, and no colors; everything is covered by black and white pebbles of approximately the same size. You may have already spotted a couple of grey spots on the screen. They are the fungi. Each fungus is about four times as big as a single pebble in diameter.

The Fungus-Eaters wandered around this huge crater desert, ate fungi when hungry, collected uranium ore, unloaded the collection when the container was full, and then set out on another tour until they became inactive either from starvation or by accident. Unfortunately, project SFE (Solitary Fungus-Eaters) turned out to be not very successful; the efficiency was not high enough to make up for the high cost of the Fungus-Eaters. Some improvements of the robot design were suggested by robot engineers, but before taking any decisive action in this direction, the government decided to send volunteers to Taros as human fungus-eaters to detect the main troubles that kept the robots from efficient uranium exploitation.

Our spaceship is now going to land on Taros. There, you, the volunteer, are expected to behave just like one of the Fungus-Eaters. You will be given a spacesuit of the most advanced type, which will shield you completely from radioactivity. The communication gadget attached to the spacesuit is not to be used except for an emergency. The cooking kit will automatically transform fungi into delicious food. You will be asked to report when you complete your mission. But forget about the report while you are a fungus-eater, and do your best to collect as much uranium as possible. A bonus will be paid proportionally to the amount of uranium you collect.

Good luck.

Along with these instructions, the subject is taught how to manipulate the controls of the spacesuit, which are actually a number of dials connected with a simulation apparatus and a recording apparatus. The subject walks, moves his head, watches a certain area, and so on, by manipulating the dials, and the scenery projected on the screen changes accordingly by means of the simulation device.

The scheme of the fungus-eater game described above is, of course, only a paradigm of the basic design. The subject may be asked to keep reporting to the base in order to obtain verbal records of his thoughts. Or the elaborate simulation device may be skipped by simplifying the task — for example, by assuming a much smaller crater so that the whole area is completely visible. This kind of experimental design is plausible if the emphasis of the experiment is one of choice rather than detection.

So much for the experimental design. The remaining part of this paper will be devoted to the derivation of a *rational* model of a solitary Fungus-Eater, or SFE, to serve for interpreting the subject's behavior in the game and as a heuristic model of human behavior in general. In other words, from now on our position is that of the robot designers at the robot factory in β-Otal System, who were asked to give the best design for an SFE.

BODILY DESIGN OF SFE

We have already assumed, in the instruction, that SFE is a humanoid; it stands erect on a pair of legs, has a pair of arms and a pair of eyes, along with a pair of Geiger counters. Having a humanoid form is essential for using SFE as a model of man, but it is not essential for the designers of SFE. So, it may be interesting to begin with a brief consideration of alternative bodily forms of SFE.

It is obvious that the major factors determining the optimal form of a robot to work on a wild planet are gravity, atmospheric and climatic conditions, temperature, topography, morphology of immobile lives (e.g., plants), characteristics of mobile lives (in particular those that may damage the robot), energy source for the robot, purposes that the robot serves, and so on. Many assumptions have already been made for many of these factors concerning Taros and SFE. Topography on Taros Crater, for example, was assumed to be flat and covered by pebbles. Wheels will probably be much less energy consuming than legs as the means of travel, if the land is completely flat, pebbles embedded in the earth, and the gravity fairly high. But if any one of these conditions is not satisfied, legs may be superior. Legs are not much affected by the smoothness or roughness of land; they can stick into soil when the surface of the land is uneven, and they may be particularly efficient means for the robot to move by jumping when gravity is low. Of course, there are other conditions (atmospheric in particular) under which wings are better, and also others that make some entirely different devices the best. Anyway, even when legs are superior to any other means of travel the optimal number of legs is another point of consideration.

For the purpose of fungus detection on a land as flat as Taros, SFE should be as tall as is technically possible, other things being equal, and should have its eye(s) on top of the body with a shelter to prevent direct exposure to the sun (and other dangers coming from above). Too tall a body should be avoided, on the other hand, if there is a possibility that strong, belligerent animals that may attack the robot exist in Taros.

It is rather hard to decide what are the optimal number of eyes and the optimal width of their visual span. If the environment of Taros Crater is completely static — no animals live and fungi grow slowly — it is needless for the visual span to cover the area behind the robot. So, if little energy is required to move the eye or the head to scan the field across the angle of 180 degrees, a single eye with a very narrow visual span will be sufficient for the purpose of detection, including distance measurement, provided it is assisted by an immediate memory field of fairly large capacity (such as a radar screen). On the other hand, a single eye with wide visual span would be preferred if the costs of large memory capacity and of the energy consumed for scanning are high. Having two or more eyes increases the precision of distance measurement and gives a greater amount of information about the shape of an object; on the other hand, the trouble of adjusting and coordinating the eyes will be added. So, all depends on technological and economic considerations of the robot construction, counterbalanced by the precision required to input information. Further considerations of the retinal structure of the SFE's eye will be given in the following section.

As for other sensory devices, a tactual organ will be most important in providing feedback information for picking up uranium and fungi. An olfactory organ will be useful if the fungi have an odor. Ears may be spared in the static world of Taros, but if the strange fungi vibrate when they grow and the air is too thin to convey the sounds, SFE should have an ear (or ears) on its sole. A magnetically sensitive device may be useful for directional orientation if Taros has a terrestrial magnetism, and so on. These things are all too obvious, and nothing interesting will come up until we get into more detailed structures of the sensory devices. In the following section, I will try to show how the detailed structure of a sensory device is to be determined in the context of the behavior program of SFE, with attention, of course, to the limitations of technological and economical feasibility.

PERCEIVING PROGRAM

We shall choose perception of SFE as our next topic because it demonstrates how the bodily design (in particular that of the eye of SFE) is to be related to the behavior program and also because the perceiving program can be dealt with relatively independently of other behavioral programs of SFE.[4] In order to discuss perception, the environment of Taros Crater must be further specified. In the foregoing instructions, we have assumed that the crater desert is covered by black and white pebbles and that the diameter of a fungus is four times as long as that of a single pebble. We will here assume that each pancake-shaped fungus covers exactly *n pits* area, where a single *pit* area is defined as the area covered by a single pebble.

The following assumptions are further added for the specification of environment:

1. The distribution of the two types of pebbles is completely random (i.e., probability of finding a black pebble at any specified position is always 1/2)
2. The distribution of fungi is also random, and the probability that any specified *l pit* area is covered by fungus is finite but very small.
3. Taking the relative luminance of black and white pebbles as 0 to 1, respectively, the relative luminance of a fungus is 0.5; the absolute luminances of these objects are given by multiplying a positive value k to corresponding relative luminances, where k is a parameter representing the absolute level of illumination on the ground.

Under these assumptions, we shall consider two problems of SFE perception, detection of fungi and cognition of patterns of pebbles. The latter is important since there is nothing else in this desert that helps identify location.

Fungus Detection

The scenery of the Taros desert will be projected, through lenses, upon an eye-screen, the *retina* of SFE. Obviously, our problem of the optimal use of the eye cannot be separated from the problem of the optimal design of the eye, in particular the optimal mode of distribution of receptors (microphotosensitive devices) over the retina. The idea that first comes to my mind is that the distribution should be denser on the upper part of the retina and more sparse on the lower part, since visual cross section of any object is roughly inversely proportional to the square of distance.[5] The uppermost band of retinal area, where the distribution is the densest, will be called the *detection-fovea,* and the lower area will be referred to as the *periphery.*

This type of receptor distribution will further be justified by the following facts. In a completely static world such as Taros Crater, any *new* object comes into the visual field from *above* (i.e., into the detection-fovea first) as long as the SFE is moving ahead and looking ahead. Consequently, efficient detection of a fungus means detection at the detection-fovea, and the relatively easy task of following up of the detected fungus will be taken up by the periphery of less capacity, leaving the detection-fovea free for further detection. So, assuming this type of receptor distribution tentatively optimal, we will proceed to the problem of the optimal use of the eye with the above-described receptor distribution. The problem may be stated more specifically as follows: What is the optimal distance of the area to be covered by the detection-fovea band? If the area is too great, each foveal receptor must cover more than *n pits* area and will report 0.5 relative luminance most of the time because of the fusion of relative luminances of black and white pebbles in the large area — that is, the frequency of *false alarm* is intolerably high. On the other hand, if the distance is too short, the detection will be more precise, particularly when the criterion of detection is taken as the multiple firing of neighboring receptors (simultaneous reporting of 0.5 relative luminances by a group of adjacent receptors), but this time the detection is intolerably slow. Eyes are useless if they cannot detect fungus before the SFE stumbles over it.

Consequently, there must be an optimal distance, which will probably be characterized by a little less than the *n pits* area covered by a single foveal receptor. No attempt will be made, however, to compute the conditional probabilities, as functions of distance, of true detection, and of false alarm when a receptor reports 0.5 relative luminance, since this requires further specifications of the density of receptors in detection-fovea and of the degree of precision of each foveal receptor. But one thing is clear here; the optimal distance will increase as either or both precision and density increase. The increase of precision and density naturally increases the cost of construction and maintenance of the eye, and whether the increased value of advance information is worth this increased cost is another optimality problem.

Here, however, we should consider an alternative design of SFE's retinal construction. If the distribution of fungi is sparse enough to enable us to ignore the probability of simultaneous detection of more than one fungus, equally high precision (and density) throughout the foveal band is superfluous. The highest precision area may be confined within a fairly narrow region in the detection-fovea, barely enough to confirm the true detection of a single fungus. This area may be located at the center of the detection-fovea and will be called the confirmation-fovea. With this confirmation-fovea, much less precision is required of the detection-fovea. The task of the detection-fovea is to detect a dubious spot, which, once detected, is then scanned by the confirmation-fovea to confirm whether it is a true detection

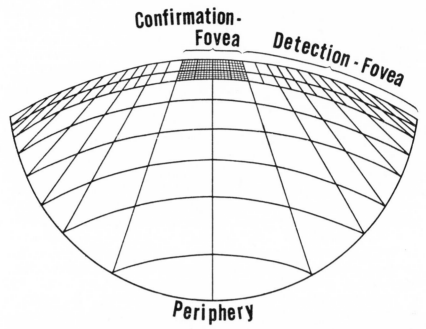

Figure 7.1. A schematic representation of receptor distribution over the retina of SFE. Each cell represents the retinal space allotted to the same number of receptors. The retina shape employed here is tentative.

or a false alarm. A schematic representation of the receptor distribution thus obtained is shown in Figure 7.1.[6] The retina shape employed in Figure 7.1 is tentative. The length of the detection-fovea band can be reduced if SFE regularly scans the environment by radarlike eye or head movements, as previously mentioned.

So far, we have simply assumed that the optimal distance covered by detection-fovea is unique. This is not true, however, if we take the problem more seriously. As pointed out by Tanner and his collaborators (Tanner and Swets, 1954), the optimal detection program can be defined only when (positive) utility of true detection and (negative) utility of false alarm are both specified. In the case of our SFE, these two utilities are both determined primarily by the fungus storage in SFE's stomach. Fungus detection is indeed a serious business when SFE is very hungry; but when it is nearly satiated, it should watch a closer area where detection is much easier, and concentrate on some other problem (e.g., uranium detection), since the need for rapid advance detection of fungus is considerably reduced in this case. That is, the perceiving program of SFE ceases to be a closed problem here and is dealt with as a subproblem of the general behavior program of SFE.

Another problem related to SFE's fungus-detection program is how the receptors can be made to measure relative luminances instead of absolute luminances. In other words, how does SFE's eye acquire brightness constancy? Here, at least two alternate methods may be considered. First, if the receptors have variable sensitivity, the level of sensitivity is always adjusted so that the mean of luminance values reported by all the receptors is always 0.5. Second, if the receptors have fixed sensitivity, the level of absolute luminance k must be measured first, either by taking the mean of all the luminance reports or by occasionally watching the area close to the horizon, where the relative luminance will always be 0.5. The value of k thus measured will then be used by the brain-computer to determine what value of absolute luminance corresponds to 0.5 relative luminance at the time. Or, the value of k may be fed back to a filter inserted between the retina and the brain-computer that passes only those receptor messages reporting $k/2$ absolute luminance. If the use of such a filter is not expensive, it is also recommended for use when the receptors have variable sensitivity, since the use of a filter substantially increases the capacity of the channel between the retina and the brain-computer. We will return to this band compression problem in the next section.

Cognition of Patterns of Pebbles

In this monotone environment of Taros Crater, the only useful clues for location identification are patterns of pebbles. So we will briefly touch on this topic.

It is intuitively clear that every pattern (consisting of the same number, n, of pebbles) is not equally useful for identification, even though it provides the identical amount of information (n bits). The reason is to be found in the differing ease of recognition of patterns. A useful pattern must, of course, be discovered and identified at a fair distance, where even foveal receptors cannot separate individual pebbles and where each receptor report is the average relative luminance of a large number of pebbles. Through this averaging operation, some amount of information contained in the pattern is necessarily lost, *unless the pattern consists entirely of black pebbles or entirely of white pebbles.* So we should conclude that extremely black (or white) patterns provide the greatest amount of information when perceived at a distance,[7] and, of course, the greater the amount of information, the smaller the likelihood of misidentification.

Now, if the patterns to be used are restricted to those that consist almost entirely of black (or white) pebbles, the task of identifying a pattern is equivalent to identifying its contour. So, the contour must be traced, probably by confirmation-fovea, and the tracing movement by the eye and/or the head must be stored in the memory device of the brain-computer. The tracing movement need not be equally precise for every part of the contour, however. Although patterns of the kind described above, which have the same area and the same length of contour line, have identical amounts of information, the same reason that made pure black and pure white patterns preferable to the others also holds here — that is, most of the information gained from microstructures of a contour is useless for recognizing the contour at a distance. Therefore, we can say that rough general features of a pattern provide more important information than microstructures. More generally, we should conclude that there is a hierarchy in the kinds of information according to their relative merits for identification. This hierarchy, however, would not be independent of the coding system employed by the brain-computer to describe contours (unless the coding system itself is uniquely determined from the point of view of optimality). For instance, if the brain-computer employs a Fourier expansion-type coding system for describing contours, the rank in the hierarchy obviously goes down from low frequency characteristics to high frequency characteristics.[8] The utility of having such a hierarchy is primarily in band compression in the broad sense — the economical use of finite memory capacity. Suppose that the employed coding system is binary, and a contour property is expanded into a series of binary digits in the order of degrading (at least, not upgrading) rank in the hierarchy. Then the marginal utility of adding one digit to the number already obtained decreases as the expansion proceeds, and a stopping rule will automatically operate when the marginal utility of adding one digit is below the cost of memorizing it.

It is rather hard to know, however, how this expansion and stopping operation of the brain-computer should be connected with the tracing operation of the motor devices moving the eye. Probably the information screening done by the motor devices can be only very loose, and the rest of the task will be done by the brain-computer itself.

The necessity for information screening of the messages provided by visual receptors is certainly much more severe. When the eye is engaged in contour identification, only a very small number of receptors are actually supplying necessary information, while the others are reporting either redundant or useless facts. The best way to avoid this waste is probably to use fewer receptors and make them mobile, with their positions controlled by the brain-computer to comply with the given situation at each moment. If these mobile receptors are technically or economically unrealizable, an *in-*

tegrator device, with fewer integrators than receptors, may be inserted in the channel between the eye and the brain-computer. The function of an integrator is to take the mean relative luminance of the values reported by the receptors under its charge. The allocation of receptors to integrators is controlled by the brain-computer, but the control activity need not be very precise and flexible. An example of the control program can be given as follows: When confirmation-fovea is engaging in contour tracing, the allocation is 1–1 for confirmation-foveal receptors, n–1 for the other receptors covering the inside of the pattern, and m–1 for the other receptors covering the outside of the pattern, where the number n is fairly large, but m is still larger. The reason for the imbalance of n and m is that the receptors covering the inside of the pattern must ensure that the relative luminance is actually "inside" zero (one), while the receptors covering the outside need only ensure that the relative luminance thereof is not zero (one). This imbalance will then give the perception of SFE a kind of "figure-ground" property.

One obvious danger that may arise from a too-simple control program of the eye movement is an endless series of figure-ground reversals. Any control program must involve, in order to prevent repetition, a stopping order operated when the eye has completed the tracing of a contour, but if the stopping order is a simple prohibition of immediate repetition, the eye may come back to the same pattern again *after* it has finished tracing an adjacent pattern.[9]

The utility of integrators to band compression is also clear when the eye is engaged in fungus detection. When the eye is looking for fungus, the sensitivity of confirmation-fovea may be cut down to the level of detection-fovea. When it is engaging in confirmation, the sensitivity of confirmation-fovea should be returned to the proper level, sacrificing the sensitivity of detection-fovea and periphery. When SFE is not hungry, some of the integrators may possibly be spared to the other sensory devices.[10]

CHOICE PROGRAM

Now we shall shift our attention from the perception to the behavioral program of SFE. We simplify the perception problem by assuming that the maximum detectable distances of fungus and of uranium are both α *futs* (a *fut* is the unit of distance SFE can travel by expending the energy supplied by a single fungus), within which detection is always perfect and beyond which, utterly impossible. It is also assumed, temporarily, that fungus consumption for the use of the brain-computer is negligibly small.

The core of the behavior program of SFE is, of course, the program of choice among alternate directions of locomotion. For instance, SFE must make a decision whether to go to a fungus or to a uranium ore when both are simultaneously detected. The choice program is a program, fed into the brain-computer of SFE by the designer, that enables the computer to solve this kind of choice problem and to make an efficient decision by taking into account various known or inferred factors that may influence the outcomes of the decision. Here a decision is efficient if it results in more uranium exploitation, as is obvious from the purpose of SFE. This does not mean, however, that SFE should always go toward uranium in case of the fungus-uranium conflict mentioned above. SFE becomes inactive when its fungus storage runs out, and this is equivalent to death by starvation of the SFE. Consequently, choosing uranium instead of fungus when SFE is very hungry is suicidal and therefore must be a very inefficient decision.

Obviously, it is impossible to work out the optimal course of travel extending beyond the readily detectable semicircular area of α *futs* in radius, if we assume, as before, that the distributions of uranium and fungus are both completely random. The only kinds of information we can draw from these random distributions are stochastic in nature; for instance, it is possible to compute the expected amount of uranium exploitation as a function of the initial amount of fungus storage *and* the choice program of SFE. Once this function is obtained, then it is possible to compute the expected amount of uranium exploitation for each alternate course of locomotion, starting from the choice point and ending at the border of the readily detectable area, beyond which the extension of the course is left undefined. Let E_r be the expected amount of uranium exploitation when SFE takes course r. Then

$$E_r = \sum_r u + f\left(v_o + \sum_r v - w_r\right), \qquad (7.1)$$

where $\sum_r u$ is the amount of uranium picked up, and $\sum_r v$ the number of fungi eaten, along the course r till the SFE reaches the border of the area; v_o is the amount of fungus storage at the choice point; w_r is the amount of fungus to be consumed to reach the border along the course; and f is the expected amount of uranium exploitation beyond the border as a function of fungus storage at the border. (Note that fungus storage must be nonnegative. So the course of locomotion should end even on this side of the border, if the storage runs out before the SFE reaches the border.) From (7.1), the choice program will be given as follows: Compute E_r for each alternative r, and choose the r that maximizes E_r.

A dilemma arising here is that the function f cannot be determined until the choice program is fixed, and the optimal choice program is given by

(7.1) only *after* the function f is specified. It may be possible to solve this dilemma by using some kind of recursive formula, but probably this is a useless adherence to rigidity. Practically speaking, the most important characteristic of a behavior program in an unknown world is its adaptability. For instance, the assumption of random distributions of uranium and fungus may not hold when SFE goes farther away from the base, or there may be a hidden regularity in the distributions that was overlooked at the time of the original inspection by the expedition crew. Therefore, the master behavior program given to SFE should include the subprograms of learning and of self-modification of the choice program, the modification of the function f in particular. So, unless the starting form of the function f is too unreasonable, SFE will be able to improve it according to its experience and will survive.

A tentative form of f will be given, for instance, as follows: Assume first that the expected amount of uranium exploitation is proportional to the expected distance traveled by SFE during its lifetime. Let p be the density of fungus distribution, which is assumed to be constant. Then it is easily shown that $e^{-2p\alpha x}$ is the probability that SFE reaches no fungus at all during the locomotion of distance x. Then the probability P_o that SFE starting with v *futs* storage dies without eating a single fungus is given by

$$P_o = e^{-2p\alpha v}. \tag{7.2}$$

The probability P_1 that SFE dies on the second trial (i.e., dies after eating a single fungus) can be interpreted as the probability of the following joint event: It succeeds on the first trial and it runs across exactly one fungus while traveling $v + 1$ *futs* distance. Therefore,

$$P_1 = (1 - P_o)\,\pi\,(1;(v + 1)\,), \tag{7.3}$$

where

$$\pi(i;(v + i)\,) = 2p\alpha\,(v + i)^i e^{-2p\alpha(v+i)}/i!, \tag{7.4}$$

i.e., a Poisson function. Analogously,

$$P_i = (1 - \sum_{j=0}^{i-1} P_j)\,\pi(i;\,(v + i)\,). \tag{7.5}$$

Therefore, the expected total distance of travel over the lifetime of SFE starting with fungus storage v, $L(v)$, is given by

$$L(v) = \sum_{i=0}^{\infty}(v + i)(1 - \sum_{j=1}^{i-1} P_j)\,\pi(\,(i;(v + i)\,). \tag{7.6}$$

Obviously, $L(v)$ is a monotone increasing function of v. Then

$$f(v) = cL(v), \tag{7.7}$$

where c is the average amount of uranium exploitation per unit distance (one *fut*) of travel. Probably it would be a plausible precaution to take the value of p a little less than the real value, since SFE must make a detour to pick uranium in cases of fungus-uranium conflict.

Now let us turn back to (7.1) and solve it explicitly in some simple cases.

Case 1. No fungus or uranium within the detectable area. *Solution:* No optimal course exists if $v_o \leq \alpha$. All the straight courses connecting the choice point and the border are equally optimal if $v_o > \alpha$. *Proof:* Straight courses minimize w in (7.1) so that maximizes f.

Case 2. Only a uranium ore is detected. *Solution:* Go straight to the detected object. *Proof:* Self-evident.

Case 3. Only a fungus is detected. *Solution:* Go straight to the detected object. *Proof:* Self-evident.

Case 4. A uranium ore and a fungus are simultaneously detected. *Solution:* Let d be the distance between the uranium and the fungus. If $\alpha \leq v_o < \alpha + d - 1$, choose uranium if $u + f(v_o - \alpha) > f(v_o + 1 - \alpha)$, and choose fungus if not. If $\alpha + d - 1 \leq v_o < \alpha + d$, choose uranium if $u + f(v_o - \alpha) > \text{Max}(f(v_o + 1 - \alpha), u + f(v_o + 1 - \alpha - d))$, and choose fungus if not. If $\alpha + d \leq v_o$, choose uranium if

$$\text{Max}(u + f(v_o - \alpha), u + f(v_o + 1 - \alpha - d)) > \text{Max}(f(v_o + 1 - \alpha), u + f(v_o + 1 - \alpha - d)),$$

and choose fungus if not.

Interpretation of the Solutions

It is obvious that the optimal course of travel depends on the fungus storage at the choice point. When $v_o \geq \alpha + d$, for instance, there are four alternate courses: (1) Go to the uranium and then go to the fungus. (2) Go to the uranium and then do not go to the fungus. (3) Go to the fungus and then go to the uranium. (4) Go to the fungus and then do not go to the uranium. (Obviously, the first and third courses are equivalent.) The SFE need not decide on one of the four alternate courses at the choice point, however. What it should decide at the choice point is the direction of travel — whether it should *start* toward the uranium or toward the fungus — and this is equivalent to choosing one out of the two alternate pairs, (1) and (2) or (3) and (4).

Here, it would be convenient to use the concepts of utility, which are defined as follows: The *absolute utility* of a uranium ore is equal to its weight. The absolute utility of a fungus is zero. The *expected utility* of a course of travel is equal to the expected sum of absolute utilities to be gained if SFE takes the course, which is then equal to E_r. The expected utility of a direction is equal to the maximum expected utility of the courses of travel sharing that particular starting direction. It is clear from these definitions that the central principle for the decision of SFE is always to choose the direction at the choice point which gives the maximum expected utility among alternate directions. As the SFE moves, new detectable area is annexed, new objects may or may not be detected, and expected utilities of directions will change accordingly (Case 5). Whether the SFE should afterward change its mind, (i.e., change its original direction) can be determined analogously to the solution of Case 4.[11]

Although choice among directions is the core concept of SFE's decision making, it may be of some advantage to replace it by an equivalent concept of choice among the alternative objects, toward one of which SFE's course will be directed at the choice point. Let us call these objects *goal-objects of the first order,* or simply goal-objects. In Case 4 the detected uranium ore and the fungus are the two alternative goal-objects. Then, it may be convenient to define utilities of goal-objects. The *compound utility* of a goal-object is equal to the maximum expected utility to be gained when SFE arrives at the goal-object. In Case 4 the compound utility of the uranium is $u + \text{Max}(f(v_o - \alpha), f(v_o + 1 - \alpha - d))$, when $v_o \geq \alpha + d$. The first component of this expression is u, the absolute utility of the uranium, and we shall call the second component the *induced utility* of the uranium. The compound utility of the fungus is

$$\text{Max}(f(v_o + 1 - \alpha), u + f(v_o + 1 - \alpha - d))$$

when $v_o \geq \alpha + d$; and this is all induced utility, since fungus has no absolute utility. Then the decision principle of SFE stated above in terms of direction can now be rephrased in terms of goal-objects: SFE should choose the goal-object that has the maximum compound utility.

Before proceeding further, I should give some intuitive interpretations to the concepts defined above, in particular to compound and induced utilities. In the context of theories of decision making, choice is ordinarily conceived as choice among objects, and each object is assumed to have a constant utility. This assumption may be approximately true in experimental rooms, where objects given as prizes have no strings attached. However, attaining an object is often not an end, but a beginning in our daily life. To possess a new car may have its own absolute satisfaction, the absolute utility. But most of the (compound) utility of possessing a new car comes from its function as a means to serve other purposes; transportation, prestige, and so on. The part of the compound utility of an object ascribed to its "means" characteristics is induced utility, since the whole utility of a fungus is induced utility originating from its only function of helping SFE reach other objects.

So, the value of induced utility of any object varies as the relations of the object to other objects change. The induced utility of a fungus is zero when $v_o + 1 < \alpha$ and no other fungus or uranium exists in the detectable area. The induced utility of a fungus is very large when $v_o < s \leq v_o + 1$, where s is the distance to a rich fungus colony in the detectable area. Similarly, the induced utility of a new car will change according to the price of gasoline, road conditions near the house of the owner, and so on. Probably the best correlate we can find for the fungus in our society is money. Almost all of the utility of a paper money disappears when the government that issued it collapses, as happened to the military notes issued by the Japanese army during the war. When his company is sound financially $10,000 might not mean very much to a factory owner. But suppose the owner is faced with honoring a bill for $10,000 or seeing his company go bankrupt. If he does not have the money, he will do almost anything to get it. For instance, he might gladly sell the factory products for a price that is far below cost, if he can find a buyer. The $10,000 is worth more to the factory owner (i.e., has more induced utility) in the latter situation than in the former situation, because in the latter situation the $10,000 is equivalent to avoiding bankruptcy. There are many less drastic examples; utility of a dime in some circumstances is not equal to the utility of a dime when one is in a public telephone booth and finds no dime in his pocket.

Once we begin to look on utilities of objects this way, it might be rather hard to find any object of finite absolute utility. Food, for instance, is no exception. Who cares for meat, if synthetic meat is much more delicious and cheaper? Even human needs may be changed by drugs. Our descendants may be satisfied by taking pills instead of real food, and later even these pills may be dispensed with. One thing is clear here, however: Utility of an object consists of various components, some of which are relatively stable and some of which are not. Utility of a paper bill as a sheet of paper is relatively stable, and as money is relatively unstable. The uranium and the fungus represent for SFE the two extreme components of the compound utility and, by so doing, they preserve the most basic characteristics of the objects.

Now we shall return to the choice program of SFE. It should be noted that the equivalence of choice among goal-objects to choice among directions only holds for the SFE living in Taros Crater, where nothing disturbs travel in a straight line. But if we assume the existence of obstacles to travel

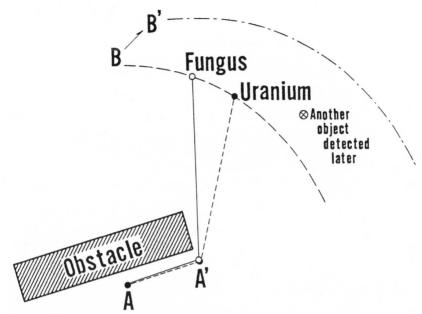

Figure 7.2. An example of choice situations arising in an environment with obstacles to travel.

(such as rocks and quicksands), optimal courses sometimes become curved or bent, and the equivalence no longer holds. One such case is shown in Figure 7.2, where there is an obstacle to locomotion but not to detection. Two goal-objects, a uranium ore and a fungus, are simultaneously detected at A; but the optimal *directions* leading to these two objects are identical at A. It should be stressed that the real choice activity concerning these two goal-objects must take place at A', instead of at A, since the border of the detectable area moves from B to B' as SFE moves from A to A'; and a choice made at A' with newly added information provided by the annexed detectable area should not be inferior, and usually should be superior, to the choice made at A. If one wishes to preserve the idea of choice among goal-objects even in this case, one should drop "objects" from "goal-objects" and call them simply *goals,* where a goal is defined as a position where there is an object or more than one alternate course. In the case shown in Figure 7.2, therefore, A' is a goal of the first order and uranium and fungus are both goals of the second order when SFE is at A. The uranium and fungus become goals of the first order when SFE arrives at A', so that the choice between them is legitimately made only at A'.

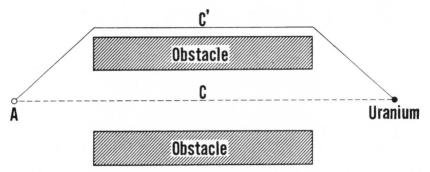

Figure 7.3. An example of choice situations arising in an environment with obstacles to travel and detection.

Figure 7.3 illustrates another interesting case that may arise in an environment with obstacles. This time, the two obstacles shown in Figure 7.3 are obstacles to detection. The uranium is the only object existing in the detectable area of SFE at A. Now, should SFE choose course C or C'? That depends. Course C' is inferior to course C, naturally, if SFE cannot find any other objects by taking course C' to reach the uranium. But by taking course C', it may find other objects that cannot be found if course C is taken. At any rate, it is obvious that the obstacles reduce the expected utility of course C, and the amount of reduction will be interpreted as the loss in *utility of information* because of the obstacles. A similar case may happen to us, too. Suppose that a temporarily unemployed physicist is offered a secret government job. If he accepts the job, he will be confined within a secret laboratory and will be isolated from the rest of the world for a couple of years. If he does not accept the job, he may find a better job later, or may not. Should he accept the job, or not? In case of SFE, a definite answer can be given by calculating the expected utility of information, which, however, will be left to the readers.

APPROXIMATION PROGRAM

So far we have dealt with cases with two objects in the detectable area. For cases with more than two objects, rigorous solutions can be obtained analogously. However, the number of alternative courses increases proportionally to the *factorial* of the number of alternative objects as the latter increases, and we can no longer expect that the negligibility assumption holds for the cost of computation by the brain-computer to obtain rigorous solutions. The cost of computation may also be measured by *fut* units, since the brain-computer uses fungi as an energy source for computation. Now imagine a case that requires n *futs* to obtain the rigorous optimal solution. Then after the computation, SFE must start with $v_o - n$ initial fungus storage, and the maximum expected utility of the obtained solution must be less than that corresponding to the initial storage v_o. Suppose that there is an approximate solution that may not be optimal but that requires less fungi, m *futs*, $m < n$, for computation. As far as it is an approximate solution, there might be some loss in expected utility but, on the other hand, SFE is left with greater initial fungus storage, $v_o - m$. Therefore, if the cost of computation affects the optimality of solution, we should say that, paradoxically, approximate solution is better than rigorous solution when the complexity of the environment reaches a certain point.

Furthermore, we have to take into account the fact that the rigorous solution (neglecting cost of computation) is not stable; as SFE travels, new detectable area is annexed and new information is supplied, and when the environment is considerably complicated, the chance is high that the solution is already obsolete by the time the computation is finished. But the recalculation of rigorous solutions for each step of travel is utterly absurd; thus SFE is almost forced to employ some efficient approximation procedures.

Here the efficiency of an approximation procedure implies the following three desirable characteristics of the approximate solution: cheap computing cost, small loss[12] in expected utility, and high stability. (High stability may be conceived as a special case of cheap cost of computation, since the higher the stability of a solution, the smaller the frequency of recalculation.) Since these three characteristics are all evaluated in terms of expected utility, it is, in principle, possible to evaluate the relative merits of various approximation programs. But this is actually hard to come by, and the following approximation programs are only those that appear promising.

1. *Approximation by grouping.* If, for instance, many uranium ores (or fungi) are concentrated within a fairly narrow area, they may be conceived as a single huge uranium ore (or a huge fungus). By so doing, the number of objects, and accordingly the number of alternate courses, are considerably reduced, and the reduction in cost of computation may be roughly proportional to the reduction in the number of alternative courses.

2. *Strategy hierarchy as means to increase stability.* A natural extension of approximation by grouping is to divide the whole detectable area into sections, and regard each section as a single object.[13] Once this section system is obtained, a rough outline of optimal course of travel from section to section will be worked out, which will hereafter be called *strategy of the first order*. The particular section involving the choice point will then be divided into subsections, and strategy of the second order will be obtained

analogously. The particular subsection that involves the choice point will further be divided into sub-subsections, and the same procedure will be repeated until each final microsection contains a single object. Obviously, these last objects are the goal-objects of the first order, and the choice among them will easily be made.

The merits of this strategy hierarchy program are the following: First, it reduces cost of computation in the same way as approximation by grouping. Second, it increases stability, since strategies of lower order are relatively immune to the influence of new information. Third, it avoids unnecessary computation; strategies of higher orders are relatively sensitive to new information, but they are to be worked out at the last possible moment with brand-new information. Fourth, it allows for differential control of computation. Since losses from improper strategies of higher orders will generally be small, the total cost of computation can be greatly reduced by making these strategies loose, while keeping total loss fairly small by making the strategies of lower orders precise.

3. *Replacing variable induced utility by its mean.* In the above program it is necessary to estimate the compound utilities of the section-objects in order to design optimal strategies of various orders. The difficulty arising here is that induced utility of an object cannot be determined before the course actually taken is fixed to the last detail, and this is the very thing that the strategy hierarchy program attempts to avoid. Furthermore, induced utilities are very sensitive to new information, and probably no computer has a large enough capacity to keep up with the ever-changing induced utilities of all the objects in the detectable area. One realistic method to surmount this difficulty is to assume step, rather than continuous, function for induced utility; if this idea is carried to the extreme, the variable induced utility will be replaced by its mean. For instance, the utility of a fungus is assumed always to be equal to $f(\bar{v}_o + 1) - f(\bar{v}_o)$, where $\bar{v}_o$ is the mean of the various amounts of fungus storage that the SFE has so far experienced. Since the mean will not change very rapidly, this is almost equivalent to giving a fungus a fixed absolute utility. If this particular approximation procedure is actually employed, the compound utility of a section-object is easily given as the sum of constant utilities of the objects within the section, minus the fungus-equivalent utilities of the minimum intrasection distance.[14]

4. *Estimating induced utility of a goal-object or section-object from past experience.* Probably a less drastic method of obtaining an approximate value of induced utility is to estimate it from the set of similar cases in the SFE's past experience. To do this, it is first necessary to categorize the experienced cases; a set of "similar" cases is then defined as the cases belonging to a single category. Here again, a hierarchical program should

be employed; when the loss is expected to be small — for instance, when SFE is satiated and there is a rich fungus colony in the detectable area — the classification need not be very precise. On the other hand, as the severity of the loss condition increases, a much finer classification must be employed to increase precision and reduce the expected loss. As precision increases, however, the cost of computation increases also, and the optimal point will be reached somewhere.

The utilization of past experience should also be done on the level of strategies. In particular, when the distribution of objects in the detectable area is simple, similar distribution will recur frequently, and it is an utterly redundant activity to recompute the same solution again and again. So, SFE should have a set of habits that enables it to decide without "thinking" in simple, familiar situations.

5. *Coordination of sensory devices with the categorization of environment.* It would greatly facilitate the ease of environmental categorization if perceiving programs that automatically coordinate with the categorization programs were given. It will not be very difficult to have a perceiving program that identifies patterns of uranium ores and fungi, like the program for identifying patterns of pebbles, in a way that makes the intrapattern distances minimum. To identify the perceived pattern of uranium ores and fungi with one of the memorized familiar patterns is the same problem as the recognition of a pebbles pattern.

It is probably also necessary to consider that the cost of perceptual identification is not negligible, and the cost will increase with the precision of perceptual identification. Here again, we will obtain a hierarchical program for perceptual identification, the precision of which will be inversely related to the expected amount of loss.

6. *Negative feedback-type travel program.* In order to go straight to a goal-object, it is necessary to identify exactly the location of the object, and the exact specification of the location of a remote object may not be very cheap. So, it will probably maximize the total expected utility, including (negative utility of) costs, not to identify the location exactly and instead to employ a rough estimate of the optimal direction. The direction employed is then modified if necessary as SFE approaches the object, and the cost of exact identification is made cheaper. The resulting course may not be straight, then, but the extra amount of fungus consumed for taking the nonstraight course will be made up by the reduced cost of perceptual identification.

7. *Backward calculation.* Suppose that SFE has detected an object or a group of objects of a very large compound utility. While v_o is not large enough to reach the object directly, it appears possible to reach it indirectly via a couple of fungi sparsely distributed in the detectable area. (This is a

much more frequent situation in our society than in SFE's world. Important objects are as a rule hard for us to obtain.) It may sometimes be useful in such a case to make backward calculations to obtain an admissible course, the course that enables SFE to reach the particular object. Here the backward calculation means, for instance, the following procedure. First, try to find a fungus within a one *fut* distance from the eventual goal, and if there is more than one such fungus, choose the one closest to the choice point. Then this fungus is established as the first subgoal of the eventual goal. The second subgoal fungus is specified analogously, then the third, and so on. If, by proceeding this way, an nth subgoal comes within $v_o - \epsilon$ distance from the choice point, where ϵ is the amount of fungus so far consumed to find out the subgoal system, then an admissible course is obtained by tracing back the subgoal fungi to the eventual goal.

There are many other methods, backward or otherwise, for obtaining an admissible solution with low cost. But, leaving them as open problems, I wish to end this section by reemphasizing the importance of hierarchical programs for approximation. The highest efficiency will be obtained when the various hierarchical programs are organized into a hyperhierarchical program, the major function of which is to control the choice of execution programs from individual hierarchies so that they are balanced (i.e., desirably from the same rank).

PROGRAMS OF LEARNING AND MEMORIZING

It is usually easy to begin, but hard to end. If I continue to proceed this way, this will be an endless paper, and I believe that I have already demonstrated that even so simple an environment as Taros Crater provides numerous interesting problems not lacking heuristic merits. So from among the remaining major problems, I will choose here only the programs of learning and memorizing by SFE, and touch upon them very briefly.

The characteristics of the environment we have so far assumed — for instance, the randomness of uranium and fungus distributions — should hold within the already inspected region near the Taros Base, but not necessarily so as SFE wanders away from the base. There are two alternative ways to keep the efficiency of Project SFE under the expected environmental change. One way is to use many cheap, and therefore expendable, SFEs with a wide variety of different *fixed* programs. Then only those SFEs that have an efficient program in the changed environment will survive and will be replicated later. The other way is to give the SFEs a flexible program, a master program of learning that enables them to modify the execution programs according to their experiences. This, of course, makes each SFE much more expensive than the former type, but, on the other hand, avoids extravagant waste of SFEs. It is hard for me to decide which is actually better, since I am ignorant of the price of SFEs. It is obvious that the programs employed by insects are rather on the side of the former, and those employed by higher mammals are on the side of the latter. Since man is one of the higher mammals and SFE is a heuristic model of man, it appears that the designer of SFE cannot evade the difficult problem of learning by employing rigid instinctive SFEs.

Three major types of learning would let SFE be successfully adaptive: learning of redundancies in the environment, in particular those in the distributions of uranium and fungus; obtaining better estimates of the function $f(v)$; and modification of approximation programs. Suppose an SFE wanders into a new environment where both uranium and fungus are relatively scarce, but where their distributions have some definite regularities. If the SFE succeeds in learning the regularities, it amounts to an extension of the detectable area, since the knowledge provides information beyond the border of the immediately detectable area. Then the advantage brought forth by this advance detection will enable SFE to survive and continue to be an efficient uranium picker in spite of the adverse environment.

Whether normal or extended, the detectable area has a definite border, and expected utilities to be obtained beyond the border can be given only in the form of the function $f(v)$. So SFE should always try to increase the precision of the estimated function $f(v)$, and when the environmental characteristics have changed, it should be revised as quickly as possible. In a new environment, approximation programs should also be revised, since the amount of expected loss is heavily dependent on the environmental characteristics.

In order to perform all these learning functions efficiently, the memorizing program of SFE must also be efficient. Here the *efficiency* of the memorizing program has a dual meaning: efficiency in remembering and efficiency in forgetting. The need for efficiency in remembering is obvious: In order to discover environmental redundancy, in order to estimate adequate $f(v)$, and in order to estimate loss,[15] past experiences must be recorded and accumulated. On the other hand, the importance of efficient forgetting is often overlooked. The capacity of the memory device of SFE's brain-computer must be finite, and it should not be flooded by useless information. This is particularly true when the environmental characteristics have changed, when the information about the old environment is not only useless but also disturbing.[16] This does not mean, however, that all the information about the old environment must be forgotten. At least the very general characteristics of the old environment are worth remembering, either to prevent a return to the old environment or to obtain a general idea about the mode of environmental changes within the Taros Crater. It is needless to point out that here we have still another hierarchical program for efficient remembering and forgetting.

OUTLOOK FOR FUTURE RESEARCH

I would like to conclude this paper by briefly commenting on the lines of research (theoretical, and not experimental — the latter has not even begun, and nothing definite can be said about it) that appear promising.

Emotion. Does SFE have emotion? The answer, of course, depends upon the definition. An affirmative answer will be given if emotion is defined as a particular state of mind accompanied by a high level of energy mobilization. SFE obviously becomes excited when it faces an important problem. Here the degree of importance will be defined as proportional to the variance of utilities of alternative outcomes of a decision. Then, if a given problem is important, the expected loss must be great, too. Consequently, a comparatively high cost of computation should be allowed to reduce the expected loss, and then the activity of the brain-computer will be excited to a higher level.

Let me take "regret" as an example of an emotional state that occurs when an SFE employs an approximation program, executes the obtained solution, and finds that the loss is far greater than expected. This is certainly an important problem, since there is a possibility that the employed approximation program is entirely inadequate in the environment the SFE is now in, and if an inadequate program is continuously employed, severe losses will accumulate. Thus failure leads to regret, and the brain-computer is activated to reconsider the failed problem and to rework the employed program.

Apparent Irrationality. It is interesting to observe that apparently irrational behavior of man can also be incorporated in the rational SFE. For instance, SFE may have a makeshift dissonance reduction mechanism. Suppose that SFE fails to find a fungus at a particular position where, according to its knowledge about the regularities of the environment, a fungus should grow. Assume that there is no indication, other than this particular failure, of either an environmental change or the inadequacy of the prediction program employed. But a failure is a failure. It will be followed by regret, and very expensive and useless activity of the brain-computer will be started *unless the* SFE *ignores this particular cognition, which is dissonant to all the other cognitive elements.* So, distorting the cognition will sometimes be more adaptive than not.

Pathology. It would be particularly promising, in a heuristic sense, to study the probable pathological traits that SFE will display when a behavior program goes wrong. Probably the commonest kind of maladjustment of SFE programs will be that of the stopping rules, since this is one of the most difficult parts of the programming. Suppose in the case mentioned above that the brain-computer starts to look for the reason for the failure of prediction and fails again. This new failure will add a new regret to the original regret, and the activity level of the brain-computer will further be enhanced. In other words, SFE will be frustrated if the stopping rules do not operate properly.

Enemies. What will happen if Fungus-Eater eaters live in Taros Crater? SFEs will be made of plastics and may have a delicious taste to these unthinkable Fungus-Eater eaters. At any rate, introducing enemies into SFE's environment gives rise to many interesting problems. For instance, SFE's behavior program must allow for SFE sometimes to trade precision and cost of computation for speed.

Social Psychology. In the "instructions" given to the player of the fungus-eater game, we have assumed that SFEs are deprived of communication devices for technological and economic reasons. It is suspected that this might be the very reason for the inefficiency of Project SFE. For instance, if an SFE comes across a land already devastated by another SFE, the former SFE will die from starvation. So, there is a possibility that even a very expensive communication device will pay if it is installed in SFEs and used as the means for cooperation among (now not solitary) Fungus-Eaters. Optimal (and admissible) cooperation programs for such Fungus-Eaters are expected to provide a heuristic for the sciences of human interaction.

Economics. There is another way to save the waste due to the starved SFEs. An SFE running into a starved SFE may save the latter by selling its fungus storage in exchange for the latter's uranium. *What should be the price?*[17]

NOTES

1. The term *design* may be used at various levels of conceptualization. In this paper, the term will be used exclusively at the levels of basic principles of design, from bodily structure of the robot to the programming of its brain-computer, and will never be used to mean actual arrangements of mechanical parts.

2. Physiological psychologists would challenge this.

3. I must beg the reader's pardon for the puns: Sapporo and Otal are the names of two major cities in Hokkaido, and Taro and Jiro are the commonest Japanese names for the first and second sons, respectively.

4. Perceiving uranium by Geiger counters will be dealt with analogously and so will not be discussed here.

5. Here upper and lower parts of retina are simply where relatively distant and closer environments are projected, respectively.

6. It should be kept in mind that the kind of receptor distribution shown in Figure 7.1 can be optimal only in an environment like Taros Crater, where there are no mountains, no trees, and nothing distinctive in the sky — where grey fungi grow on a black and white land, and the flickering pattern of the ground melts into a homogeneous greyness near the horizon. In other environments, where any one of these assumptions is violated, the optimal retinal arrangement should have another periphery above the foveal band. It is needless for me to pose a question that must have come to the reader's mind: What type of environment makes the human retina optimal?

7. Note that this reasoning holds only in Taros Crater, where the distribution of black and white pebbles is completely random. In an environment where black pebbles are far more abundant than white pebbles, a bright grey pattern may provide a greater amount of information than a perfect black pattern.

8. Obviously, the coding system employed by man for intuitive description of contours is not Fourier nor any known set of orthogonal functions. Furthermore, dimensions in the functional space of the human coding system will not be made completely orthogonal in order to prevent miscoding (i.e., there will be a little redundancy in the set of "elemental descriptions" of contour property). This would be an interesting area for experimental investigation.

9. Note that these are only heuristic arguments and not models of figure-ground property and figure-ground reversals.

10. If an SFE stands in the midst of a rich fungus colony with a full stomach, it may be permitted to enjoy the luxury of looking up at the sky and enjoying the beauty. But, even if an SFE should be observed in this posture, it must just be accommodating its visual receptors to the pure whiteness of Taros clouds. The robot designers would not dare to implant the sense of beauty within this practical robot, and the poor SFE, even then, would not stop to look for a grey spot that looks like a fungus in the cloud.

11. It may be interesting to remember here that, in classical mechanics, behavior of a particle can be described equally well by integral equation or by differential equation. This bears some resemblance, therefore, to the decision rules of SFE, which can be described either in terms of courses or in terms of directions. So there may be a way to define Lewinian "force" for SFE on a rigorous ground, although I am not sure if this is worthwhile.

12. Loss is defined as the difference in expected utility between the approximate solution and the solution that is optimal when the initial fungus storage is $v_o - m$, where m is the cost of computing the *approximate* solution. The amount of loss must be estimated to evaluate an approximation procedure, but, obviously, the optimal solution in the above sense cannot be known at the time of choice. So, to improve its approximation program, SFE should spend

some fungi, when it is satiated and induced utility of fungus is nearly zero, to rework its past choices and to estimate how much loss was incurred by its approximation program.

13. As the number of sections is fixed, one of the criteria for optimal partition will be the minimum intrasection distance (i.e., the minimum distance to be traveled to reach all the objects in each section, starting from one of the objects in the section).

14. As to the minimum intrasection distance, see footnote 13. I think it is needless to demonstrate the heuristic merits of these considerations, since they are so obvious. Ample examples are found in Miller, Galanter, and Pribram (1960) illustrating how "plans" of man resemble the strategy hierarchy of SFE. Giving constant utility to fungus is a typical case of means turned into ends. This is certainly a useful approximation procedure, but it also involves a danger of maladaptation. If the capacity of the brain-computer of SFE is too small to allow for flexible control of approximation programs, it may be very difficult for an SFE to give up a rich fungus colony even after its stomach is full.

15. See note 12.

16. Consider, for instance, the approximation program of replacing variable v by its mean, v_o. This approximation becomes particularly harmful if the mean is impartially taken across the whole previous life history of SFE; an SFE coming from a richer fungus distribution will be too optimistic to be adaptive (like a boy born in a rich family put in an environment where he has to make his living for himself), and an SFE coming from a poorer fungus distribution will be too pessimistic and will behave like an abnormal fungus-lover in a rich fungus colony.

17. As an afterthought, I think it is probably worthwhile to point out that the Fungus-Eater is made equivalent to a creature whose only purpose is survival, *if it is assumed that uranium distributes everywhere.*

REFERENCES

Miller, G. A., E. Galanter, and K. H. Pribram. 1960. Plans and the structure of behavior. New York: Henry Holt.

Simon, H. A. 1956. Rational choice and the structure of the environment. *Psychological Review* 63:129–38.

Tanner, W. P., and J. A. Swets. 1954. Theory of visual detection. *Psychological Review* 61:401–09.

8 EMOTIONAL FUNGUS-EATERS

Years ago I created a robot by the name of Fungus-Eater, though only, of course, within the realm of the printed page. This was a biological robot — or an android, if I am allowed to use science fiction jargon — that was sent to a planet deep in space to mine uranium and sustained itself by eating wild fungi, pancake-shaped mushrooms. That argument dealt with logical problems concerning optimal decision making; the robot's tasks could have been carried out with mathematical derivations alone, if one so wished. My preference, however, is for working with concrete images, and the experimental subjects with whom I tested my hypotheses also loved to work within this science fiction type of cover story (Toda, 1962; 1968). The same spirit applies to the approach of this paper, which may be called the emotional Fungus-Eater's approach. My intention is to demonstrate that a group of experimental humanoid robots, sent to some biologically wild environment, would have to be programmed to be more emotional than intellectual

This paper is a revised and expanded version of the lecture I gave under the title of ''A System Theory of Emotions'' at the XXII International Congress of Psychology held in Leipzig, DDR, in July 1980. Although couched in the Fungus-Eater terminology, this paper is to be taken as a sequel to Chapters 10 and 11. It was Hans Crombag who prompted me to revive Fungus-Eaters in this new context; I am also indebted to Charles Vlek for his comments on the earlier version of this paper.

in order to survive there. Of course, the robot fiction is again a cover. When the model is tested by computer simulation for its alleged survival value, all of its robot guises will have to be transcribed into cold symbols.

Before beginning this story of emotional robots, let me first explain my motivation for initiating this kind of approach. Recently, my empirical decision-making studies drew my attention to the issue of emotions, the relevance of which to decision making should no longer be left neglected. The greater the importance of a given decision problem, the more likely it is to stir up intense emotions. It is one of the well-known characteristics of an intense emotion that it disturbs the thinking process and makes it difficult for one to pay a balanced, detached attention to all the possible aspects of a complicated problem. In particular, it is likely to put long-term consequences of possible decisions outside the scope of one's awareness (Toda, 1980; 1981).

While ruminating over these depressing aspects of emotions, I came across an article on the human respiratory system in the science section of a newspaper. It was written by a physiologist, who began his argument with a cynical comment on nature's faulty design of the human body. He contended that the mouth, or more exactly, the gateway to the respiratory system, should be located on the breast rather than on the face. Thus, he argued, the shortened passageway would eliminate most of the problems that our current tracheal system has to cope with. However, he went on to describe (this being his major point) the marvelous way nature handles this task of coping, how ingenious and meticulous are the solutions nature has provided to overcome the deficiencies caused by the original faulty design. It impressed me deeply, as any story about the wisdom of the body unfailingly does. But this time I was nagged by a question. Why is the wisdom of evolution, viewed as the biological designer, always limited to the body and not applied to the mind? Why should only the mind suffer from such vexing appendages as emotions? How could such an awful partiality exist in nature? When the sense of wrongness goes beyond a certain limit, however, it is usually the time to begin doubting one's original assumptions. The Gordian knot may be cut simply by reversing the evaluation of emotions and regarding them as another manifestation of the wisdom of evolution — and why not?

Note that evolution has certainly not designed the human mind to fit contemporary industrial society. Unlike Japanese automobile manufacturers, evolution produces its new models rather sparingly. When the new biological model called human being was brought on to the market perhaps millions of years ago, the market, or the biosphere, in which the new model was supposed to thrive and multiply was a wild environment of forests, savannas, or prairies. So if the sales point of this biologically computerized new model called human being was to be found in its biologically programmed wisdom, it should have been the wisdom for survival in the wild. If, for the moment, you take this assumption for granted for the sake of argument, it is not too difficult to imagine how the wisdom of the wild begins to backfire in the relatively recent, man-made modern society. In contrast to the stable, simple wild environment, the large-scale, tightly organized technological society has peculiar system characteristics that tend to create repercussions to the decisions made there, repercussions that spread out across a wide space and are very slow in dying out. Who knows to what fate a single gun-shot, or a simple statement made in a wrong place, may eventually lead the society as a whole? Confronted with such awesome possibilities, which could never have occurred in the primitive society of the far past, it is no wonder that the ancient wisdom of the mind in the wild should now create problems rather than solving them, in the same way that the wisdom of the body is now showing signs of helplessness in the face of industrial pollution.

The only thing we can, and should, do is to find a way to live with emotions more harmoniously than we do today, since we cannot backtrack the course of history and discard civilization entirely. And this goal can be achieved only by gaining a better understanding of the nature of emotions. If emotions reflect the wisdom of the mind in a wild environment, as I assume them to do, their nature and functions can be uncovered only by looking at their mode of operation against a wild background.

So I decided to beckon Fungus-Eaters back onto the stage, instead of making wild speculations about wild human beings in a wild environment, since Fungus-Eaters are better suited for the kind of deductive task I am interested in. What kind of mental routines *should* Fungus-Eaters have in order to be able to solve effectively, without too much intelligence, the survival problems they would encounter in a wild environment, such as unexpectedly meeting a predator known to prey on Fungus-Eaters? Only after I have successfully deduced these built-in mental routines for Fungus-Eaters, which I call "urges" rather than "emotions," will the whole system of Fungus-Eaters' urges be compared with the whole system of human emotions. So I want you to keep in mind that no one-to-one correspondence between individual urges and individual emotions is intended at this stage, even though names of individual urges are often borrowed from the names of emotions, when such a transference appears justifiable. Of course, the borrowing of names suggests more than just mnemonic convenience; it will indicate tentative hypotheses concerning the direction in which our urge-system model would eventually grow. For the moment, however, this suggestive connotation of urge names is all there is that pertains to human emotions.

In any case, I found this rationality-based deductive approach quite promising and am now preparing a lengthy progress report of this "emotional Fungus-Eater" project. Here, I will discuss only a few topics sampled from the whole work, in the hope of conveying the spirit and potentiality of a deductive approach such as this.

First, I have to make a few assumptions. Since the goal of the approach, at least in its first stage, is to uncover the operating logic with which the characteristics of a wild environment determine desirable mental routines, those human attributes that are not directly relevant to the immediate issues will have to be neglected. For example, even though the new Fungus-Eaters are much more humanoid than the original one, they are still sexless, and there will be no reproduction or childrearing. One may, of course, doubt the wisdom of making such a vastly simplifying assumption, as many human emotions are known to be closely related to such sex-related issues as mating, reproduction, and childrearing. However, because of this dependence, I believe that it is crucially important first to determine the extent to which emotions can be dealt with disregarding sex, since otherwise the theory of emotions could easily fall prey to some all-embracing, sex-based theoretical construct. We can then gradually introduce, step by step, more complicated (though not necessarily advanced) Fungus-Eaters, which engage in childrearing, reproduction and mating, perhaps in this order.

EMERGENCY URGES

The new Fungus-Eaters are omnivorous, love to eat fungi, but eat other foods just as well. I also decided that their bodily appearances and functions should be similar to those of humans, despite a strong temptation to make a few improvements therein. Their intelligence is underdeveloped by present-day human standards, but their basic cognitive faculties are assumed to be essentially the same as ours, except that their language is very primitive.

Now let me consider a few concrete cases. Our first example is the one already referred to, an emergency situation caused by a sudden appearance of a predator, which might have been silently stalking up to a solitary Fungus-Eater. Note that the critical survival element in this situation is time. A split second will separate life from death. Nevertheless, an action, such as fleeing, should not be taken blindly. There are a few important cognitive appraisals to be made. Is there a fair chance of outrunning the enemy by fleeing? If the answer is no, the next question to be asked is whether the powerful beast looks satiated and not in the mood for hunting, as is sometimes the case? If yes, the best thing to do might be to stay frozen stiff so as not to stimulate the beast unnecessarily. If this answer, too, is negative, the last, though very small, chance of survival may be found in attempting a desperate attack.

So at least some information processing must take place. But the important point is that the type of information to be processed must have been *predetermined* by the cognitive appraisal of the situation to expedite the whole process, and it should be done in the most concentrated way, since the situation can support no distraction. Depending on the outcome of this concentrated information processing, the action to be taken must also follow almost automatically because of the pressure of time.

So now we have established the first *urge* of Fungus-Eaters, which may be called *Fear Urge*. This urge will be activated by a cognitive identification of an object implying an immediate, serious threat to the survival of the individual. Fear Urge, once activated, will initiate two parallel processes, the first being bodily activation, or warming up of the bodily energy-discharge system, which is needed because most of the actions to be carried out in an emergency will require a high rate of energy consumption. The second process is that of concentrated attentional control to carry out the minimum necessary information processing required to select one action, such as fleeing in a certain direction, from the predetermined list of actions appropriate under the class of situations activating Fear Urge.

Perhaps it is better to consider another urge, which precedes the activation of Fear Urge, the one to be called, tentatively, *Startle Urge*. This urge will be activated by any unexpected detection of a potential danger signal, such as a loud noise, an unfamiliar smell, or a furtively shifting figure. Such a detection does not necessarily imply the presence of an enemy, but the likelihood of it cannot be ignored. So the survival logic dictates the following three parallel processes to be triggered immediately under this urge: (1) stopping all actions currently engaged in, (2) bodily arousal, and (3) concentrated cognitive effort to identify the source of the disturbance. If the third process in fact reveals an enemy, Startle Urge will be switched over to Fear Urge.

At this point, let me introduce an important urge parameter called the *intensity* of an activated urge. The cognition that has activated an urge will also determine the intensity of the urge, depending mainly on the appraisal of the *importance* of the urge activities in relation to the survival or welfare of the individual. For example, the intensity of an activated Fear Urge will be a function of the estimated degree of danger, determined primarily by the power difference between the enemy and the self, the distance from the enemy, and so on. Once so determined, the intensity of an urge will function as the urge-regulating parameter. It will control, among other things, the decision-time pressure to be reflected in reaction time, the strength of bodily arousal, and the degree of attentional concentration. All of these will be more intensified as the urge intensity increases.

This last aspect, the attentional concentration, may deserve a further explanation. Note that once an urge is activated by a cognition, further cognitive information processing will take place under the control of the activated urge. Usually, such urge-based environmental cognition has a target object such as an enemy, and no attentional distraction from the target object is allowed when the intensity, and thus importance, of the activated urge is at its highest. However, when its intensity level is much lower, complete attentional concentration on the target object will be more detrimental than beneficial in that it will make the Fungus-Eater miss the possible occurrence of more important urge-activating events or objects. Intensity will then be utilized in determining the proper amount of attentional relaxation; the less the intensity, the more diffused the attention will be. The same consideration also leads to another very important role for intensity to play. When more than one urge-activating cognition is made simultaneously or in succession and the corresponding urge routines are in conflict, only the routines of the most intense urge are allowed to operate.

Now let me go back to the emergency urges again. Remember that Startle Urge makes one concentrate on identifying the possible source of danger. What if the source of danger cannot be identified immediately, even though the sign of danger, such as the strong smell of a predator, persists? Obviously, what needs to be done is to continue the concentrated search for the exact location of the enemy, though the attention should not be allowed to dwell on the same location for any extended period of time since the predator may have a nasty habit of falling upon the victim from the most unexpected direction. The routine of *Anxiety Urge* will thus be characterized by a constant shift of concentrated attention from one potential source of danger to another, and this routine will often have to be carried out under a high bodily arousal.

Note that when the danger signal that causes the activation of Anxiety Urge is very strong, it will also activate Fear Urge, and the intensity of the latter will inevitably increase as time passes without a successful identification of the enemy. So eventually, by taking over anxiety, fear will make the potential victim flee in whichever direction appears at the moment to be the least dangerous. Since the Anxiety Urge routine has not yet been successfully completed, any additional partial clue to the location of danger will be enough to make the victim abruptly change its fleeing course. Even this haphazard running behavior of *panic*, caused by a joint operation of intense anxiety and fear, may still be the most reasonable behavior in this extremely desperate situation, definitely superior to behaving as a sitting duck. In addition, the openness of the environment is critical in giving this panic behavior a survival merit. The same characteristics of panic that often enable animals to escape successfully from a forest fire will only invite disaster in an artificially closed environment, such as a burning building.

In a similar vein, consider the human emotion of anxiety. Though human anxiety takes place under various guises, its invariable activation characteristics seem to be a realization that something important to oneself is at stake and a large amount of uncertainty either about the source of risk or about the proper course of action to take. A hasty, intense search of the most probable cause of failure, which will be attempted with quick shifts of attention under high arousal, will make it very difficult to analyze the given situation in a detached, holistic, and long-range manner. If the expectancy of failure to cope with the situation also activates fear, the person may panic and be led either to make a rash decision or to succumb to a state of cringing helplessness. At least in this case, the cause of dysfunction of human emotion is obvious: In modern society the majority of important and dangerous emergency situations cannot be coped with simply by locating a single enemy and fleeing from it.

At this point let me summarize a little more systematically what an urge really is. An urge is a built-in "motivational" subroutine that links cognition with action. A separate set of cognitive contents is responsible for the activation of each urge, while each member of the set is characterized by a value corresponding to its estimated *relevance* to the issue of survival. Whenever one of the members of this set is brought into cognition, the urge subroutine is activated or "called," with the relevance value of the cognition transferred as the urge intensity, and the subroutine will be immediately executed if no competing urge with a higher intensity exists. This set of cognitive contents and relevance values characteristic to each urge are subject to modification through learning.

Strictly speaking, estimating the real survival-relevance value for each cognitive content is a hard cognitive task and, furthermore, it is context dependent. In order to relieve the not-very-advanced cognitive system of Fungus-Eater from possible overload, we will employ the following strategies. First, the baseline value of relevance of each cognitive content is primarily determined through learning (allowing generalizations), and second, the context-dependency element will be dealt with through a device that may be called *mood control*. The mood of a Fungus-Eater is a vector variable representing, partly, the state of the Fungus-Eater, bodily and environmentally. Depending on the value of this mood variable, the relevance of some cognitions will be heightened and others lowered. The value of mood is controlled by *mood-operators*, each of which, being activated in a similar way as an urge by a certain characteristic set of context-affecting cognitions, modifies the mood value according to the rules characteristic of each mood-operator. To make the complicated story short, mood control operates under practically the same principle as the control dials you have on your stereo set. When a Fungus-Eater is told the sad news that one of its fellow Fungus-Eaters has been attacked by a nearby predator, its "dangerous context" dial is turned up, and it will be startled by even a slightly anomalous signal received by its cognitive pickup.

Mood, defined this way, is quite obviously contagious. Since the environmental context should be the same for all Fungus-Eaters staying in the same place, the perceived mood of others, especially when it is strongly shared, will naturally operate as a powerful source of context-determining cognition. This contagion effect of mood will also have an important role to play as a cohesive agent within the coalitional setup discussed later, even though no further discussion of the role of mood as such will be attempted.

Now let us get back to urges. When an urge is activated, it will initiate three different types of parallel routines under the operational mode defined by its intensity: cognitive information processing, attentional control, and bodily arousal. The second process selectively supplies data to the first process, and the outcome of the first process, newly acquired cognition, may further modify intensity and thus the operational mode. However, the major function of these new cognitive data is to aid the choice of an *action plan* from a preselected ordered set of alternative action plans characteristic to the urge.

Each action plan, such as escaping from the enemy by climbing a tree, is characterized by a set of conditions for its executability, such as "if there is a tree to climb," or, "if the enemy is not a tree-climber"; unless all these executability conditions are satisfied, that action plan ought not to be employed. So, for the sake of efficiency, the alternative action plans for an urge ought to be priority ordered, though modifiable, again, through learning and mood. Once an executable action plan is chosen, this decision-making phase of the urge process will be switched over to the next phase of execution of the action plan, which calls for the corresponding new information processing and attentional control routines. When all the routines in this phase are completed, the urge is finally deactivated, with the exception of the postmortem cognitive appraisal of the entire, just-completed urge process, upon whose outcome all urge-related learning routines will depend.

When a successful completion of an urge process is blocked or aborted for some reason, the cognition of failure will activate either another urge or a mood-operator. For example, if no executable aggressive action plan is found under Anger Urge, to be discussed later, the frustration may activate an anger mood-operator, making the individual oversensitive to Anger Urge activating cognitions; he would thus on a later occasion respond to some such cognition with unusually high intensity unless the mood had been changed during the period to a more moderate level.

Obviously, this is only a rough sketch of what the urge programming is going to be like. This is perhaps a good place to give a brief overview of the whole problem of Fungus-Eater programming, of which urge programming is only a part. Note first that, as mentioned previously, urges are built-in motivational subroutines for making decisions and executing the chosen action plan; the system of urges as such encompasses a much broader domain than the system of so-called human emotions. Also, because of its preprogrammed nature, it leaves out all the other motivational routines that each Fungus-Eater may develop for itself through the aid of its own cognitive system and through learning. Note also that we have not yet discussed in any detail the two large boxes in the structural map of Fungus-Eater's mind, the cognitive system and the learning system; we will soon come to need a more detailed specification of them for the programming of the urge system because of their mutual interdependence. It is also quite clear that Fungus-Eater should be given a value system defined over its possible states, since not only is value cognition the essential ingredient of the initial cognitive appraisal, but also without the value feedback at the end (how much reward or how much punishment), no urge-related learning could ever take place. In concluding this overview, let me emphasize that all these structural filling-in tasks ought to be carried out primarily on a deductive basis as in the case of the urge system, on the basis of judgments of the best ways to enable the species of Fungus-Eaters to survive in a wild environment with a minimal amount of mental resources.

All the urges I have so far discussed in some detail belonged to the class of emergency urges. There are, however, at least three more important classes of urges. The first one may be referred to as the class of *biological urges*, represented, for example, by Hunger Urge. Biological urges have mainly to do with the maintenance of bodily welfare and are rather independent of each other. Their major characteristics are similar to those of emergency urges except that they require a relatively low level of arousal due to their nonemergency nature. With extreme intensities, however, maintenance problems turn into emergencies and require correspondingly high arousal. The second class may be called the class of *cognitive urges*, represented by Curiosity Urge. Further discussion of this class of urges had, perhaps, better be postponed until I take up the issue of Fungus-Eater's cognitive system elsewhere.

SOCIAL URGES

All the remaining urges seem to be subsumed under a broad class of *social urges*. Social urges are the urges needed mainly to help Fungus-Eaters engage in a cooperative social life. Remember that the goal of the present Fungus-Eater project is to find a program that guarantees the highest survival probability for Fungus-Eaters as a species, and such a goal can be achieved only if they cooperate with each other. Or, to put it differently, we must let them form a coalition in the survival game played by all the participants who live in the wild biosphere of Fungus-Eaters' world. The term coalition is, of course, used here in a sense similar to the one used in game theory: a subgroup of game players operating as if they were a single player for the purpose of increasing their game-playing power, which thereby makes their joint gain greater than the sum of individual gains without cooperation. In game theory it is customary to assume that each game player is a complete individualist who maximizes only his or her own gain. The crucial point to be noted here is that cooperation and individualism can be compatible. Because coalitional cooperation produces an extra joint gain, this additional resource can be distributed over the coalition members so that the net individual gain of every member can be greater than his or her baseline gain without coalition. Any distribution rule for dividing the joint gain that guarantees extra gain for every coalition member will be called here an *admissible distribution rule*. Thus, as long as the employment of an admissible distribution rule is ascertained, even an individualist has a motive for joining a coalition; if the distribution rule is not admissible, a coalition will break down because underpaid individuals will have no reason to stay in the coalition. This is the well-known condition of *individual rationality* in game theory.

Of course, game theory cannot be applied directly to real groups. Yet, as we will see, its clear-cut logic, such as the above, could provide us with a pervasive insight into the logical structure under which real groups operate. So, rather than blaming game theory for its unrealistic assumptions, let us see what modifications of game theory are needed in order to develop a more realistic, but still deductive, theory of groups. For example, the most unrealistic is its implicit assumption of the unlimited information-processing capacity of game players. They are assumed to know immediately where the greatest benefit lies so that the problem of how to let them form a cooperative coalition never arises as long as cooperation is beneficial. In reality, however, people or Fungus-Eaters may not always be able to see the benefit of cooperation because of their limited cognitive competence. Moreover, the fact must be taken into account that cooperation does not necessarily pay each time because there is a chance element involved; a greater joint gain can be ascertained only in the long run. Considering all these reservations, the only way to let Fungus-Eaters cooperate is *first to force them to cooperate by means of urges, and then to let them see for themselves that cooperation does pay in the long run.* Such must be the basic guiding spirit under which social urges are programmed. However, this is a difficult task, beset with numerous pitfalls, solvable only with the use of an intricate system of urges, designed and tuned like a precision machine. Let us now consider a relatively simple concrete example.

Again we will take up the same example of a hapless Fungus-Eater who unexpectedly meets a predator. Note that the predator can be subjugated if the individual in distress can summon enough rescuers. Such a rescue operation is undoubtedly the most apparent case in which the benefit of cooperation is demonstrated. Still, to implement the rescue operation we need to pay attention to at least the following aspects of the situation: First, the individual in distress must send out a loud distress signal to broadcast its predicament. What would be the natural response of the fellow Fungus-Eaters who hear such a distress signal, if they are not deliberately *given* a helping urge? As the distress signal indicates the presence of an enemy, it will most likely activate Fear Urge in the receiver of the signal; the receiver would then run, not toward, but away from, the individual in distress. So a counterurge, which we will call *Rescue Urge*, activated by receiving a distress signal and making one run toward the distressed individual for help, is needed. The intensity of this urge must be *fairly high* in order to overcome fear, but must *not* be overwhelmingly and blindly high.

Why? The reason is simple. If the intensity of the activated Rescue Urge is always blindly high, rescuers may arrive at the trouble spot one by one, only to be subjugated by the enemy one by one. We certainly cannot allow them to sacrifice the whole group to save just one individual. This difficulty, however, can be taken care of automatically if the intensity of Rescue Urge is of a moderate value. Note that the intensity of Fear Urge, which would certainly have been activated under the circumstances, is a function of the distance and the power difference between the enemy and the self. So as a rescuer approaches the enemy, the intensity of Fear Urge will monotonically increase to balance out at a certain point with the intensity of Rescue Urge and cause the individual to stop. Only when the rescuer sees others will the estimated power difference between the enemy and the group of rescuers be reversed, effectively beating down fear.

At this point let me reemphasize that no issue for Fungus-Eaters is so important that it demands a blind urge all the time. Cooperation is no exception. Even though cooperation is the primary goal to be achieved by social urges, it does not mean that a blind, unconditional cooperation is to be achieved. If it did, it would certainly be much simpler to consider building a single, all-powerful Super-Fungus-Eater instead of plural, less powerful Fungus-Eaters. Even such a super-robot, however, may occasionally commit a fatal mistake, or the environmental conditions may undergo an unexpected twist that undermines the ability of the super-robot, and then all is lost. On the other hand, by having a number of less powerful Fungus-Eaters with considerable individual differences, by design or as an outcome of different experiences, the whole colony of Fungus-Eaters will be made much less vulnerable both to individual errors and to changes in the environmental conditions, by virtue of variation in opinions, propensities, and abilities. At the same time they can be collectively very powerful when the need for cooperation arises.

These are, however, only possibilities. In order to turn the possibilities into reality, still many more problems have to be solved. For example, in the above example of rescue activity, since the helpers would suffer from energy losses and physical harm as a result of their helping activities, Rescue Urge of the rescuers might easily be unlearned if no reward were given to more than compensate for those losses. This problem is obviously common for any helping activity. Helpers must sacrifice at least something in order to help, be it labor, time, a possession, or whatever. So all Helping Urges need a backup rewarding mechanism of some sort to maintain their intensity. Note first that this problem can have a solution because there is a resource for rewarding, the extra gain that cooperation creates.

One obvious means of implementing rewards is to program an urge process that facilitates favor-reciprocation. Design *Gratitude Urge* in the following way: First, its activation condition is cognition of oneself being helped. Once activated, it will urge one to present coded "gratitude" expressions according to the intensity of the urge and to activate reciprocation mood-operator, which sensitizes (increases relevance) those cognitions that signify a chance of favor reciprocation. When any such cognition occurs on a later occasion, it will activate Reciprocation Urge to consummate reciprocation. Thus both this coded gratitude expression and the expressions of joy (to be discussed later) of the helped will operate as a *promise* (secondary reinforcer) of a later reward.

The question is if this is enough. The answer, of course, will depend on the resourcefulness of the helped. If the helped is not very resourceful, the reciprocation will in any case be a delayed gratification, and if the delay period is too much prolonged the grateful mood of the helped may be diminished or even disappear. Let us consider that, in order to enhance the robustness of the all-important helping urges of Fungus-Eaters, a booster urge that more directly cashes in the extra resource created by cooperation, an urge that may be called *Love Urge.*

Perhaps "love" is a little too loaded a word to apply to Fungus-Eaters; "camaraderie" or "friendship" may better describe the real mode of operation of this urge among Fungus-Eaters, amongst whom no mating or childrearing takes place. However, such a distinction is only a matter of intensity, and intensive cases, even though relatively rare, will usually reveal more of the essential characteristics of an urge. So I will retain the name of Love Urge and consider what it does, especially under high intensity.

The primary function of Love Urge is to form and to maintain a coalition, typically an intragroup one. This is also another step we take beyond game theory. Game theory considers only one kind of coalition, which presupposes complete cooperation among coalition members. Such a simplification results from the fact that game theorists deal only with single-facet games, while the survival game is multi-faceted and coalitions can be conditionally defined. There may be a loose coalition; members may cooperate only under certain situations and in certain types of activity. Or it may be very tight, and the members will cooperate under almost any circumstances. The whole group of Fungus-Eaters represents a grand coalition of a comparatively loose kind, and within the whole group there may exist intragroup coalitions of various degrees of tightness.

Undoubtedly, the tighter a coalition, the greater the potential that the coalition will entail a greater excess gain. However, a tight coalition is hard to come by because close cooperation implies strict coordination of coalition members' activities, realizable only under the condition that the "personalities" and abilities of coalition members satisfy a rather severe criterion of matching. Because of the large potential gain, each individual will seek such an ideal coalition partner, and Love Urge will be activated when an individual thinks that such an ideal potential partner is found. The activated Love Urge will then lead the individual to offer all kinds of helping and favor-giving activities to the target individual, since such activities will help to establish the image of the first in the eye of the target individual as an attractive potential partner. If, for whatever reason, Love Urge activation is reciprocated by the target individual, a coalitional *bond* is established between the pair, substantiated by continual *exchange* of helping activities and cooperation. And if all things go well, such a cooperation will produce a large joint gain to be shared by the coalition members.

What exactly is this "coalitional bond"? It is similar to the heightened relevance distribution Gratitude Urge entails over the subset of cognitions signifying favor-reciprocation possibilities to the particular other. In contrast to the case of Gratitude Urge, with which this relevance-elevation effect is only temporary and often nullified by the execution of reciprocation, the relevance elevation caused by the establishment of a bond is far more permanent because a bond is essentially a sustained reciprocation relation.

This does not mean, however, that the maintenance of a bond is automatic. It can be unlearned. For example, what may happen if the exchange of favors takes place rather unilaterally? Then the cost of helping the partner may exceed the benefit one receives from the partner, and the bond may be weakened on the side of the disadvantaged. And, naturally, a bond is no stronger than its strength at the weakest end. Under such circumstances the repair of a weakened bond can be effected only through the helping behavior of the overadvantaged. This logic for maintaining a bond through helping actually holds true in a much broader context than suggested in this example since, no matter what, a bond tends to be uniformly weakened by the constant coordination cost between coalition partners. So the bond as a favor-exchange channel must be used constantly to maintain its effectiveness as a device for producing extra gain, and therefore any significant helping activity will create a reward of its own through the cognitive appraisal of a fortified bond.

Note that a coalition, in particular a tight one, also contains a large potential risk: the risk of *defection* by a coalition partner. A coalition member may be tempted to join a more profitable coalition of another kind; defection would be the inevitable outcome, since it is often impossible for one individual to be a member of more than one tight coalition. The loss the deserted partner then suffers may not be just giving up the coalition-based gain. Since real-world coalitions are more or less permanent, due to the mutual coordination and adaptation costs, the loss of a partner may sometimes inflict irrecoverable damage on the deserted member, particularly when the coalitional coordination is almost entirely habituated on the side of the deserted partner. So some safeguard measures may be needed to stand against the occurrence of such disasters, and urges like suspicion and jealousy may be needed as such preventive agents. (Suspicion is a variant of the cognitive urge of hypothesis testing, and jealousy is a variant of anger, to be discussed shortly.)

Obviously, there is a lot more to be said about the broad class of Helping Urges. However, since this is an inexhaustible topic, I will move on to my next topic after making a brief comment on helping motivations in human beings. Recently, I have often heard voices deploring the lack of helping motivation in man. I believe, however, that these arguments are not always based on a correct premise. Genus Homo is a particularly group-oriented species, and groups cannot be organized without presuposing mutual assistance. So human beings should never be thought of as lacking helping motivation as long as they are eager to form groups and coalitions. The real major change concerning human helping behavior that has taken place historically seems to be its institutionalization under organizational control; a social welfare system is certainly more efficient than individual helping behavior. On the other hand, however, such institutionalization will decrease the cognized *need* of individual helping behavior. So problems will remain: Shall we, with our weakened motivation for individual helping activities, be able to deal with possible crises that we may face in the near future as a result of, for example, a global economic collapse and the ensuing collapse of social welfare systems? Are we not losing the robustness of a cooperative society for the sake of efficiency? Of course, this is not the kind of question answerable by a simple yes or no; much more is involved here than just helping motivation. Large-scale, organizationally implemented, efficiency-based institutions are more and more taking over the functions that were, presumably, once served on a far smaller scale by emotions. And here we see the inexorable workings of the basic principle represented by the *condition of group rationality* in game theory, which assumes that a coalition behaves in a way that maximizes its joint gain. Obviously, here again, game theory is neglecting human limited information-processing capacity, and what is really taking place in human society is to be considered as a rather blind, groping search toward optimality; if a societal change improves the total gain, that change will be stabilized, and if it turns out to be detrimental, an attempt will be made to nullify the change. Usually, any such stabilization of new societal innovations will take place through their institutionalization.

A close similarity between this societal process and the numerical computational procedure called iterative optimization is to be noted. The latter is a computational technique to arrive at the optimal set of parameter values for a mathematical model too complicated to be solved directly. First, a set of parameter values is arbitrarily chosen, with which the value of a certain criterial evaluative function concerning the performance of the model is computed. Then, on each iterative step, some small change in the parameter values is systematically introduced. If this improves the criterial value, the same change will continuously be applied. The most recent change, however, will be canceled if the criterial value worsens, and a different type of change will be attempted on the next step. Of course, the real technique is much more complicated, and various procedures have been proposed concerning, for example, how to avoid being trapped at local maxima of the criterial function.

The major difference between this technique and the societal process seems to lie in the fact that the changes in societal parameter values are not completely controlled. So the state of a society cannot stay indefinitely at any optimal spot (local or global) because of the unavoidable drift. Furthermore, the obtained value of the societal evaluative function, however it may be defined, will strongly influence the choice of the change to be introduced at the next step, so that the societal process is usually irreversible and untoward changes are often uncancellable. Thus there is absolutely no guarantee that the whole societal process is steadily moving toward the direction of optimality, in spite of so much effort and local successes. The risk of a total breakdown of our societal systems will never be completely removed unless we successfully remove the "blindness" in our efforts first.

SOCIAL STRUCTURE

So now let us turn to the problems pertaining to the structure of the far simpler Fungus-Eater society. The need for some societal structure is apparent, since cooperation need not be restricted to individual helping activities. The greatest benefit of a cooperative society *should* come from organized actions, and organized action requires at least some temporarily effective, mutually agreed-upon rules for regulating the activity of individual members. Consider, for example, group hunting. In hunting, environmental conditions change so rapidly that there is hardly a chance to hold halfway meetings to decide what to do next. Each member has to be given a role in advance, with a leader and subleaders to give orders whenever necessary. Of course, there are many alternative role systems we can impose on Fungus-Eater society, depending very much on their assumed level of intelligence. I will describe only the simplest of such possible systems in order to consider its implications, and none seems simpler than a linear rank-order system. According to this system every member of Fungus-Eater society is ranked from the top member, the leader, to the bottom-ranking member, and in any group (subgroup) operation the highest ranking member gives the necessary orders while the others obey. Many urges are needed to implement and maintain any such basic social system. Since a social system can be represented by a set of rules that the members of the society should follow, let me first assume a generic class of urges to be called the *Rule Observance Urges*, which includes, for example, the urge to comply with the orders of higher-ranking members. Like any other urges, this urge does not presuppose absolute compliance.

The rule for assigning ranks to individual members seems to be rather straightforward: Ranks should be determined according to each member's *socially recognized power,* which henceforth will be called the individual's *social status.* To simplify the argument, let me put off giving an exact definition of this notion and consider first only the baseline gain of each individual as a determinant of status. Note that this baseline gain (the gain one can secure without help from others) will generally represent one's individual power. Remember the condition of individual rationality discussed earlier. The joint gain of any group operation must afterward be distributed over the group members, and each member's share should not, in the long run, be less than the member's baseline gain. Because higher ranking implies greater control power of the individual over fellow members, any rank order uncorrelated to the order of baseline gain will tend to lead to a breakdown of this condition of individual rationality, particularly on the part of higher-ranking members.

However, this correlation by itself will not be enough, since the same condition would also be broken on the part of lower-ranking, weaker members if the powerful ones always tried to monopolize all the spoils. In order to protect the integrity of the whole group, weaker members must be protected from the greed of and persecution by the powerful members. This situation creates a need for a special social rule, *Protect-the-Weak Rule,* with a backup *Protection Urge.*

Note that this Protect-the-Weak Social Rule can be invoked only by a weaker member against a stronger, by means of the former's "display of weakness" — that is, by giving a special weakness signal, such as the Fungus-Eater equivalent of crying. This display will then activate Protection Urge in the latter, which causes it to stop persecution or to give the weak a curried favor. There is a pertinent Japanese saying translated roughly as "Against a crying child or a sheriff, everyone is helpless."

As an outcome of any such exchange, a *confirmation* of the status difference between the strong and the weak will result, which is both the cost the weak must pay for invoking the rule and the reward for the strong for protecting the weak. We will come back to this topic of confirmation after we have discussed the implications of rank in terms of personal benefits and costs.

On the basis of the previous arguments, Fungus-Eaters must have a rule for distributing the group gain, and though its exact formula is up to them, the rule should be of a *parity* type (i.e., the proportions of individual shares should correlate with individual ranks provided that the condition of individual rationality is observed on the average). So as long as the gross gain is concerned, higher rank is more lucrative and thereby provides a general basis for motivation to improve one's rank. This motivation requires no special urge for its existence; it is only a special case of the fundamental individualistic urge of Increase-One's-Own-Gain Urge, which makes one take whatever action one can to increase gain whenever a chance to do so presents itself, provided that there is no stronger counterurge operating. Thus, the point of argument is whether this competitive motivation, which *may* be called Ambition Urge, is something to be discouraged by a special counterurge. Competition and cooperation, however, are not necessarily contradictory activities; we can let Fungus-Eaters compete for their contributions to the benefit of the whole group. So we will rather leave this competitive urge at that and look more closely at its implications.

Now, what would one do if one really wished to improve one's rank? There are two obvious courses: either to increase one's own power or to impair deliberately the power of someone else, in particular, of the individual immediately superior to oneself in rank. Obviously this latter alternative could do tremendous harm to the welfare of the whole group if its use were allowed freely. So some basic social rules, such as do not kill, do not steal, and so on, are needed to effectively prevent positive attempts to harm other group members, and they must be backed up by corresponding Rule-Observance Urges and also by some other measures to be discussed later.

On the other hand, one's own power can be increased without harming others' powers, for example, by inventing a hunting tool or by improving one's hunting skill. Most of these personal improvements will be beneficial from the point of view of the whole group, too, because they are assets in any group operation.

An important point is that such an increase of personal power has to be made known to fellow group members so that it reflects upon one's rank, as the rank order is a system whose effectiveness depends on the shared recognition by group members. This is why status, as the primary determiner of ranks, must be a socially recognized power rather than raw power. Recognition of one's new incremental power requires a demonstration, and so there will be a *Demonstration Urge,* again a corollary of the fundamental individualistic urge, activated when one gains in power.

Though I cannot dwell on this topic too long, I will briefly mention some related topics. Whenever one recognizes an appreciable improvement in one's state, it will activate *Joy Urge.* Joy Urge is an urge primarily for consolidation of the improved state, and since the improved state is very often brought about by an increase in one's (control) power, Joy Urge will also activate Demonstration Urge. As discussed earlier, it will also activate Gratitude Urge if there exists an individual who contributed to the occurrence of the joyful event. In contrast to Joy Urge, an appreciable degradation of one's state will activate what may be called *Frustration Urge.* Frustration Urge, however, had better be considered as meaning either of the following two (coexistable) urges: *Anger Urge,* to be activated when there is some target object that is so attributed as to have caused the damage *in violation of some social rule*; and *Grief Urge*, when no such target object exists. The primary function of these two urges is to attempt to deconsolidate the damage, and we should note that this deconsolidation task will usually be carried out under a time pressure because the damage, usually concomitant with a power loss, will be consolidated through its social recognition as time passes and will possibly entail a rank demotion. Note also that the importance of the issue itself and the time pressure will jointly produce a rather high level of arousal and the accompanying attentional concentration.

Let us consider Grief Urge first. Its major activities for deconsolidation will be carried out mainly in the area of a cognitive search for a means of achieving a quick recovery from the damage; the attentional concentration of this aspect may tend to make one take a rather "desperate action." When no appropriate action for recovery is found, the next alternative could be a defensive move of hiding the fact of damage, such as avoiding fellow members while staying out of action. The activation for this last course of action, that of hiding from fellow members, is the opposite of the Demonstration Urge routine; it thus will be referred to as *Hiding Urge*. Note that a particularly severe power loss might engender not just a status degradation but also the need to entirely reorganize one's cognitive system to adapt to the diminished level of personal power. Where such a drastic cognitive reorganization is impossible, a pathological situation might develop; the depressed Fungus-Eater may live partially in a fantasy world and, as far as the circumstances permit, behave as if its status remained as high as ever before. Some Fungus-Eaters have *pride* as well.

Yet one more important class of alternative actions to be employed under Grief Urge remains to be discussed; this is the act of calling for help by invoking Protect-the-Weak Rule. Cry loudly enough and help may come to compensate for the loss. Note that at this point we return to an aspect of the previous topic that was left open — that is, the cost for the weak of invoking this rule is confirmation of his low status. If the individual's rank is already low, nothing is lost by confirming it. If the individual's rank is rather high, however, the possible loss in status must carefully be weighed against the value of help to be obtained by invoking the rule.

Now we come to Anger Urge. Even though Anger Urge is also activated by frustration, its primary function as one of the key social urges is to operate as a universal watchdog for social rules. Since social rules are the major fabric of the social structure, they must guard against possible infringements; infringement could take place in spite of Rule-Observance Urges because no urges are absolute. The most natural way to guard social rules against infringement is obviously to administer punishment to the rule-breakers, so that they learn to inhibit such acts. To implement this punishment, the following points are to be considered: First, the act of rule infringement must be detected and reported by someone. Note that in the majority of cases, a rule-breaking act is committed for personal gain. It will then most likely follow that there exists a victim whose welfare is harmed by the act. As the victim will usually be the first to detect such an act, it is simplest and most convenient to allow the victim to administer punishment directly to the rulebreaker; at the same time the victim is given a chance to recover his loss. Such a direct punishment can be implemented, however, only when the victim is more powerful than the rulebreaker. If the victim is not, he may then appeal for help to those who are more powerful. This appeal will activate Protection Urge in those appealed to, and often Anger Urge as well, as any rule breaking is a potential threat to the stability of the social fabric upon which their own high status depends. A question may arise: What if the rulebreaker is the holder of the highest rank, the group leader? Even the king of Fungus-Eaters can be punished, however, as we will discuss shortly.

So this is what Anger Urge does. Remember that the cognition of an infringed social rule is a necessary condition for Anger Urge activation. Therefore, even in the case of a weak member tormented by a strong member, the urge to be activated in the weak could be Grief rather than Anger as long as the weak sees no rule infringement committed by the strong. For example, in the case when the weak broke the rule, the strong was only punishing the weak as the victim would. Note that Anger Urge would be programmed to guarantee by and large that the severity of the punishment be reasonable by making it proportional to the intensity of the activated anger, which in turn would be a function of the degree of infringement and the damage done to the victim. Still, a social rule may be needed to delimit the severity of punishment, since any unjustly severe punishment will activate anger in the punished.

At this point let me briefly comment on Rule-Observance Urge. This urge is a typical *inhibitive* urge and is activated by a recognition that the action one is planning to take involves an infringement of a rule. If the intensity of the action-inhibiting Rule-Observance Urge is stronger than the intensity of the action-promoting motivation or urge, the execution of the action will be canceled. (Inhibitive urges actually require special treatment because of the inherent difficulty of their postmortem appraisals.)

The function of Anger Urge as an external watchdog against rule infringements will be supplemented by *Guilt Urge*, which is an internal device of the corresponding function. This urge will be activated by a recognition of one's own rule-breaking act. The operation of Guilt Urge is quite similar to that of Reciprocation Urge, and it seeks a chance to balance out the loss inflicted upon the victim. Guilt Urge thus charges the cognitive input space with a search problem through a mood-operator, a cognitive load that must be removed quickly so as not to inconvenience other cognitive activities. This urge will then make the rulebreaker ready to accept a punishment when the rule-breaking act is discovered or prone to make amends to the victim in whatever way available.

One may wonder why we should take all this trouble, instead of employing the simple measure of making Rule-Observance Urge irresistible. Again, the reason is plain. We are opposed to making any urge absolute because it will create an Achilles' heel in the adaptability of Fungus-Eater's urge system. In the present case, no social rules need be absolute. They can be invented, modified, and abolished according to social needs, and a good rule at one time may turn out to be bad at another time. A means, therefore, must be open to allow a bad rule to be proven bad by its being unobserved by majority.

It is, on the other hand, a tremendous task to maintain the "sanity" of as flexible and complicated a system as this one, since as yet no principle has been found to help the system to recover its proper operation and to make it impervious even to drastic change in environmental conditions. Consider, for example, what would happen if the size of Fungus-Eater society increased enormously. The need to regulate and coordinate the members' activities would multiply, requiring more and more social rules for the purpose. Eventually the social rules might become so numerous that no individual would know exactly what they were. This ambiguity regarding the correct interpretation of rules would then seriously hinder the proper execution of the role of anger; not only would the frequency of anger activation increase, but its function of punishing rulebreakers would also be made impotent. Suppose that a Fungus-Eater named Aefe were to be angered by another named Befe, as Aefe thinks that his right has been unjustly infringed by Befe. But from Befe's viewpoint, what he did may be entirely within his domain of rights. According to Befe, therefore, it is Aefe's anger toward Befe that is unjust, and this will naturally make Befe angry with Aefe. So by making both parties angry with each other, Anger Urge will only contribute to creating and exacerbating a conflict. Even if an overt fight were avoided, their aborted Anger Urge would be likely to activate an anger mood-operator, precipitating onsets of further conflict implicating other members of the society as well.

It is no more than my guess that something similar is taking place in human society today. But if my conjecture is right, there may be a way to find a remedy for this issue of impotent anger, as well as for the issue of an impotent Helping Urge discussed earlier. Though I can hardly go into details, an emotional hygiene program might be developed and implemented through education on the basis of the following points: Since emotions depend on cognition, emotional processes may be controlled by changing cognition. If the nature of emotions is better known, cognition of others' emotions will be changed and the cognitive skill of empathy will be made easier. A new a posteriori urge (motivational process) could be *designed* and taught — that is, a cognitive urge to make clear the differences in the interpretation of a social rule, such as the one concerning the role relationship between a parent and a child. Unfortunately, a much more fundamental measure of making social rules simpler and unequivocal seems unexecutable at the moment, when the whole of human society, in particular its societal value system, is apparently undergoing a drastic transformation.

STATUS-RELATED ISSUES

Let us now move to our final topic and discuss issues related to status, including the problem of how to demote a bad group leader. As I discussed previously, the rank-order system of Fungus-Eater society depends on the status of each member of the society, while status varies with the individual's power and how the power is socially recognized. Concerning the social recognition process, I have already introduced Demonstration Urge and Hiding Urge, activated by a personal gain and loss in power, respectively. In the same vein, we should also consider *Confirmation Urge*, which urges one to demonstrate one's power occasionally even without a change in power, since the lack of this demonstration may make others suspect that one is hiding a power loss. The intensity of this urge will usually be stronger with high-status members, since the spontaneous decay of power will naturally be greater with them; this is why the confirmation of strength works as a reward when the strong gives protection to the weak. For the same reason, higher-status individuals will be more sensitive than lower-status members to a possible status infringement; some ritualistic rules will thus evolve, which lower-status members are supposed to comply with to satisfy the Confirmation Urge of high-status members. Harassment of lower-status members by one of higher-status members may also take place within limits when a rather intense Confirmation Urge is activated in the latter. If a high-status individual overdoes this, or neglects to give protection to lower-status members, however, there is a way for others to punish such an individual and degrade his status, thus depriving him of his high rank, even if the individual is the group leader.

The major apparatus for implementing such social control is the organizing and disbanding of *support coalitions*. Note that coalitions provide a possibility of nearly limitless power increase, in contrast to the apparently limited means of personal power gain. So the powers of the top-ranking members of Fungus-Eater society would almost all be based on public support coalitions, where the supporting members would be willing to offer help according to the needs of the supported in exchange, of course, for the protection the supported would provide for them in turn. So if one of these higher-ups fails to fulfill his obligations, neglecting to provide protection or persecuting lower-status members beyond the limit, this undesirable oppressor can be punished by the majority by disbanding the supporting coalition or simply by changing the target of support from the undesirable one to another, more suitable leader-candidate. In spite of the autocratic appearance of the linear rank-ordered society of Fungus-Eaters, it really is quite democratic. The danger of real oppressive autocracy begins only when a means is created for the top leaders to organize a comparatively small but powerful supporting coalition, such as an army, whose power is artificially augmented with some kind of arms not available to the general public. Fortunately, Fungus-Eater society is yet far removed from reaching that stage.

Note also that such social control over an individual's status can be exercised in a much broader context and not restricted to the election and demotion of leaders. Any individual who contributed significantly to the welfare of the whole group might be rewarded, most likely under the initiative of high-status members, by being offered social support, which automatically promotes the individual's status. Such a social procedure may be called the *honoring* of an individual, and the honored one will naturally activate Demonstration Urge. Analogously, one who significantly impaired the group welfare would be punished by the withdrawal of support, by depriving to some extent the individual of his group member privilege of being helped by others. This *dishonoring* or social blaming procedure will automatically degrade the individual's status, thereby activating Grief Urge in the blamed, which in this special circumstance may be referred to as Shame Urge and which will in turn activate a rather intense Hiding Urge.

Perhaps this is as good a place as any for ending my presentation, as there obviously is no real end in the description of Fungus-Eater's urge system. Note, however, that any more detailed arguments can be given only on the basis of knowledge of the related subsystems of the mind of Fungus-Eater, among which we should count at least the cognitive system, the learning system, and the value system. Descriptions of these other major subsystems, which are to be designed under the same survival-oriented deductive principle, will be given elsewhere. If you feel that the combined subsystems may make the whole system too complicated to be useful, let me point out that even with that much ramification, the system of Fungus-Eater's mind is still far simpler than the mind of a human being; further, there is absolutely no reason to believe that the structure of the human mind is any less complex than that of the human body.

Yet let me emphasize that, despite its complication, the system of Fungus-Easter's mind is designed under a single deductive principle; even where the choice of design may appear ad hoc, the appropriateness of the choice can still be testable through computer simulation by computing the chance of survival under the design as well as under alternative designs. And such an attempt will never lack heuristic merit because it makes one *think* about the proper, original functions of characteristically human ways of doing things and the possible causes for their malfunctions. As a result of such thinking, we may expect to obtain otherwise unobtainable clues to ways of solving the individual and social problems we have to cope with today.

REFERENCES

Mandler, G. 1975. Mind and emotion. New York: Wiley.

Strongman, K. T. 1978. The psychology of emotion. Second ed. New York: Wiley.

Toda, M. 1962. The design of a Fungus-Eater: a model of human behavior in an unsophisticated environment. *Behavioral Science* 7:164–83.

———. 1968. Kinokokui robotto no Jikken [The Fungus-Eater: an experiment]. *Sūrikagaku* 6, no. 1:22–29.

———. 1980. Emotion and decision making. *Acta Psychologica* 45:133–55.

———. 1981. What happens at the moment of decision? meta-decisions, emotions and volitions. In Human decision making. L. Sjöberg, T. Tyszka, and J. A. Wise, eds. Lund: Doxa.

IV THE COGNITIVE SYSTEM AND DECISION MAKING

9 THE DECISION PROCESS:
A Perspective

A PERSPECTIVE FROM DISTANCE

The answer to the question "What is decision making?" may vary according to the distance one takes from the *event* called *decision making*. Take any elaborate decision process as an example and imagine a mural that somehow depicts all the aspects of the process in their temporal order. Exactly at the center of the mural, one will find the critical event, the *moment of deciding*. If he stands close by the mural at this very spot with a magnifying glass in hand, he will observe that a discrete shift in the state of the decision-making system (hereafter abbreviated as DMS) takes place at this moment; something clicks somewhere and the operational mode of the DMS undergoes a sudden change. In order to see more clearly what goes on before and after this moment of deciding, one must walk backward in order to take in more distance. Then in the "before" area, he will see a familiar

This paper was published in *International Journal of General Systems* 3 (1976):79–88. Copyright © 1976 by Gordon and Breach Science Publishers Ltd.; used by permission. This is a revised version of the paper read at the IIASA Workshop on Decision Making with Multiple Conflicting Objectives held at IIASA, Laxenburg, Austria, in October 1975. I acknowledge my gratitude to the help offered by Charles Vlek, George Klir, and Ralph L. Keeney.

scene, corresponding to the phase of decision analysis. As this area has been fairly well lighted, exposed and focused upon, it is not difficult to identify what is happening there. Several alternative courses of action, which I shall call *plans* in this paper, are neatly organized into a form of decision tree. All the alternative plans branch out from the node, representing the current decision situation. Each of the plan-branches fans out at a chance node over which is assigned a probability distribution. Then at the end of each finger of the fan one will find another subdecision node from which subplans branch out further. After repeating these branchings several times, each route will end up at a certain *terminal state*. Utilities are assigned to various locations all over the tree, and also to all the terminal states.

Given this fully worked out decision tree, it is a simple matter of computation to determine which plan produces the highest expected utility, and the end of computation is followed immediately by the moment of deciding. What happens at the moment of deciding may be described in such a way that each of the subdecision nodes relevant to the chosen plan is gated to one outgoing path only. This is the well-established part of the decision analysis process. Looking further back, however, we find a busier under-construction area, where assessments of probabilities and utilities are under way. Roads are not as well paved there as in the final phase, and one may inadvertently fall into the mouth of some murky pit opening up in this area. The magnifying glass will then reveal that each of these pits (or, singularities) is itself another decision problem, concerning, for example, which method is to be used to estimate the utility of a multi-attribute outcome. These are the decision problems nested within a grand one, and they should also possess their own predecisional phases as well as their own further nested decision problems. Of course, this may go on indefinitely as far as the logical possibility is concerned. The possibility also extends in the opposite direction; the given decision problem may be a nested one within a grander decision problem that is nested within a further grander problem and so on. Formally, therefore, any decision problem is situated within an infinitely self-embedded hierarchy of decision problems, which shall be referred to as the *decision hierarchy*.

Before going any further, let me make it clear that in this paper my major concern will be the normative question of how to improve the performance of a DMS, and, being an empiricist by trade, I will tackle normative problems mainly from an empirical point of view. I view, therefore, a decision process as essentially a process going on inside one's brain. As long as it is strictly internal, however, much relevant information may be lost through the process due to the limited information-processing and storing capacity of the brain. Man, however, invented a means to externalize some of his internal processes. Once externalized, that part of the process can be polished and elaborated through applications of also externalized normative principles, without being hindered by individual human limitations.

The major emphasis of this paper will be that most of the internal cognitive processes pertaining to decision making have yet to be externalized. The complete externalization will perhaps be a goal that is never reached. However, it is still possible to externalize far more than we have so far, to improve normatively the newly uncovered processes, and, in turn, to upgrade the whole decision process. Though needless, let me stress the obvious. The quality of performance of a DMS depends on the *whole* decision process, not just a part of it, however beautifully the latter may be worked out with formal analysis. The strength of a chain is equal to the strength of its weakest link, and all the effort of elaborate decision analysis will go down the drain if, just to mention two obvious cases, the employed decision tree does not properly represent the reality or the chosen plan is not correctly executed. Even though the externalization of internal processes is primarily a task for empirical investigation, it will not free normative decision theorists from their responsibilities of finding good decisions, which can be achieved only by paying balanced attention to all parts of the decision process, in particular to the hitherto unexternalized internal processes.

NESTED SUBDECISIONS

There are two major problems concerning nested subdecisions. The first is related to the infinitely nested structure of the decision hierarchy mentioned previously. Of course no real DMS can work with an infinitely open system, so that nesting must end somewhere up and down the hierarchy. In this section we shall discuss only subordinate decision nodes, leaving supraordinate ones to later sections.

To end nesting down the hierarchy means that at a certain low level of hierarchy, subdecisions are made *automatic* so that potential subdecisional nodes cease to be decision nodes any longer. This automatization may hereafter be referred to as *closing a node*. Of course, closing a node is not just a necessary evil. Subdecisional processes are costly and time consuming as all decision processes are, and a sensitivity analysis[1] (external or internal) may demonstrate that DMS will profit more by closing down some nodes than by keeping them open. Perhaps without exception the majority of potential subdecisional nodes are virtually closed with any real DMS; in case of an individual DMS, these closed nodes are often referred to as "habits." Obviously nothing is inherently wrong with having habits; only by virtue of habits can we *smoothly* carry out our *routine* functions. On the other hand, the dangers lurking under their smooth cover are also to be noted. Once a node is being closed down, its existence as a potential node is likely forgotten, and as a result, the possibility of reopening it may be lost forever. This is important because the real world changes with time, and what is a good habit at one time may not continue to be so over a long period of time.

If all the once-closed nodes can never be opened again, the DMS may not really be adaptive, let alone creative, and its future most likely is doomed. However, keeping the possibility of reopening once-closed nodes will be a difficult task, not only because of the multiplicity of closed nodes but also because automatized responses are kept beyond conscious control for good reasons. In the case of a corporate DMS, however, it may not be entirely impracticable to keep a monitoring activity over at least some of the closed (habituated) subdecisional nodes and to run occasional sensitivity analyses, or even to tentatively reopen some of them to observe the results. Perhaps one may need a monitoring activity one level higher, which decides (automatically, perhaps?) how much of the lower-level monitoring activity is really needed in view of the general level of performance of the DMS. If this could be carried out successfully, it would help to rejuvenate corporate organizations. Because of the great value of rejuvenating old systems, the possibility certainly deserves serious attention despite the apparent difficulty of the task.

GOAL SETTING

The second issue concerning the subdecisional nodes is related to the following point. It is customary to assume in formal decision analysis that all the relevant subdecisional nodes in the decision tree are closed once and for all at the moment of deciding, implying that the chosen plan is complete. This is, of course, a simplification. No actual plan spells out every detail and provides for every possible contingency. Suppose that a decision tree contains a subdecisional node of, for example, whether or not to write a certain letter to a certain person, and also that the question is subsequently decided affirmatively. The decision, however, does not in general mean that details have been all spelled out, details such as word-by-word construction or how to deal with contingencies like failure in recalling a certain important date to be mentioned in the letter. The subdecision of writing the letter is therefore, at best, categorical; what it really implies is that a goal is set — a letter of a certain nature should be written when a specific stage is reached during the postdecisional phase of execution of the grand plan.

So the subdecisional node concerning the letter writing has not been strictly closed by the grand decision in a way that only one (sub) plan is singled out to be executed then and there. However, the important point to be noticed here is that the DMS can regard the node as being *virtually closed* once a goal is set, since the DMS can proceed to plan ahead from that goal-state on and leave the details of the *sub*plan unfilled. (Provided, of course, that the probability of actually achieving the goal can be estimated and various alternative states are specified in case of failure in meeting the goal.) So let me call a subdecisional node being *G-closed* if the subdecisional problem is made context bound by the preselected goal (or goals). As a matter of fact, we may safely postulate that subdecisional nodes are G-closed only in a decision problem of a sizable magnitude.

Now let me consider why goal setting is apparently so popular a strategy in human problem solving. It is often pointed out that goal setting makes the working-out of plans considerably easier; with a fixed goal added to the fixed current state, one can engage in a two-way search, forward and backward, for a workable plan connecting the two states. To this reason we should also add another of similar importance: A fixed goal makes it enormously easier to deal with unexpected contingencies that will occur during the execution phase. One watches the goal and tries to maneuver himself so as to steadily shorten an appropriate "distance measure" between his state and the goal state, a well-known negative feedback technique.

While these are very nice features of having a fixed goal and often are the only manageable search strategy for workable plans, it should also be remembered that these nice features of having a fixed goal are brought about by the fact that a fixed goal drastically narrows down alternative plans. So by setting a goal one is running a risk of overlooking much better plans, and the evaluation of goal-setting strategy depends highly on one's ability to find good goals. Are there any reasonable normative rules for finding good goals? A tentative answer to this question will be discussed in a later section.

These considerations have been dealing with the efficiency aspects of goal setting. However, there is a much more compelling reason that makes goal setting almost a necessity in any decision problem that contains subdecisional nodes. As already argued, goal setting enables the DMS to G-close subdecisional nodes without bothering about details, and this is the only way for the DMS to structure the decision situation hierarchically and concentrate on *major issues* first. Note that solving minor issues can wait, and whatever part of the decision problem that can wait should wait, since it is the general rule that the DMS is better provided with more relevant information as the execution phase approaches. On the other hand, the DMS cannot postpone everything. If he does, then there will be no plan to execute. Putting these two propositions together, the great advantage is to be able to separate hierarchically the aspects of the given decision problem into those that require immediate attention and those that do not. The grand plan thus represents the skeletal structure of the whole plan and leaves many unfilled gaps that are G-closed only at the time of grand decision making. The gaps are filled and the whole plan is fleshed out by subplans only when the time becomes ripe for these subdecisions.

The fact that a decision tree represents only the major aspects of the given problem means that the hierarchical structuring of the given decision problem has already been completed when the tree is given. If we think further about the decision process as a whole, we will get a recurrent feeling that most of the important works of decision making are virtually over before a decision tree is ever produced. In order to proceed further into the realm of *predecisional structuring*, we need to pay a short visit to the epistemological question of what the decision tree really is.

COGNITIVE SIMULATOR

A decision tree is a representation of the structure of the external world that pertains to the given decision problem — not only the real world at the moment of decision, but all the possible worlds that will develop over time, conditional on the actions taken by the DMS. When probabilities are assigned to the chance nodes in this decision tree formulation, what is then achieved is a *simulation* of the world process relevant to the DMS's decision problem.

It is a simulation indeed. Not only should the formulation be valid, but it should also simplify the infinitely ramifying structure of the world into workable form without missing anything important.

Let us first consider the issue of valid representation, for which no word will be needed to point out how formidable a task it is. Still, people, each of whom is a DMS, seem to cope with this task in making their own decisions. It is unlikely that a simulation model is constructed afresh for each decision problem; each person should already have a general model of the world, a *cognitive simulator*, which will be applied to each decision problem, supplemented by some necessary additional pieces of information. As far as the use of a cognitive simulator is concerned, there seems to be little difference between individual and corporate DMSs; the latter may aggregate more than one cognitive simulator of its personnel to form the decision tree for its own use.

Obviously, a systematic externalization of this process is a formidable undertaking. Each person is supposed to be working at building his simulator almost all his life, and it therefore cannot be anything but an enormously elaborate system. Still, the task is compelling, and to uncover just the major framework of the system may not be impossible with the available data alone, once we focus on the fact that it is primarily a simulation-oriented system.

Apparently, a person does not genetically inherit a full-fledged cognitive simulator, but only its very basic components, which specify, perhaps above all, how sensory inputs should be processed to obtain the structural and relational information concerning himself and the environment. The main edifice of the cognitive simulator must therefore be built a posteriori on the basis of this type of acquired information. Thus we may view the cognitive simulator, as well as other components of the cognitive system, as a self-organizing system.

At a certain stage of development, however, the primary activity of any self-organized system should be switched from self-organization to production, if the system is to have any practical use whatsoever. Even though self-organization and production are not incompatible, running the two functions simultaneously will not be efficient. Just imagine how troublesome it would be to use a system that is constantly changing itself for more-or-less routine work. Furthermore, the type of information needed by a system for each of the two functions is generally different; in the self-organizing phase, structural information is more important than situational information, and vice versa in the production phase.[2]

The advantage of a self-organizing system is that it can develop adaptively to fit itself to the given environment. This adaptive development should imply that some of the structural invariants of the system are matched to the corresponding structural invariants of the environment, a characteristic that we may call *structural matching*, where the matching rules may be very sophisticated in the case of human beings.

Until the structural matching is carried out to some extent and the system begins to perform satisfactorily in the environment, the system will be of little use in production. The system not only lacks sufficient representational validity but is also unstable; some environmental event may at any time give an impact at a deep level of the system. Therefore, whenever such a system starts functioning satisfactorily (under some given criterion), it would probably be better to *freeze*, or *harden*, the structure of the system then and there.

This freezing effect may be achieved by closing inputs for certain types of information, particularly for those that may affect the deep structure of the system. The closing will then give the system room for more inputs for situational information — input data — to update and to operate the cognitive simulator. Perhaps that still may not be enough to stabilize the system. Even situational information may occasionally have a far-reaching effect. For example, one may get information that is so out of range of his expectation that the validity of his cognitive simulator may be seriously doubted. Nonetheless, the overall performance of his system may still be smooth and satisfactory. The dilemma that will then arise is whether he should embark on the costly business of restructuring his cognitive simulator, which will for some unknown period of time impair his performance, or just ignore the troublesome information. The latter alternative also includes, in case the information obtained cannot simply be ignored, a cognitive strategy of inoculating it by distorting its interpretation. Festinger's cognitive dissonance (Festinger, 1957) and other, known or unknown, cognitive defense mechanisms seem to be relevant to this issue.

Considering man's limited information-processing capacity, one cannot unconditionally blame the cognitive defense strategy. Depending on what a DMS is supposed to produce, it could be thrifty and therefore good as long as it is evaluated within a relatively short span of time. On the other hand, the structure of the environment, particularly that of society, may not remain the same in the long run, and the validity of a frozen cognitive simulator will be degraded accordingly. So once one starts to "defend" his cognitive simulator, the need for defense will increase in frequency following the validity degradation, which will in turn decrease the real information input, and this may very well be the beginning of a vicious cycle.

Note also that the costliness of restructuring applies equally to externalized systems of a corporate DMS, the more so as the externalized structure grows larger and more elaborate unless, of course, the externalized system is self-organizing without human help. No such system, however, seems to exist at present.

LEARNING OR EXPERIENCE-FEEDBACK STRATEGY

The activity of a DMS begins when it is given a decision problem (i.e., when a person finds himself in an open decision node). In general, the problem itself will not dictate the alternative plans over which a person should make comparisons. Note that the preselection of alternative plans that are subsequently put to decision analysis out of virtually infinite possibilities cannot be made on the basis of strict expected utility maximization, for the obvious reason that preselection precedes expected utility calculation.

This is a place, therefore, where at best a heuristic principle is applicable. The question of what heuristic principles could exist is important and challenging for both normative and empirical investigators. One obvious candidate for the heuristic is to set a goal, if it has not been done already by a supraordinate plan, and then to work out alternative plans more or less analytically. This "metaplan" only shifts the object of search from plans to goals, as goals are also something to be discovered and evaluated. Sometimes the chosen goals may be very ambiguous, hardly pointing to any specific plans at all — for example, when they are mere manifestations of the DMS's desires. These are the cases that are traditionally dealt with in psychology under the general heading of *motivation*. So there are a wide spectrum of possible goals, from very specific to very diffuse, and what they all do in common is to put additional constraints on the nature of adoptable plans. As the original set of constraints is provided by the decision situation itself, we may lump them together and call the total set the *decision context*. Of course, the more stringent the total constraints, the narrower the sphere of possible plans.

Our current problem, then, is to consider the ways of generating a set of plausible alternative plans, given a decision context, without recourse to piecewise calculation of expected utility of any specific plan. Barring analytical calculation, an alternative mechanism that will come to any psychologist's mind is the response selection model employed in learning theory. Stripping the notion of the learning system to its bare essentials and applying it to our problem, it suggests the following heuristic: Associate plans to decision contexts with varying degrees of strength. Then let the decision context generate alternative plans according to the order of their associative strengths. Obviously, then, the plausibility of each plan in each decision context is borne by its associative strength, which is established through environmental feedback in the following way: If the performance of a plan in a decision context turns out to be satisfactory or (unsatisfactory) in the DMS's experience, the association holding between the two is immediately incremented (or decremented).

The underlying assumption that supports this "reinforcement" system is undoubtedly the overall stationarity of the world processes; if a plan worked satisfactorily in a particular context, then it will work well again, more often than not, in the same context to be encountered in the future. Granting this assumption, which is plausible enough, the system is still incomplete, since no two decision contexts will be exactly the same. To mend this weakness, the notion of similarity must be introduced and another assumption about the nature's homogeneity must be invoked: A plan that worked well in one context in the past will also work well, more often than not, in a *similar* context, though the validity of this expectation will be reduced as the similarity decreases. To consolidate this and similar assumptions, learning theories are usually fortified by the notion of "generalization gradient.'' A touch of perfection will then be added; important discontinuities in the world, breaches of the similarity principle, can still be learned as discrimination learning.

In order not to commit oneself to any particular type of learning theory, let me call the above-stated type of associative-inductive principle based on reinforcement and generalization the *environmental feedback strategy* (abbreviated as EFS). EFS is, as a strategy of life forms, to be viewed as biological rather than cognitive, since it can be found in fairly lower animals.

Apparently, in the case of man, EFS cannot be the sole determiner of behavior, as some of the learning psychologists have claimed, and its superficial generalization to analytical, constructive mental activities will be futile, if not impossible. Still, it will be tremendously important to point out the ubiquity of EFS in human mental processes, particularly to normative theorists who, in contrast to some psychologists who are preoccupied by it, often seem unaware of its existence. So let me now evaluate EFS as a strategy rather than an empirical theory. Its greatest advantage is apparently that it can operate in very thin air — under an almost complete lack of the relevant information required for analytical thinking — as long as the given context has even the remotest semblance to some context experienced in the past. Almost as important as this is its low operation cost; once a system, like the human brain or a computer, is given for handling a rather large bundle of associations, its operation can be automatic and no specific case-by-case information processing is required.

On the other hand, the demerit of EFS is also apparent. As long as the associative strength representing the worth of a plan can be updated only on the basis of the frequency with which the same (or similar) situations are encountered, the solution provided by EFS can hardly do justice to important and rare decision problems, even more so as the importance and the rarity are often highly correlated. It was perhaps exactly for the need of mending this grave defect that, at some point in the history of evolution, an analytical, constructive problem-solving routine was born, which human beings have since greatly elaborated.

We may say that the living organism began to make decisions only after the birth of this routine, for the plan-selection mechanisms based on EFS alone hardly deserve the name of DMS, even though the chosen plan for a context is not fixed and is adaptive. We may call the decision node L-closed if the plan selection for the node is taken care of by means of EFS. It is, of course, far better to L-close a node than to S-close (strictly close) it, as long as the small running cost of EFS for the node can be neglected. Still, the running cost is not zero, and it is expected that L-closed nodes will gradually be transformed to S-closed nodes once the same plan is *overlearned*. These are, however, details. What I would like to emphasize here is the importance of externalizing EFS, not as a descriptive learning theory, but as a practical normative strategy to be employed by the corporate DMS to keep relatively less important, semiroutine decisions adaptive, with relatively low costs.

Now let me hypothesize a bit about how this new thinking routine could ever have emerged from the powerful, prevalent reign of EFS. For anything new to emerge, there must be a temporary vacuum in the system, such as the complete inability of EFS to produce a plan in a totally unfamiliar situation. The vacuum can be enlarged by setting up a threshold for the associative strength of an adoptable plan to reach; if the strength of even the most tightly associated plan to the given context does not exceed the threshold, its otherwise automatic execution is temporarily inhibited. We may as well call this occasion *problem detection*, since it implies that there have been no plans in one's past experience that were good enough.

Of course, this is only the beginning. But let me digress a little at this point. The inhibition of immediate execution of the first-come plans will be deliberately used to generate alternative plans in analytical decision making even if they all exceed the threshold. The plans successively generated according to their order of associative strengths will then be subjected to decision analysis, whereby the expedient measure of associative strength will be replaced by the more rigorous expected utility. Also note that setting up thresholds for passable associative strength can be a natural predecessor to setting up goals. They both establish a criterion for a plausible plan to meet, and the preselection of goals will again be performed by way of EFS.

Returning to the main issue of the new thinking routine, we may simply argue that the only way to cover the failure of EFS is to utilize the types of information that are not used by EFS — mainly more structural information concerning world processes. For example, unfamiliar decision contexts may be analyzed into more familiar components. Plans may also be likewise decomposed. Then, utilizing structural constraints discovered among these components, a new representation of the decision context and a workable new plan corresponding to this reconstructed decision context may be recomposed.

All of this is pure speculation, unjustifiable as a descriptive hypothesis, but let me leave it at that and mention, instead, a little more about EFS. Note that EFS could be used as something like a universal plaster with which one could fill almost any gap left by analytical thinking, if the EFS principle were separated from its direct application to the context-plan associations. For the separation would make EFS almost equivalent to induction. And induction can be externalized; the best example of externalization is Bayesian inference. When objective probability cannot be analytically calculated, it is replaced by subjective probability, and Bayesian posteriori probability is a normative version of the latter.

Why should it be only probability that is to be learned? Utilities that appear in decision analysis are, in actuality, mostly expected utilities — expected utilities of a special kind, those that cannot be calculated by the analytico-constructive formula of mathematical expectation. The expected utilities of the *terminal states* of a decision tree and of the preselected plans can, by definition, be estimated only through induction or by EFS, on the basis of one's past experience (direct or indirect). Let me call the hypothetical cognitive system that generates these inductive estimates of utilities ULPS (Utility Lookup for Plans and Situations).

It is quite true that our individual ULPS seems to work well in solving our personal decision problems. It is deplorable, however, that due to the lack of impersonal, externalized ULPSs, even big corporate DMSs, whose decisions might affect the welfare of millions of people, could depend only on some individual ULPSs; individual experiences are so much impoverished in comparison with the sheer magnitude of the decision problems in their hands. In my opinion, the interpersonal incomparability of utilities is not an insurmountable obstacle to the development of an externalized ULPS. A formula very similar to Bayesian inference may work here, too, and the initial disparity among people's utility estimates is expected to diminish (perhaps not necessarily to disappear) as collective experience accumulates.

DECISION SCOPE

Once a set of alternative plans has been selected, they may be put to the cognitive simulator to develop a decision tree. A "plan" works as if it is an operator applied to the "context," and the simulator will produce a set of new situations as the possible outcomes. If the preselected plans end there, these outcomes may become the terminal states of the decision tree. One can, however, proceed further by generating futher plans, taking these outcomes as interim subdecisional nodes. Even though one can go on indefinitely this way, the need to keep decision tree tractably small forces him to stop somewhere and to regard the last outcome thus generated along each path as the terminal state. The set of terminal states will be called the *horizon*. The background field upon which the decision tree lies, defined jointly by the preselected plans, the horizon, and the structure of the tree network produced by the hierarchical organization of the decision situation, will be called the *decision scope*. Note that each of the three major determiners of the decision scope has a large freedom of choice, and normative principles (which could be at least heuristic) concerning the choice of plausible decision trees should be the target of intensive investigations (see Toda and Shuford, 1965; Toda, 1968). Also let me point out in this vein that the studies done in relation to the cognitive information processing of expert chess players and the chess-playing computer programs are particularly relevant to the topic of decision scope, even though no direct reference to them will be made in this paper.[3] As a matter of fact, the issue of decision scope is so great that I shall discuss only a few aspects of the problem concerning, primarily, the size of the decision scope. Consider first the horizon of the terminal states. Obviously, there is usually nothing really terminal about terminal states, unless some special condition is met, like Savage's small world condition, which implies that all the terminal states are equivalent concerning the DMS's future prospect beyond the horizon (Savage, 1954). In reality, these conditions are seldom met; each terminal state is a separate beginning. The utilities assigned to these terminal states, therefore, must reflect the differences in the corresponding future prospects, and thus they should be "expected" utilities estimated through inductive inference. This consideration, therefore, sets one criterion for the choice of terminal states: Other things being equal, one should choose as familiar a state as possible for the terminal state so that the expected utility estimate is reliable. What, then, are "other things?" There are in fact quite a few other things, and the chess player studies are particularly relevant here. We shall, however, consider only a very general question: If we can neglect the cost of decision analysis (which includes decision time), is it, in principle, always good to set the horizon as far away as possible? Considering the precision of analytical computation of utilities in comparison to that of its inductive estimation counterpart, the answer may appear affirmative (i.e., long-range plans are always preferable to short-range plans). However, there is one important factor never to be overlooked — the dependability of information the DMS has concerning future affairs. As discussed in a previous section, the quality of relevant information is monotonically degraded as the time interval increases between the moment of decision and the moment of execution. It is true that a decision tree can cope with this problem to some extent; it may contain chance nodes corresponding to possible alternative sets of information one might acquire in the future. However, it is certainly impossible to provide for every imaginable contingency. The whole point is that a plan brings into one's flow of behavior a certain amount of rigidity as well as consistency. So if one makes a very long range plan based on rather unreliable information, he will perhaps lose more in the form of diminished freehand in unexpected situations than he gains from consistency.

Therefore, the crucial factor here is the speed of information degradation in the direction toward the future. If one lives in a very unpredictable world, it will be better to set the horizon rather near to ensure his future freehand. If, on the other hand, the world is quite stable, as in the world of expert chess players, long-range plans may turn out always better.

This, however, is not the whole story. The speed of information degradation should also affect the optimal hierarchical structuring of the decision situation. By setting up long-range "goals" and leaving detailed planning as much as possible to subdecisions in later periods, one may be able to obtain a long-range and still fairly flexible plan. The load for properly executing any such plan, however, would be great. No simple-minded evaluation of these alternative decision scope-building strategies appears possible.

The other critical determiner of the nature of decision scope besides its horizon is the variety of preselected plans. I can give only a commonsense suggestion here to increase the variety, though that alone would scarcely do justice to this important topic: One may be able to increase the variety of preselected plans if he can deliberately change his decision context. Note that a decision context is always subjective as long as no one can grasp the whole implication of a given situation. So it is not impossible to change the conception of a given situation, and different conceptions will generally lead to different plans. Of course, this is not as easy as it may sound, but systematic training will certainly help increase the ease of it.

POSTDECISIONAL PROCESSES

The postdecisional phase of the decision process is by no means a straightforward execution of the decided plan, since a plan is, in principle, incomplete, and details are to be filled by subdecisions to be made during the process of executing the grand plan. These subdecisions are characterized in the following way: They have preset goals that the DMS tries to meet since failure in meeting them may often disturb the whole plan. Their decision scopes are in general smaller than that of the grand decision, and the solution of these subdecisional problems needs rather narrow but down-to-earth types of information. These characteristics will require narrower but more focused attention of the DMS for the information search than in predecisional phase, where attention should be rather broad and diffused to encompass a much larger decision scope.

The focused attention will serve two purposes. The first is the one just described. The second purpose is more subtle, but is equally important — that is, to defend against disturbing information.

Note that the optimality of the chosen plan at the moment of deciding may no longer hold as its execution begins and a more up-to-date set of information comes to hand. Of course, the DMS may change his mind; he can abolish the whole plan and do the grand decision making all over again. This is, however, costly. Moreover, one might not be able to get any single plan executed to the end if he changes his mind every time a new set of "disturbing" information turns up. One should, in addition, consider the inertia effect. Once the execution of a plan starts, it will begin to involve external factors like other people, other social systems, and so on, which cannot be stopped without some cost; the cost will be especially high in the case of the corporate DMS.

Once the execution process is started, the DMS has more or less committed himself to carry out the chosen plan even if it may turn out to be a rather bad plan. If DMS is so committed, then why bother? Why can't he just neglect all the disturbing information (like outsiders' criticisms) that is not directly relevant to the execution?

He should bother, however, to some extent, since he should retain the freedom to abolish the plan if it turns out to be extremely wrong. The point of dilemma arises concerning the evaluation of badness. Deliberately deciding whether or not to abolish (or even to revise) the chosen plan every time one obtains disturbing information would be in itself very "disturbing" and costly, indeed.

Narrowing his attention during this phase suggests a compromise solution. DMS can set up a threshold and neglect all information whose disturbing value does not reach this level. Apparently individuals apply this strategy in their plan execution; the threshold seems to correspond (though indirectly) to the "will" of carrying through a plan.[4] Threshold or barrier, to set it up apparently implies a sort of defense mechanism, and the corresponding argument concerning defense mechanisms given in relation to the cognitive simulator applies here too.

Interestingly enough, the switchover of the cognitive simulator from its self-organizing phase to the production phase may be regarded as a very grand decision one makes usually just once in one's life, even though the moment of deciding in this case may appear as a rather gradual shift. This brings us to the topic of supraordinate decisions, which has been left open.[5]

SUPRAORDINATE DECISIONS AND CONFLICTING GOALS

It is quite true that most of the decisions a person makes are subdecisions of some supraordinate decision process. The scope of such a supraordinate plan is in principle bigger than that of its subdecisions, and as one goes far up the decision hierarchy, he will meet a very grand decision that rarely occurs in his life. So most of the time these grand decision nodes are in the state of G-closed, defining partially the decision context DMS has to deal with in his everyday life, whether or not he is aware of the existence of such constraints. On the other hand, the subdecisional nodes down below the hierarchy are either S-closed or L-closed, as discussed previously. So we may say that most of real, analytical decisions we make are in the middle range of the hierarchy.

Now suppose that a need arises to relinquish or revise a higher plan because of severe overall performance deterioration, which can no longer be tolerated. Apparently something is wrong with one of the higher plans, but how high would it be? The error of choosing the wrong hierarchical level may very well occur, and one would be apt to choose too low a level. Very high level decision nodes have usually been closed for a long time, and any long-closed decisional level tends to escape the DMS's awareness of its existence (or they may be too well emotionally defended against reconsideration, like one's belief system). At any rate, a mistake in choosing the proper level for the "trouble" plan will create an insoluble decision problem and may well lead to a pathological mental breakdown.

This is not the matter only with individuals. For corporate DMSs the problem tends to be more serious, since their decision hierarchy generally has more layers. A small policy decision may be bound by precedents, which may have been created under a general policy of the company made up a long time ago. Such a general policy might have been established in accordance with the general tradition in the economic system of the society, which would in turn be a product of the cultural background of the society, and so on. Of course, all these very high order constraints are outcomes of "collective decisions" and can be subject to change only under the utmost pressure. There are, however, many supraordinate decisions on intermediate levels, which can be changed if the DMS is really up to it. However, for the same reason applied to the individual's case, the goals set by these past high decisions are often just "blindly" accepted.

In this vein we should also consider the common situation in which more than one conflicting goal is set either by different supraordinate plans or by external agents. When the goals are given in the form of gradable objective functions, the optimal compromise solution may be found through their tradeoff relations, the topic now being one of the most popular in normative decision theory (Humphreys, 1977). Of course, there is nothing wrong with the compromising strategy. Practically every decision, whether it is individual, corporate, or societal, can be regarded as a product of compromise one way or another. However, one should never think that compromise is the only way out in case of conflicting goals. A possibility is always open for finding a better plan by which the conflicting conditions may be bypassed, by enlarging one's decision scope or by revising some of the supraordinate plans whose inadequacy has yet to be suspected.

NOTES

1. I am not suggesting a particular form of sensitivity analysis here. The issue of cognitive sensitivity analysis, however, has a tremendous importance as it will play the most dominant role in cognitive decision problem solving and calls for a good working hypothesis to begin with.

2. From Piaget's works, we know that children have to go through the stages of learning various conservation laws — of matter, of volume, and so on — on an intuitive level. Having learned all these, a housewife's concern will be shifted to more concrete issues, such as how much a litre of liquor will cost next month (see, for example, Flavel, 1963).

3. There are numerous documents in this area. To know how the notions fit together, see de Groot, 1964.

4. In Japanese, "decision making" is translated as "will forming."

5. It is also noteworthy that, at the opposite end of decision hierarchy (i.e., in the visual perceptual process), almost parallel arguments seem to apply to those given in this paper. See Neisser, 1967.

REFERENCES

de Groot, A. D. 1964. Chess playing programs. *Proceedings Koninklijke Akademie van Wetenschappen*, Series A, 67, no. 4:385–98.

Festinger, L. 1957. A theory of cognitive dissonance. Stanford, Calif.: Stanford University Press.

Flavel, J. H. 1963. The developmental psychology of Jean Piaget. New York: Van Nostrand Reinhold.

Humphreys, P. 1977. Applications of multiple attribute utility theory. In *Proceedings of the Fifth Research Conference on Subjective Probability, Utility, and Decision Making*. G. de Zeeuw and H. Jungermann, eds.

Neisser, U. 1967. Cognitive psychology. New York: Appleton-Century-Crofts.

Toda, M. 1968. Problems concerning decision models in applied psychology. In *Reviews, Abstracts, Working Groups: XVIth International Congress of Applied Psychology*. Amsterdam: Swets and Zeitlinger.

———, and E. H. Shuford. 1965. Utility, induced utilities, and small worlds. *Behavioral Science* 10:238–54.

10 WHAT HAPPENS AT THE MOMENT OF DECISION?
Meta-Decisions, Emotions, and Volitions

In spite of the numerous articles written on the subject of decision making, I have yet to be enlightened on one critical question: What is it that is *made* at the moment of decision? This is a strictly psychological question, neither semantic nor philosophical; some "internal" event must occur to mark off the moment, and that event need not be the onset of overt behavior. A prime minister may make an important political decision while smoking his favorite cigar, without displaying any external sign of the event. The nature of the decision will be made apparent at a much later date, when the premier begins to implement it. Some circumstances that arise before the implementation, however, might make him abandon the decision. It may then appear to a naive observer that no such decision had ever been made. So in this case the successive events, the decision making and its subsequent abandonment, remain strictly within the sphere of the premier's cognitive universe without being manifested in the domain of his overt behavior. Nevertheless, being

This paper is to appear in *Human Decision Making,* L. Sjöberg, T. Tyszka, and J. A. Wise, eds. (Lund: Doxa, 1981). Copyright © 1981 by Doxa; used by permission. This is a revised version of the paper read at the Sixth Research Conference on Subjective Probability, Utility and Decision Making held in Warsaw, Poland, in September 1977. I am indebted to Adam Biela and his colleagues from the University of Lubin, Poland, for useful suggestions.

important cognitive events, they will have significant aftereffects on his cognitive processes at a later time and, in turn, on his subsequent overt behavior.

Consider another example. Imagine a person engrossed in conversation while eating. Eating is usually a choice situation, as there may be more than one kind of food on the plate — meats, carrots, potatoes, and so on — to be picked up for immediate consumption. The person might find out, when the argument is over, that he has somehow eaten everything on the plate; that is to say, the choices have been made and his overt behavior successfully carried out the motor activities necessary to consummate the choices *without any conscious effort to make decisions.*

Note that, in this latter example, it is not correct to regard the choices made as habituated effortless decisions; the person could certainly have indulged himself in deliberate decision processes, had he not been engrossed in an interesting discussion. He might have found on the plate, for instance, one of his favorite delicacies and could have asked himself: "Shall I eat it first, or save it for a while to prolong the pleasure of looking at it?" He might have eliminated carrots by their "aspects" because he believed himself to be allergic to carrots, and so on — if only he paid enough attention to the foods. But he didn't, and the topic of conversation was so exciting that he had even eaten the carrots. So the choices made are hardly habituated decisions.

It is true that these choices were made automatically because of the lack of conscious attention, but the term *automatic* requires clarification because the same sequence of choices seldom repeats itself in similar circumstances. Note also that most of our daily choices are made on this "automatic" level; only occasionally, comparatively speaking, do we engage in elaborate decision making with its characteristic decision processes. The rest of the choice situations (and what situations are not choice situations?) are coped with by a more-or-less automatic (subattentional) choice that is quite competent. Its capability is enough to guarantee our survival; however absentminded, however engrossed in conversation, one would not eat something inedible that happened to be on the plate for ornamental purposes, nor would one eat carrots if one really abhorred them. So this subattentional choice device of ours must be equipped with very well developed software, which produces fairly adequate responses given circumstances and given perceptual inputs.

There apparently are two types of processes that entail making choices: one that requires little attention and is usually followed by an immediate action and one that requires conscious attention and is characterized by a predecisional information processing including, most importantly, the appraisal of more than one *possible* action and possible outcome. For the sake of conceptual clarity, let me restrict the term *decision* to the latter type of choice process. Since these two types of choice processes are most likely supported by two different neural hardwares with correspondingly distinct softwares, let me set the purpose of the present paper as being to propose a tentative model for these subsystems of the brain, called *System I* and *System II*, respectively. As the reader will see, I am including a far wider spectrum of functions than making choices within the jurisdiction of each of these subsystems, and my arguments are bound to become highly speculative because of oversimplification and the insufficiency of pertinent data. The major purpose served by such a highly speculative global model is stimulation to produce more empirically testable hypotheses from hitherto unimagined dimensions.

To the above two subsystems of the brain, a third, *System C*, should be added, where *C* stands for either the consciousness or the control center. All three will be discussed one by one, with special emphasis on their functions as they pertain to making choices.

SYSTEM I AND SYSTEM C

According to my assumption, System I is the subsystem of the human brain that takes care of all the *basic* functions the brain needs to carry out for the subsistence of an individual as a warm-blooded, gregarious animal. In comparison to this basic subsystem, System II is a luxury subsystem specifically developed in the genus Homo, probably highly dependent on its tremendously enlarged forebrain as the supporting hardware. Viewed this way, undoubtedly it is this information-processing power of System II that has given the genus Homo a special dominant power over the other mammal species and allowed it to develop its own artificial environment called civilization. Once this artificial environment is created, and in order to survive within it, a well-developed System II becomes a necessity and no longer a luxury.

However, this may not alter even slightly the position of System I as the basic core subsystem of the brain of any animals as well-developed as mammals, the system being assumedly self-sufficient. As such, it must be an enormously elaborate system, supposedly brought to near perfection through evolutionary processes over hundreds of millions of years. Compared to it, System II has a very short history, and it is not surprising that we may find this new subsystem, however powerful, to be full of flaws and requiring the constant coordination of System C.

So in the awareness or consciousness of the genus Homo, the activities of System II appear disproportionally large and important, standing as the "figure" in the content of awareness, and we tend to disregard the activities of System I as the "ground," which, in spite of its real importance, may require little monitoring. Even so, I believe that System I must have emerged earlier than System II in evolution's creative process. Note that System I, as a self-sufficient information-processing system for survival, must constantly engage in closely coupled parallel activities — perceiving, responding, and so on. Then, as discussed by Simon (1967), a serial central processor becomes a necessity to temporally regulate these parallel processes.[1] Perhaps the role of this central processor, or System C, may not be restricted to simple temporal sequencings. However elaborate System I is, there may arise occasions of accidental operation jam — perhaps more serious as the system gets more elaborate. In that case the operations of the relevant parts of the system must be temporarily halted and reset after appropriate troubleshooting. Note that a troubleshooter must have a backup that is for all practical purposes basically independent of the system being served; only an untroubled system can shoot a trouble in another system. It could quite well be the case that System II was originally developed as such an independent backup of System C for its troubleshooting of System I.

In order to pursue this hypothesis, we need to clarify my view of System I a little further. First, let me touch very briefly on what System I supposedly does in perceiving the external world as one of its major routine tasks. It seems that today the proposition is widely accepted that we can draw information from incoming simuli only insofar as our *perceiving schemata* allow them (see Neisser, 1976). The perceiving schemata provide us at each moment with what we may anticipate perceiving by virtue of the information concerning environmental redundancies and our bodily motions, so that the really novel information the perceiving system needs to process is rendered manageably small. Needless to say, for this program to operate effectively, relevant information concerning the environmental redundancy and the current motion of the body must constantly be fed to the system. The part of the bodily motion information feedback would not be difficult.[2] In contrast, feeding constantly relevant and useful environmental information is a tremendous task. It requires not only a really large amount of preprocessed information but also a very efficient organization of the System I memory, in order that the relevant environmental context can be simulated in the form of appropriate schemata nearly all the time.

Note that perception is the task that allows one no breaks while awake. There should be no time allowances for leisurely memory hunting for all the objects one encounters every moment. But if one does not identify virtually everything one observes from moment to moment, one would not be able to identify the environmental context one is in (i.e., one would not be able to *understand* one's position in the world). Consider an imaginary experiment in which one's sensory input is completely disarrayed; each object may be familiar, but a person is hung upside down in midair grinning, a fish is flipping in front of his eye, and a hat is apparently making a loud noise. If any such Alice-in-Wonderland sensory distortion could be produced by some experimental gimmick all of a sudden and without reason, it is quite sure that the poor experimental subject would at least panic, lose consciousness, or go mad. Interestingly enough, however, no theory in experimental psychology predicts such an effect. Learning theory should predict that the subject should respond to whatever part of the stimuli he sampled by observing the fish, for example, in the manner to which he had been conditioned in the past. According to the theory of perception, the subject will do the feature analysis, which will come out right, and every object will be correctly identified in the proper perspective. In neither case is any difficulty anticipated, and the subject will remain serene and sane. This is because neither theory incorporates the dire need of constantly identifying the current context for the person, which I interpret as identifying his position in his cognitive world. This is needed because the perceiving mechanism of System I is keyed to this knowledge, without which it cannot produce perceptual anticipations necessary to process perceptual information.

What we should deduce from this is that the *primary memory*, or the information store of System I, must be a conditional simulator that produces the perceptual schemata for the input to be received at the next moment, depending upon the current input and the bodily motion feedback. In order to perform the task without a moment's delay, the primary memory must be a tightly organized network and cannot afford to be a leisurely random-access memory (Toda, 1975).

The point of my argument here is that, even though such a system will function very efficiently as long as it does not misinterpret the input, it might easily lose its own correct position within the maze of the primary memory once a mistracking has occurred. Ordinarily, however, the resetting of the perceptual mechanism would not be too difficult; it requires backtracking the wrong simulation course in the primary memory network until the correct restarting point is discovered. However, any such procedure cannot be a part of the routine work of the perceptual subsystem of System I, which allows no break. Since the task should include many test phases and reorientations of the course of search, the job properly belongs to System C. Through these operations, and as an outcome of them, it is conceivable that System C develops another auxiliary memory to assist in the task, whose content may consist of common causes of perceptual misidentifications and possibly in due time of an ensemble of higher-order redundancies of the environment, independent of the spatio-temporal organization of the contents of the primary memory.

Now let us turn our attention from perception to response control, but first note that the two activities are closely linked together, as are all System I operations. As mentioned earlier, the feedback of one's bodily movements is indispensable for the operation of perceptual schemata. This is, however, not a one-directional operation; perceptual inputs will also control bodily movements according to some well-established response schemata. In other words, the response schemata and the perceptual schemata are both operated by System I under close coordination, and the source material for the response schemata, the *primary response memory*, should also be considered as tightly interwoven with the primary perceptual memory. Combined, they form a substantial body of System I, and the term *memory* seems too awkward to apply to it. This primary memory grows through learning, not in that new elements are just added to it, but as a self-organizing *system* that keeps its integrity as a coherent system all the time. The real nature of this self-organization process is still largely obscure, except that it is apparently guided by some still not too well specified genetic programs. It seems obvious, however, that one of the ground principles for the self-organization process of System I is to achieve survival efficiency by means of acquiring *automatic* connections between the given conditions and the response.

For the purpose of survival efficiency, the bodily needs should apparently constitute the major input to the response selection mechanism; combined with the perceptual input, the needs direct the type of responses to be made. Human beings and animals are creatures who satisfy bodily needs through environmental objects, and perceptual inputs indicate the existence (or nonexistence) of specific objects. Now, the survival efficiency of this scheme will be acquired, in spite of the lack of System II for any elaborate information processing, by making the formation of cognition-response connections depend upon the *frequency principle*: Strengthen the connections that were effective in satisfying the bodily needs, and weaken those that were not. In other words, let the frequencies of success and failure be the critical determiners of the strength of the cognition-response connections.

To cut a long story short, we have now arrived at the reinforcement-type learning principle for the System I response-evocation mechanism. In spite of the general adverse approach of cognitive psychologists and decision theorists to traditional learning theories, I should point out the merit of the frequency principle in the economy of information processing. In view of the fact that we can hardly afford detailed cognitive information processing for everything we perceive or detailed predecisional processes for every response selection we make (which are luxuries entertained only after System II is developed), System I must make do with completely routinized processes. By default the frequency principle is the best suited to the purpose of automatic adaptation to the environment. (For a rationale, one may regard it as a loosely applied Bayesian principle.)

Of course, this does not mean that we should accept all the dogmatic parts of traditional learning theories; in particular, the "stimulus" parts are the weakest element in the theories. Even a rat should be aware of the context in which its response is taking place, and its behavior must be keyed to the context; it should hardly be able to survive otherwise in a natural environment where very often the input configurations are novel. This implies that the perceptual side of its System I is well developed; the real difference between human beings and rats should show up only in the capabilities of their respective System IIs.

What I have been arguing may be modeled, either by expanding the notion of stimulus into a far more elaborate set of cognitive registers or by introducing self-modification routines working under the frequency principle into the production system–type models of Newell and others (Newell, 1973). By so doing, these two approaches will turn out to be equivalent in their essential features.

In spite of the above argument concerning the economy and efficiency of the frequency principle, the principle also has a grave flaw. It may work quite well, fortified by the standard equipment of learning theories such as generalization and discrimination, as long as it deals with familiar occasions in a stable environment. However, when the animal encounters an entirely novel situation where the frequency principle is inapplicable, or when the instability of the environment makes the frequency judgment powerless, System I is in real trouble. And even though these occasions may be relatively less frequent than familiar occasions, they are nonetheless often critically important. These are the times when System II is called on to engage in an elaborate decision process. Before going into that topic, however, we should consider a superstructure of System I, which may be called System I +, the realm of desires and emotions.

SYSTEM I +, DESIRES AND EMOTIONS

In the previous section I stated my hypothesis that the response-evocation mechanism of System I operates under the bodily need input in such a way that, if the perceptual input indicates the existence of a means-object with which the need can be satisfied (food, for instance, under the hunger need), it evokes the response to consume the food. It is, however, more than likely that the perceptual input indicates no possibility of food. What, then, shall the system do? One strategy is to wait for a food input to turn up. Note that quite a large variety of lower-order organisms employ this strategy. Most of these organisms may be supposed to be constantly hungry, and their food is usually distributed fairly abundantly and homogeneously. The probability may then be relatively high that the waiting strategy will pay off for them.

For more highly developed organisms, however, the probability will be lower because their foods are more specialized. They must positively search for food, and the searching behavior is hardly a single response; it is a rather complicated system of routines including suppression (or inhibition) of irrelevant routines — irrelevant under the currently aroused pressing needs. Perceptual schemata must also be replaced by special ones that pay selective attention only to possible food. Bodily chemical balance might also be altered to accommodate a rapid energy discharge, for instance, to chase a fleeing prey. Remember that I am assuming System I to make no decisions. Instead, this special conative orientation that System I is put under by a special bodily need generally makes appropriate choices automatically to satisfy the need. If we call these need-instigated special states of System I *primary desires*, then we may view them as the System I version of "decision system." Since such a specialized program is not needed for lower-order organisms, which employ the waiting strategy and eat whatever edible turns up, primary desires are to be regarded as jointly forming a higher stratum of System I, which may tentatively be called System I +. Apparently, System I + is completely integrated with the other parts of System I and shows no sign of internal inconsistency.

I do not regard the primary desires as the sole constituent elements of System I +, however. There exist higher-order desires that, as desires, function in a similar way to primary desires but are not directly based on primary bodily needs. Instead of primary needs, these higher-order desires are typically driven by a special class of System I states called *emotion*. Let us consider anger as one of the typical emotions. Most commonly, anger is aroused in a certain context (i.e., when the organism's cognitive interpretation of itself within the surrounding world has taken a malevolent turn). So the arousal of the emotion of anger is very much keyed to the cognitive input. When it is aroused, characteristic physiological changes take place and certain types of behavior, most typically aggressive ones, become more likely to be evoked than other types of behavior, just as the primary desire of hunger instigates food search behavior. Perceptual schemata are tuned to the target of potentially aggressive behavior; when such a target is missing, the person will look for a likely one. So the emotion of anger, as well as other emotions, is to be considered as a part of the System I + version of the choice system; exactly as do the primary desires, emotions select types of behavior under the conditions of the given cognitive input.

The major differences between primary desires and emotions thus seem to lie in their respective arousal conditions; primary desire can be aroused by a bodily need alone, even though the arousal may be stronger when combined with a suitable cognitive input, while the arousal of emotions is more strongly keyed to the cognitive input, though the possibility that some physiological condition alone creates a certain emotion is not excluded.

Another important point to be discussed in this vein is the survival merits of these "choice systems" of System I + . The survival merit of primary desires is quite obvious for a wild creature whose repertoire of behavior is just far enough advanced to allow for different routines on different occasions. The survival merit of emotions is far less obvious. It is more in line with traditional thinking to consider emotions as primarily disruptive, and no doubt anger, say, may sometimes be very disruptive to a person's self in our contemporary civilized environment. If a man lets loose his aggression every time he is angered, he will most likely be an outcast from his community and end up in a correctional or reformatory institution of one kind or another. To temper anger is the critical skill one has to acquire in order to survive in the modern world.

Nevertheless, anything so flagrantly counter-survival could hardly have "survived" in the evolutional process if it had been counter-survival to begin with. As emotion is undoubtedly a much older system than our higher information-processing abilities represented by System II, we may entertain a hypothesis that emotion *was* an efficient pro-survival system at the time when System II was only rudimentary or in a burgeoning state, when, obviously, we had no civilization, which presupposes rather sophisticated information-processing capabilities.

Take anger, for example. Consider a situation in which an organism has succeeded in getting hold of a big chunk of food after hard labor. Another creature, of the same or of a different species, passing by and watching this, may try to steal it. What should the rightful owner do to this stealthy intruder? If he does not wish to be robbed of his food, which is counter-survival, he should fight if the thief is willing to put up a fight or chase if the latter tries to run away. In either case, it is imperative that his physiology is geared to bear a high rate of energy discharge and that his perception is primarily tuned to the thief. In a world where there is no law enforcer who may take up the task of bringing back the spoil to the rightful owner, the rightful owner must do this job all by himself. As long as all these activities — fighting, chasing, and the preparatory physiological and perceptual phases — are routine, the creature in such a situation had best be preprogrammed to do them automatically, through the emotion of anger.

One foreseeable danger in this automatization arises from the possibility that the food snatcher is much stronger than the original owner, and fighting for the rightful ownership may be a suicidal act for the latter. A safety valve for this danger may then be supplied by another emotion, fear, which, through its contrary commands, may keep the risky aggressive tendencies at bay.

In this paper I cannot attempt any further considerations of the organization of various emotions as a behavior guidance system aimed at efficient survival with a minimal cognitive effort. I will take up the project elsewhere and will show, among other things, that the system of emotions was apparently developed *after* our ancestral species had achieved a considerable number of successful social interactions.

COGNITIVE DECISION SYSTEM

Now let me turn finally to System II and concentrate especially on its conscious, cognitive, decision-making activities. Remember that I pointed out earlier the grave flaws of System I choice routines based on the frequency principle: first, it cannot cope with novel situations and second, it operates in too narrow a context of the immediately given environment. System II apparently overcomes these shortcomings of System I primarily by two means: first by extending the context from that immediately given to an ensemble of *possible* worlds and then by conducting extended simulation within this enlarged context.

Note that one of the most salient aspects of the System II's predecisional information processing is to generate alternative plans of action for comparison. In this phase, apparently, two System II activities are called for. One is to trace the *possible outcomes* a plan of action may entail. The other is to suppress any immediate action that System I will tend to evoke. Note that the latter, if successfully enforced, automatically serves the purpose of generating alternative plans of action, as System I should have the tendency to produce an alternative plan of action if the first is suppressed for whatever reason. During the suppression, which is rightly in the power of System C, possible outcomes of alternative plans of action must be produced for comparison, and this, too, can be done with the resources of System I alone. As I have already discussed, the primary memory of System I has all the materials for simulating environmental processes given the bodily movements. The perceptual simulation, however, is not free; it is bound also by immediate perceptual input, and the simulation waits moment after moment for its confirmation. What happens if the simulation is run free

without waiting for confirmation? If System C could run the same simulation device in this way, supplying it only with the *possible* bodily movement
and the current context, one could arrive at a rudimentary form of anticipating possible outcomes of a possible action.[3]

Of course, it is anybody's guess what really happened at the very beginning of the emergence of such System II routines. However, it seems very
important to me to demonstrate that only a very small "push" in the right
direction was needed to create System II routines, since it is hardly credible
that System II had been designed out of the blue with an entirely novel set of
ideas. The original gap between System I and System II must have been very
small, but once it was crossed, an entirely new vista of "possible worlds"
was opened up for the human mind to operate in.

Coping with novel situations may be considered in a similar vein. Note
that primate infants have a notorious tendency toward exploration
activities, which often have to be restrained by mother in the interests of
safety. Physical exploration is, of course, the most direct means of turning
the novel into the familiar. When cubs are no longer under protection of the
mother and fear prevents direct exploration, they *can* still do cognitive
simulation, since parts of the novel situation may still be familiar even
though the total configuration of the situation may not. To extract parts
from the whole may be included in the repertoire of System I, notably in the
perceptual schemata, so that an organism can analyze the whole into parts
and then synthesize the characteristics of the whole from those of the
parts — but this must be done in the cognitive universe with simulative
skill, and this is no small feat at all.

Something like this, however, must have happened in the course of
evolution, and these two processes — making inferences about future
events and analysis-synthesis — are undoubtedly the two major founding
blocks of System II, upon which, at a much later time, were to be erected
the two pillars of System II operations, *externalization* and *symbolization*.
By externalization I mean the action of transplanting internal constructs
onto the external world. Note that simulating possible future courses of action internally would be useless unless some of them were acted out later in
the external world. The transition from this stage of action planning to the
stage of object designing is a small step, though it requires additional supporting hardware, which human hands provide. The symbolization undoubtedly originated from the survival merit of communication; if one can
analyze a novel situation into familiar components, the possibility arises
that one can *describe* it with vocal symbols, and the listener may be able to
reconstruct the situation from the symbolized sounds. This process, too, requires supporting hardware, a signaling system of a rather large capacity,

and human beings had this too in their vocal cords. Undeniably, very favorable conditions had existed for the human System II to emerge and develop, though it might have taken millions of years for the original vestigial System II to attain its almost supernormal proliferation in modern times.

What has this development of System II brought to human beings eventually? Has System II finally succeeded in entirely dispensing with System I? Some people — those who were deceived by the obvious preoccupation of our System C with System II routines — were led to believe that we were almost on the brink of that stage. Until very recently, System I routines such as emotions have been considered as irrational, awkward but something to be tolerated, since they look as if they are the very essence of human beings who, unlike cold-blooded machines of System II type, act foolishly and commit errors.

Apparently, this view contains two major misconceptions: First, System I is not an irrational system but is based on a principle of rationality different from that of System II. Second, System I is not something ordained to be subjugated under the control of System II; on the contrary, the latter has been developed as a subsystem to aid the former. An aid, however, may sometimes become overly powerful and attempt to control its master, and this seems to have happened here, too. In consequence, some conflicts seem to have emerged between the two systems particularly because of the disparity in their respective guiding principles and the tremendous amount of self-organization of System II through the use of symbols and language. Nevertheless, the fact remains that System II is, and will remain, a proper subsystem of System I, albeit a special one. Despite a slightly jarring relationship between the two in the post-Eden period after cognitive evolution, System II will keep providing System I with better and detailed information than the latter could have obtained alone, due to the former's special faculty for operating not just with the real world but also with an ensemble of *possible worlds*.[4] On the basis of this improved set of information, System I can choose actions whose capacity for providing satisfaction is correspondingly upgraded.

Note that it is this property of action-elicitation belonging to System I that deprives System II of the possibility of ever superseding System I and becoming itself the master of an individual. System II may make a decision, but its execution belongs to System I. In most cases we do not feel this separation of respective jurisdictions; when we decide on something, like eating one food rather than another, we usually do as we decided. However, suppose that one has *decided*, for one reason or another, to walk across a slippery log-bridge over a deep gorge and has found immediately thereupon that one's foot refuses to step upon the bridge. What System II can do then is to try to coax System I, by imagining, for example, how attractive the goal beyond the bridge is, how shameful it would be to appear cowardly, and so on, at the same time avoiding looking at the depth under the bridge. (We shall consider later a similar example in relation to abstention from smoking.) All these observations point to the hypothesis that System II can manipulate System I to some extent, but only indirectly, in this case through arousing counteremotions to overcome the fear emotion; any direct control of the actual behavior is beyond the reach of System II.

As seen in this example, at least one of the major sources of recent conflicts between the two systems may be ascribed to the extended horizon of advance planning put forward by System II. Planning is obviously the most important asset of System II, whose advantage tends to increase as it becomes more elaborate. However, the advantage can be gained only if the plan is executed, and whether it is executed or not is up to System I. Note that planning itself is not an innovation of System II. System I is guided, among other things, by genetic plans, manifested prominently in animals in the cases of procreation, childrearing, migration, and so on. Since they are System I plans, they are naturally under the full support of other System I routines, with specific hormones and so on, and are executed to the letter as long as the external environment permits.

System II plans, on the other hand, cannot expect any such unconditional support of System I; System I, by its own nature, is triggered by things in the immediate environment unless it is driven by some superior forces like a genetic plan. So System II must control not only the external environment but also the internal environment for the execution of its plans and must devise ways to let System I avoid unforeseen temptations, impulsive desires, or being sidetracked. All the strategies that System II conjures up for the purpose may be subsumed under the name of *volition* or *will*, and any decision, or selection of a plan, must accompany the setting up of a volitional scheme for the execution of the plan.

PLANS, DECISIONS, AND VOLITIONS

Before going into the volitional processes, a little clarification of the notion of *plan* may be called for. A plan is, as I see it, a system of conditionally linked subplans whereby the smallest unit of a subplan is a fixed action. A plan to pick up a pencil without using one's eyes, a pencil that should be near the telephone, will be executed by first extending one's hand in that direction. The movement will be continued until the fingers touch something. If the tactile sensation tells that the touched object is the surface of the table and not the pencil itself, the fingers will grope around until they touch the pencil, and then the hand will grasp it. So by being conditional to environmental contingencies, a plan can acquire flexibility and efficiency in coping with environmental uncertainties within a certain limit. If the environmental vagary goes beyond this limit — for example, if the hand does not touch the pencil after a period of search — this plan is terminated and linked to another plan, like searching the place with the eyes or calling out to somebody to fetch a pencil, since these plans are undoubtedly conditionally linked subplans of a higher plan.

Apparently, a plan in this sense can be viewed as a hierarchically organized sequence of executions and tests (Miller, Galanter, and Pribram, 1960) or as a form of flow chart; computer programs are only plans of a special kind. Not only computer programs, but the behavior of humans and animals, are all organized as plans in this most general sense; perhaps the only major distinction of human behavior from that of animals is the greater depth in the hierarchical organization of the former.

When a notion becomes so broad that it encompasses almost everything, its usefulness is partly reduced, however. So let me call hereafter a plan in the general sense discussed above HOCLIR (Hierarchically Organized, Conditionally Linked Routines), and a material system that embodies a HOCLIR a HOCLIR system. A programmed computer is a HOCLIR system, and an organism in general may be viewed also as a HOCLIR system as far as its behavior is concerned. By this I save the term *plan* for a HOCLIR that is *to be imposed on* a material system. Thus a computer program per se is a plan. With human beings a plan is something created by System II that is imposed on System I for execution. (The Systems I and II referred to here may not belong to the same person.)

Note that System I is itself an *adaptive* HOCLIR system made of habituated subHOCLIRs. Its linking probabilities may be modified through experience. However, insofar as the modification is done only through some principle like the law of effect, most of its subHOCLIRs will remain nearly stable, making the whole system a rather dull one that never does anything particularly new. On the other hand, System II can compose entirely new subHOCLIRs out of old elements through experimenting in imaginary possible worlds and can also stock them in the form of information for later use. In any case, it can provide System I with a nonhabituated subHOCLIR *to be used only once*. Or, it can improve System I's HOCLIR by adding to or severing its habituated conditional links.

The imposition of plans by System II on System I cannot be done directly, as the former has no direct control over the latter. This does not, however, mean that the task is difficult in general. On the contrary, under usual circumstances the two systems will cooperate in perfect harmony as they should. First, a desire may be aroused in System I + . If the environment does not permit any immediate gratification of the desire, like in a novel situation, System II takes over. Perhaps a standard System II operation may be summarized as follows: First, by utilizing a special HOCLIR, it will look for a state in one of its possible worlds that satisfies the desire and will set it up as the goal. Then it will work out an execution plan to reach the goal. When this mission of producing a workable plan is completed, the plan will be submitted to System I to see if the excitatory input created by the image of the plan, presumably corresponding to its expected utility, exceeds the restraining threshold. If it does, the decision is made, meaning that the desire aroused in System I is channeled into the execution of the plan as the means of satisfying it. System II is permitted to set up a control HOCLIR called *volition*, which is in the simplest case nothing but a set of cognitive routines to *revive* the desire at critical links. Note that this control HOCLIR is needed for any not-too-simple plan to be executed, since System I desires may undergo a spontaneous decay when they are not based on some basic physiological needs. Revival itself, however, will not be too difficult. For example, just linking to critical junctures a cognitive routine of bringing up the image of the goal will do, since desires are known to be aroused by images as well as by real sensory inputs.

A problem arises, however, when a strong counterdesire, working against the execution of the plan, is expected to arise in the future, when the original desire has lost its strength. A typical example is given by the case of the decision to stop smoking.

META-DECISIONS

The decision to give up smoking is perhaps one of the most frequently made, most difficult to execute decisions and has thus contributed to making the world a little happier by being an inexhaustible source of jokes. Besides jokes, it also presents quite a few theoretical puzzles and paradoxes. Let me examine these one by one.

Note first that the plan chosen by this decision is not meant for once-only use, in contrast to the once-off decisions customarily dealt with in contemporary decision theory. Even though some plans may be stored in memory for repeated use, these one-shot decisions are meant to end at a certain moment in success or in failure. At that time the volitional control HOCLIR is disbanded,[5] and the person may gain a feeling of relief. On the other hand, the plan to give up smoking consists of an indefinite number of repetitious choices, an endless loop, the only exit from which is the failure exit. Of course, in actuality there is a semblance of an end; the goal of this plan is to replace habitual smoking links in System I with habitual nonsmoking links, and this can be done through repeated identical choices forced upon System I, since automatization of repeated linking is a part of System I's learning program. So as long as one sticks to the abstention plan long enough, its execution will be virtually over. On the other hand, if one dissolves the vigilance HOCLIR prematurely, one might easily relapse into the old habit, since a new habit formation does not necessarily mean complete obliteration of old habitual links, but may mean only that a makeshift bypass was set up to circumvent a dangerous link.

In any case, the control HOCLIR set up at the moment of the stop-smoking decision is meant to be used repeatedly whenever the temptation to smoke arises. It is a decision preempting all the future decisions belonging to the same category. In this sense, any such decision as the stop-smoking decision, accompanied by a control HOCLIR that tries to enforce the same plan whenever a certain condition is met, may be called a *meta-decision.*

Note that meta-decision making is not only intended to either form or to unform habits, but it also constitutes one of the most important classes of real-life decisions. If one is young or still can remember the time of youth vividly, the reader may recollect having made numerous important-sounding meta-decisions especially in adolescence, those that were meant to be kept for life: "I will always be kind to old people." "I will always imitate whatever my idol so-and-so does." "I will never hurt the feelings of my mother." "I will never doubt the correctness of my choice of life goal." And so on. Some of these meta-life-decisions may be downright unexecutable and soon abandoned. Some, however, will be executable and become integrated within one's habituated lifestyle. The extreme lifestyles of some, like those of truly religious people, could hardly be accounted for without assuming some such *self-shaping* process of lifestyles.

In order to discuss the implications of this hypothesis, we need to find a rationale or rationales for making meta-decisions, as there must be one even though formal decision theory appears to be incapable of supplying any. However similar to each other some decision situations may appear, they should differ in their long-lasting implications, and finding an optimal decision in each individual situation should never be inferior to making a blanket decision lumping all the similar situations together. This is true, however, only with an ideal information-processor cum decisionmaker with whom the predecisional analysis is instantaneous and costless.

Because of the importance of this issue, let me discuss it first within the traditional context of the tree-form plan or the *tree plan.*[6] Put in the tree plan context, the argument made above leads to the problem that worried Savage, which he expressed in the form of two contradictory proverbs: "Look before you leap," and "You can cross that bridge when you come to it" (Savage, 1954, pp. 16–17). Suppose that decision analysis is costless. Then the conflict between the two precepts advocated by the above proverbs will disappear. Note first that, even though the decision concerning crossing a certain bridge is better made, theoretically at least, on the spot rather than in advance, *one may not be able to reach the bridge in the first place* if one has not planned appropriately in advance. And one is always entitled to *reconsider* one's previous decision in its entirety when one reaches the bridge, or when a new set of information becomes available, if reconsiderations are cost free.

Practically the same argument provides at least one rationale for meta-decisions. In advance planning of any kind, we can treat individual future situations only categorically; the lack of information that differentiates individual situations within the same category will make it imperative to assign the same decision to all the members of a category, thus producing a meta-subdecision. Of course, this rationale for meta-decision making is a very weak one, as the assumption of free reconsideration makes the meta-decision only tentative in nature.

Now, by dropping the assumption of cost-free decision making, the rationale for meta-decisions is fortified in one aspect and weakened in the other. Consider first the weakened aspect. With a finite decision cost the reconsideration of a grand decision or meta-decision at each subdecisional node may not be justified and, therefore, the decisionmaker is made more strongly bound by the advance decision. This may in turn exacerbate the loss caused by a possibly inferior advance decision. The consequence would be especially grave in the case of meta-decisions, which are meant for keeps. In this respect, this is the weak point not only of meta-decisions but also of all the *habits*. Once a behavioral link is automatized under whatever mechanism, there is a risk that it can hardly be brought into attention even in the situation where a modification of the link will more than make up for the reconsideration cost (Toda, 1976).

When a meta-decision has not yet been entirely habituated, however, meta-decisions as well as grand decisions can be reconsidered for a certain price. The problem is that it is impossible to determine precisely whether the given on-the-spot information makes reconsideration worthwhile until the costly reanalysis has been completed. Apparently, what one can do to overcome this dilemma is to develop a makeshift evaluation scheme for the implication of information, based on past experiences or on some heuristic. Any such makeshift evaluation scheme, when employed, will be incorporated within the control HOCLIR of a grand decision or a meta-decision, most likely in a form of an *escape clause*: only under such and such conditions may one reconsider the previous decision, but never otherwise. Obviously, the setting up of a good escape clause requires highly sophisticated cognitive skill, and thus we may expect to find a fair variety of types of escape clauses actually employed by individuals. A person who tends to set up overly stringent escape clauses will behave like a person of high will-power and of low flexibility, and a person whose escape clauses are overly lax will behave impulsively and be always under the sway of immediate circumstances. These are, however, not the only alternatives. With skill one may be able to develop an ingenious escape clause, which is almost precisely tuned to the necessities of the decision and the environmental contingencies. Nevertheless, just having this escape clause itself gives the volitional control HOCLIR an Achilles' heel, often bringing an eventual doom, as we shall discuss in the next section.

In spite of these possible shortcomings and weakness, the potential usefulness of meta-decisions also increases tremendously with the increasing cost of the predecisional analysis. Note that, even though it is theoretically possible to prepare for all the foreseeable possible future contingencies in drawing a decision tree, no one does this in practice because it is practically impossible. For example, suppose that an executive manager is drawing a plan for a big construction project he is responsible for. He could certainly foresee many subsection chiefs coming to see him with requests to raise their budget. If he incorporates all these incidents in his decision tree, which may happen at any time, and considers all possible grounds for the requests as chance alternatives, the decision tree will immediately become unmanageable. Adding just one subdecisional node to the tree, even the simplest binary one, will double the number of subdecisional nodes from that point. A most common practice to overcome this difficulty is to remove all these "common" subdecisional nodes from the decision tree by virtue of a meta-decision — a meta-decision such as "I will handle it on the spot when it happens, with the best of my ability, to achieve the goal of completing the construction successfully with minimal cost." Note also that this is one of the most popular and most important classes of plans in stock in everybody's cognitive repertoire; it might be called *goal-directed maneuvering*, only by virtue of which can one make a grand plan without bothering about details. (See also Toda, 1976.) Note also that meta-decision making does not necessarily mean to employ the same action in the same situation, but it means to apply the same *plan* whenever the same class of decision situation arises. In the above example, a well-seasoned manager's plan may be to have a hearing, evaluate the necessity of a budget raise according to a certain criterion of his own, refuse or haggle the claim depending on the assessed necessity, and then draw the necessary minimal amount of money from the special reserve fund.

This goal-directed maneuvering, however, is not the only meta-decision applicable to the present case. The manager, for example, may decide to flatly refuse all such claims. This meta-decision is certainly much cheaper to execute but, on the other hand, it may be dangerous because some of the claims may not be a bluff. So an escape clause — such that he will apply the goal-directed maneuvering plan if and only if the same claim is made for the third time after two refusals — will be needed.

One should not see the benefit of meta-decisions just in the aspect of saving decision costs. In the case of individual decision making, the most important limiting factor is the capacity for information processing rather than the cost. If we can approximate the capacity of making plans from the maximum number of subdecisional nodes involved, then only meta-decisions allow one to explore far into the future and make long-range plans. This conclusion is consistent with the previous hypothesis that quite a number of meta-decisions seem to be made in one's adolescence and much fewer in later years. Even though I know of no objective study relevant to this point, I feel positive about this supposition. For those who are inclined to make plans, adolescence is the time to make approximate life plans, and how can one make such a super-long-range plan without severely reducing the uncertainty created by his own uncommitted future decisions?

This, therefore, is a good enough rationale in support of meta-decisions. There is another, however, equally strong one, more psychological in nature, to which we shall now turn our attention.

CAN YOU REALLY GIVE UP SMOKING?

Honestly speaking, I do not think myself qualified to discuss the ordeals accompanying the meta-decision to give up smoking, since I made a meta-meta-decision to "never make a meta-decision to give up smoking" in my adolescence and have kept it since then. I made that decision thanks to my awareness of the futility of the attempt in my case; I am not the type to carry through a meta-decision with sheer willpower. The meta-decision to give up smoking really requires willpower, as everyone knows and as is clearly demonstrated in the study of Sjöberg and Johnson (1978). They recruited volunteers who were willing to make the attempt to give up smoking and followed up the consequences of the meta-decision made by the ten subjects they recruited with repeated interviews. What they found was that nine of the ten subjects failed within a rather short period of several days. They also found that the breakdown occurred under twisted rationalizations, mostly when the subjects found themselves in a sort of depressive mood. So they write:

> It is suggested here that strong mood states brought about by stressors are the cause for a decrease in quality of information processing. The reason for this assumption is as follows. In order to carry through action in an orderly manner according to plans — and in the face of strong, often conflicting wishes — it is necessary to allocate some of the available mental energy to regulating the order of processing of wishes. Hence, some energy which otherwise would have been available for the cognitive system is lost. This is called mood pressure. The effect is selective which means that the withdrawal of energy first affects more sophisticated cognitive mechanisms leaving the more primitive ones. This may leave the door open for a corrupt, twisted, and shortsighted reasoning which generates excuses for changing the initial decision. This is the final and most proximal reason for a breakdown of the will. As we shall see later, there seems to be no limit to the variations of excuses brought about by this type of twisted reasoning. [Sjöberg and Johnson, 1978, p. 151]

Before going on to discuss their hypothesis, we need to pay attention to the psychological factor, the reversal of preference, which makes meta-decisions like giving up smoking so much more difficult to keep. At the moment when the meta-decision was made, the person preferred nonsmoking to smoking, with some good reason. When some time later a desire to smoke arises, many succumb to the desire, preferring smoking to nonsmoking. The person's preference has thus been reversed within a rather short period. Our daily experience is apparently full of similar examples. Is there anyone who can boast of never having faltered at the moment of initiating a difficult or embarrassing task that one's mind was made up to carry out under any circumstances, like undergoing a surgical operation or divorcing one's spouse? The factor common in all these cases is the immediacy of a desire-arousing situation, be it either a consumption desire or an avoidance desire.

This strong pulling (or pushing) effect of immediate possibilities, which arouses an unusually strong desire or emotion, has been known as "temptation," to which one should resist but only with difficulty. Recently Ainslie (1975) has proposed a hypothesis to explain this paradoxical preference reversal: the assumption that the effect of a reward is a strongly upward concave decreasing function of the time interval between the moment of the effect being measured and the moment when the reward is given. Since Ainslie's notion of reward is apparently broad enough to be identified with utility, this is nothing but a version of the discounting-future-utilities hypothesis popular in economics and dynamic programming. As Ainslie correctly puts it, however, the exponential temporal attenuation function used by economists does not produce the reversal of preference. The function must be more strongly upward concave than the exponential function to produce the effect, and he uses the function U/T for illustration, where U is the "reward" and T is the time interval.

I would not bother to refute the unrealistic U/T function, not just because it takes the value of infinity at $T = 0$ but because any mechanical application of a simple formula appears futile, done for no other purpose than accounting for the preference reversal effect. There are two reasons. First, making a preference concerning any nonimmediate events or objects is a cognitive activity, and one has to begin by keeping the alternatives (or their aspects) in mind for comparison. The relative attractiveness of alternatives produced through these operations can hardly be a function of *objective* temporal distance. (The subjective temporal difference, of course, can be *one* of the *many* aspects that jointly determine the attractiveness.) Second, the preference reversal does not necessarily occur every time; it occurs usually only when a rather strong desire-provoking object is present in one's immediate environment, supplying its characteristic sensory stimulations, and when a direct action to get hold of the object is also immediately possible. (The same can be said for the temptation to avoid a situation that one ought to face, in which case the object or the situation has a tendency to approach the person rather than vice versa.) All this suggests that what really is responsible for the preference-reversal effect must be an intervention of System I desires.

As I have discussed in earlier sections, System I characteristically responds to immediate inputs, leading often to the arousal of emotions, affects and desires, which in turn give pressure for the employment of habituated actions learned to be associated with gratifications. So unless System II does something quickly to countermand the desire aroused by the immediate stimulation, any person is bound to give way to temptation. From this argument, one should not identify System I with the Freudian id-system; not every potentially desire-arousing stimulus actually creates a desire in System I, as System I can learn to restrain desires if they are detrimental to survival. Not everyone feels temptation every time he sees a beautiful woman, a liquor bottle, deliciously flavored food, a stack of banknotes, and so on. The temptation desire occurs most notably when there is a habituated act leading to gratification through the object. Therefore we expect that the difficulty in resisting temptation would be most acutely felt when System II is tampering with habituated actions with a meta-decision, and the role of volitional control HOCLIR becomes especially important in this case. The control HOCLIR is supposed to execute a plan to influence System I by stimulating it with counterdesires.

It should not be difficult for the reader to imagine what this volitional control plan is like, since most people should have gone through, at least several times, a habit control process of some kind. When a desire to smoke arises after the meta-decision of giving up smoking has been made, its control HOCLIR will fill up the working storage of System C with images and notions that may arouse fear and counterdesires for the act of smoking, such as the image of lung cancer, of the improved bank account due to giving up smoking, of the air pollution he has been contributing to, and so on. Often the combined force of counterdesires thus created will turn out to be too weak to be effective. So on the next attempt after a failure, one may take the precautional measure of implicating the people around the person by notifying them of the meta-decision made. This would then add to the repertoire of the control HOCLIR the powerful weapon of the shame of failure. Ainslie discusses in the same paper the notion of *private side bet* as a means to combat temptation: The bigger the stake that one will lose if one succumbs to temptation, the more effective will the decision become. Among the various tactics discussed by Ainslie to make the stake bigger, the joining of different bets together into a single bet seems to require special attention because it may mean that, if one loses on one meta-decision, the subjective probability will increase that one will also lose on other meta-decisions, as the inefficiency of *his* volitional control HOCLIRs is implied by the failure. The expected utility loss that ensues could be very great since the inability to keep meta-decisions should seriously impair one's capability to make long-range plans that hold fast.

However ingeniously armed one's control HOCLIR may be, its escape clause never fails to be its softest spot. As also discussed by Ainslie, though in different terms, escape clauses must be very sharply defined in advance in order to be effective; otherwise, as Sjöberg and Johnson found, System II apparently invents a new interpretation of the escape clause before it concedes defeat to temptation. Probably having a legitimate escape clause is of paramount necessity, lest the credibility of one's entire control HOCLIR system should fall.

In this interpretation I am at variance with Sjöberg and Johnson; I believe that the will has already failed when one begins to search for an excuse. The de facto failure makes it imperative to find one — any excuse at all that System II under pressure can somehow sanction as a valid case to which the escape clause applies.

The mood pressure discussed by Sjöberg and Johnson could very well be the real cause of failure in many cases. I am a little skeptical, however, about the causal relationship between mood and mental energy, if the latter is meant in the sense of real energy. It is known that someone can change his or her mood very quickly. Could the level of physiological energy discharge in the brain shift so suddenly in an apparently eventless environment? It is possible but unlikely. Low mood seems to act as a diffusely operating suppressor of higher brain activities (tantamount to increments in restraining thresholds) that results not only in sluggish cognitive activities but also in downgrading any positive evaluations done by System II. High moods, on the other hand, which diffusely lower restraining thresholds, often result in rush overt activities and overestimation of positive outlooks. In either case, too strong a mood is detrimental to System II activities and apt to ruin the effectiveness of volitional control HOCLIR.[7] Viewed in this way, the functions of mood are similar to those of System I + activities, those of primary desires and emotions, and in fact mood must be a proper member of System I + activities. The state of mood may depend on either the System I evaluation of mental energy and/or the global cognitive assessment of the cost of cognitive activities. The effect of the latter is demonstrated by the fact that a high mood generally follows the emotion of joy and a low mood the emotion of sorrow. Note that, as far as emotion is keyed to the "evaluation" of mental energy rather than the mental energy itself, it can be swayed from one direction to another by cognitive input alone.

Before closing this section, let me mention an ironic observation. In an attempt to abstain from drinking, one may employ the tactic of going home by a different route to avoid encountering the direct visual stimulation coming from the bar that one frequented. This avoidance of direct confrontation with a tempting object could have been very effective should System II not inadvertently belie its own intent. System II, however, is habituated to exploring the consequences of possible courses of actions. As the bar is still not very far from the new route home, there may be ample clues in the sensory input to trigger System II's simulation process — "If I turn the next corner to the right and go one block, there is the bar and I will . . ." and the imagination would even produce a sensory image of the whisky going down his throat. Images are just as strong stimulations to System I as direct sensory inputs, and the person would have to fight the temptation as bitterly as he would have on the old course of going home. So System II's role in volitional control is really multifold. First it makes a meta-decision and sets up a volitional control HOCLIR. Then it fights with temptation by producing counterdesires, during which time it must also *control itself* to not inadvertently create images that might strengthen the desire to succumb to the temptation. A modern individual with an overdeveloped System II is indeed a complicated being!

CONCLUSION

By having started my argument with the question of what happens at the moment of decision, I have so far presented a crude model of the process taking place around the moment of decision making, under the assumption that the decision process always follows a certain pattern. It is as if we had once made a big meta-decision about how to make decisions. Apparently, however, this is a contradiction. Vlek and van Raaij (1977) have described how predecisional analyses are done according to some hierarchically organized plan; even a very young child can apparently execute goal-directed maneuverings without much thinking. So the basic structure of the plan with which we make decisions, together with the predecisional structuring and the major execution subroutines, must have been determined genetically. The surprising richness of the repertoire of nature's plans under which human beings operate, including those for making decisions, is impressive, particularly so since they mostly take the form of *meta-plans*, supplying only the skeletal structures of plans and letting each individual supply the details, also according to a meta-plan. So not only can we *learn* to make decisions better through experience, but we can also make meta-decisions about the way we make decisions, thereby creating the possibility of making tremendous shortcuts in the process of improvement (with a comparable risk of inviting dangers and instability), which the mechanical means of learning alone would take a long time to attain, if ever at all.

This particular human faculty of volitional *self-shaping*, however, seems to have been deliberately neglected by contemporary psychology, probably because of a false supposition that assuming anything that may imply an initiative on the part of an organism is an unscientific attitude and thereby creates a mystic agent beyond rational explanation. There is, however, nothing unscientific at all in imagining a system that organizes itself and takes "initiatives" by itself in starting a new stage of development. Nonetheless, as exemplified by the nature-nurture controversy, psychologists have apparently been under a common agreement that a person is shaped only by something other than himself. In my opinion, this false assumption has done a great deal of damage to the image of a human being, making it a sort of entirely passive entity, made up from genes and shaped exclusively by the direct bombardment of environmental influences. This is, however, an extreme vulgarization of nature's exquisite and elaborate ways of manufacturing its "systems." It is true that self-shaping is also influenced and determined by genes and environments. Just because this is so, how to shape oneself well can be *taught*. In order to teach correctly, however, the self-shaping process must be *studied* in the first place.

Self-shaping is an activity of System II, to which, as we have seen, major obstacles are set up by System I, in particular by its impulsive desires, emotions, and moods. How much do we already know about this aspect of System I? Clinical psychologists have been dealing with desires and urges, learning psychologists with drives and needs. It strikes me, however, that individual desires and emotions are almost always dealt with as if they were separate, independent phenomena, serving thus as *primitives* in psychological theories. Even though many emotions and desires are known, they have not yet been properly catalogued, let alone systematically analyzed to discover their interdependencies as the meaningful parts of a whole scheme, a system with its own rationality. This strange lack of curiosity, or aloofness, is most prominent in decision theory, where utility, nothing but a projection of desires upon preference, is dealt with entirely as an extraneous variable whose values must be measured but could not be analyzed.

Whatever the real cause for this peculiar "aversion" may be, there is a dire necessity to know System I more deeply, as in the time of mass communication twisted reasonings are going around with ever stronger influences. Twisted reasonings are produced not only when one gives up giving up smoking. They are manufactured whenever System II tries to cover up the fact that a person is behaving under the pressure of System I and not according to the rational plan System II openly claimed to execute. A lie given under a criminal intention may be uncovered. But a twisted reasoning made with skill *but without awareness* is really hard to detect, unless we learn more about the interplay of Systems I and II to discern tacit signals of emotional distortions.

As a final remark, let me reflect upon meta-decisions and their relevance to very long range plans. By very long range I mean to imply that the plan-maker is in a situation where he has to handle a decision scope too large to allow the possibility of drawing a reasonable decision tree. One such case may be found in a youth contemplating his course in life, and another in a government that is pressed to cope with a tremendously complicated world, which moreover changes rapidly and unpredictably. In the first example, the youth cannot really plan, since most of the consequences of whatever he or she does today would hardly survive uncertainty over many years to come. Still, the youth can set a life goal, such as becoming a renowned scientist, a jet pilot, or a movie star, and may mean it, even though the youth is unable to draw for the moment an exact tree plan to reach the goal. With or without an exact plan, the choice of a life-goal is undoubtedly a decision-making process, full-fledged with the characteristic phase of predecisional information processing and the postdecisional setting up of a volitional control HOCLIR. Indeed, a youth can be very *determined* in achieving his goal. So, even though an exact tree plan is missing, there must be some plan, the execution of which the control HOCLIR is to watch over.

A plan that is likely to be employed in such a case, and in many other cases as well, may be referred to as a *policy plan*, consisting of a goal and a collection of disjointed conditional plans, which are not sequentially organized so as to form a tree. Many of these conditional plans will take the form of meta-decisions since they are to be executed whenever their characteristic conditions are met. I often like to imagine a youth's view of his or her own future as something like a panoramic scope seen from a high mountain. The view will be filled mostly with the white clouds of uncertainty, with occasional distant peaks of mountains jutting out shining among the clouds representing alternative life goals, though revealing no details because of the distance. A girl may yearn to reach Mt. Movie Star, and the fact that she cannot make out any exact route may not distress her a bit. Being a pretty girl, she is certainly entitled to choose the goal and she will set forth by making a meta-decision that she will always proceed toward the direction of the goal *whenever possible*, meaning that she will take whatever action that will keep up her beauty and polish up her charm, and she will grab any chance that may make her acquainted with a movie director, producer, and so on. Even though such a policy plan may not always work out as intended, the point to be emphasized is that the consistency produced by a meta-decision is almost the only *simple* means of ensuring progress toward the chosen goal while overcoming uncertainties.

In other circumstances more than one well-chosen meta-decision will be needed to guide behavior, and blind effort alone will hardly do the job. Nevertheless, it remains true that only with consistent, constant actions one can set a finite-probability course over a wide expanse of the ocean of uncertainty, where turns of events may toss one to and fro, but seldom with any sort of consistency.

The goal, however, need not always be located in the distant future. In the case of a government, or of any social organization, the goal may often be to maintain a certain state of the system under its care. When the environment of the system, internal as well as external, is rather complicated and unpredictable, a fixed tree plan, however well provided for possible contingencies, would turn out to be obsolete sooner or later. A policy plan in a form of loosely organized meta-decisions and conditional decisions, the main function of which is to kick the state of the system back toward the ideal state whenever a danger signal is observed, would be far more viable. This, of course, is what most social organizations are de facto doing, on the basis of what has been learned through history and experience and not, unfortunately, on the basis of well-founded normative principles of policy making. So to externalize the process of policy planning and to develop a set of sound principles should be one of the most important and urgent tasks of the decision theorists. (And, I suspect, the study of policy plans might lead us back to System I again, since this control mode smells of the *old wisdom* all over.)

NOTES

1. Simon argues that the whole central nervous system must work in a serial fashion and conjectures that, when CNS appears to execute parallel routines, it would be doing so through frequent time-sharing operations. For me it is hard to imagine the whole CNS operating in a time-sharing mode, though possibly with System C alone.

2. This reminds me of a comment made by a driver who used to drive on an icy road: "When you go into a skid, as long as you think you still have the car under control then everything around you seems steady, but as soon as you feel that the car is getting out of control the outside world turns round you rather than the other way around."

3. This operation may be called the hypertemporal simulation. See for more detail Toda, 1975, 1978.

4. This reminds me of the remark by a famous Japanese mathematician, S. Takagi, who marveled in his famous book on introductory calculus: "What transparency and lawfulness has the introduction of imaginary numbers brought to the nature of real numbers!" Abstraction and the acquisition of higher-order lawfulness, the finest products of cognitive activities, appear to be achieved only through putting the real world within a much broader context of possible worlds.

5. The disbanding of an important volitional control HOCLIR will usually be followed by the postmortem HOCLIR, the primary function of which is to reflect upon the plan just executed.

6. By association and for the sake of the fun, the plan employed in a meta-decision may be called an "avenue plan" as it consists of a disjoint alignment of identical tree plans.

7. Note that impulsive juvenile crimes would perhaps occur more frequently in a high mood than in a low mood, suggesting that in a high mood a general, diffused activation of System I is taking place, thus lowering the restraining threshold for *any* activity. So the relationship between mood and volitional control should be rather complicated, and we need more data concerning other types of meta-decisions; smoking and drinking are minor activities indeed, requiring minimal mental and physical energy, and thus can be performed even in a depressive, inhibitory mood.

REFERENCES

Ainslie, G. 1975. Specious reward: A behavioral theory of impulsiveness and impulse control. *Psychological Bulletin* 82:463–96.

Miller, G. A., E. Galanter, and K. H. Pribram. 1960. Plans and the structure of behavior. New York: Holt.

Newell, A. 1973. Production systems: models of control structures. In Visual information processing. W. G. Chase, ed. New York: Academic Press.

Savage, L. J. 1954. The foundations of statistics. New York: Wiley.

Simon, H. A. 1967. Motivational and emotional controls of cognition. *Psychological Review* 74:29–39.

Sjöberg, L., and T. Johnson. 1978. Trying to give up smoking: a study of volitional breakdowns. *Addictive Behaviors* 3:149–69.

Toda, M. 1975. Time and the structure of human cognition. In The study of time II. J. T. Fraser and N. Lawrence, eds. New York: Springer-Verlag.

———. 1976. Decision process: a perspective. *International Journal of General Systems* 3:79–88.

———. 1978. The boundaries of the notion of time. In The study of Time III. J. T. Fraser, N. Lawrence, and D. Park, eds. New York: Springer-Verlag.

Vlek, C. A. J., and W. F. van Raaij. 1977. Analyzing values for decisions; an exploratory exposition. Paper read at the Sixth Research Conference on Subjective Probability, Utility and Decision Making, Warsaw.

11 EMOTION AND DECISION MAKING

Whatever the philosophers claimed, the main use of logic was to justify your emotions.

—Philip José Farmer (1978, p. 173)

Imagine a boy at the breakfast table on a merry Sunday morning; he is contemplating whether he can get away with not eating the detestable spinach on his plate. He looks surreptitiously toward his mother. Noting that she already appears to be a bit irritated by his hesitation to eat his spinach and that any more delay in eating it may result in a spanking, he resignedly stuffs all the spinach in his mouth and tries to swallow it in one gulp in order to shorten the loathsome act. While he is not particularly afraid of the pain

This paper was published in *Acta Psychologica* 45 (1980):133–55. It is a fundamentally revised version of the original paper presented at the Seventh Research Conference on Subjective Probability, Utility and Decision Making held in Gothenburg, Sweden, in August 1979. Copyright © 1980 by North-Holland Publishing Company; used by permission. I am indebted to Lennart Sjöberg and W. M. McKenzie for many valuable suggestions.

of being spanked, he feels a spanking would be very humiliating and would certainly spoil his expansive Sunday morning mood.

It is basically a decision process that the boy is involved in. All that is described above in emotion-relevant terms can be transcribed into such decision theory expressions as utility, subjective probability, and information. For example, it is the information obtained through the boy's observation of his mother's apparent state of mind that causes an increase in the subjective probability of the worst outcome contingent upon the alternative course of action of not eating the spinach. This increase results in the other alternative, that of eating the spinach as quickly as possible, as having the highest expected utility, and therefore the boy chooses this alternative.

I began this paper with this simple family scene in order to make a few points. What the boy has undergone is a very common kind of decision process (the reader may observe how touches of various emotions guided the process in a decision-theoretically proper way), and he has hardly been "emotional" in carrying out the process. One may argue that this is just a "description" of a decision process making heavy use of emotional terms, which could be far removed from the boy's actual decision process. Admitting this, let me point out the fact that this "emotional" description is a natural one, which anyone can understand without difficulty. It is also much richer in content than the more decision-theoretical description of the process that followed. That is, the emotional terms used seem to tell us about far more than just the decision process itself; they convey information about the characters of the boy and his mother, about the family atmosphere, and about the things the boy might do after breakfast. This richness in content, as well as the implications underlying emotional concepts, must be the reason why fiction writers use such concepts almost exclusively in telling the reader how the characters in a story went about making their "decisions."

So there seems no doubt that every one of us has, as a major component of "common sense," a cognitive framework, or a system of schemata, consisting primarily of emotional notions for describing, comprehending, and predicting human behavior and human relations. Let us call this cognitive system *commonsense psychology*, and I am an admirer of its efficacy. It may not be an overstatement to say that only with its assistance are we able to cope with the complicated interpersonal relationships we are confronted with in modern society.

Perhaps this commonsense psychology is no more efficient than the commonsense physics we use for dealing with familiar objects in our surroundings: the type of physics that tells us, for example, that heavy objects will fall faster than light objects. In physical issues, however, we can resort to the real, nearly infallible laws of scientific physics whenever the issues become complex — for example, when building a building, constructing a dam, or designing a rocket. With the complex issues of human relations, however, we have nothing even remotely comparable to modern physics. Thus we depend exclusively on commonsense psychology, whether the issue at hand is simple (for example, a little family strife) or complex (for example, diplomatic negotiations between nations). In case of the more complex issues, politicians and diplomats are expected (besides having other qualifications) to be expert commonsense psychologists, particularly in the manipulation of other people's emotions. It is easy to demand that these people, who are responsible for the safety of millions of lives, behave in a very rational manner. They are rational in their own ways. They try to manipulate the emotions of their constituencies or of their opponents because such a strategy pays off; this is part of the game they play, and the emotion-based nature of the rules of the game has hardly been brought out into the open for the more rational mind to scrutinize. So, if we really want to realize a world in which rationality prevails over emotions, we should, first of all, *externalize* (Toda, 1976) the nature of emotions. Dismissing emotions as just noisome irrationality and pretending that we are beyond the sway of emotions are both sure ways of making ourselves susceptible to emotional manipulations.

EMOTION AND VALUE

Before going into the issue of rationality, which I will do in the next section, let us take a brief look at the relationship between emotions and values (utilities). As in the case of the spinach-hating boy, when we say someone fears something bad might happen if he does a certain thing, the person himself is often not in a state of fear; rather, he is *anticipating* a fear he might feel as a consequence of an act he may perform. De Rivera quotes from Truman's memoirs to demonstrate how such an anticipatory emotion might influence important political decisions: "In deliberating whether or not to resist the invasion of South Korea, President Truman reports considering how he would feel about himself if he, as President, failed to resist the aggressive action of another nation" (de Rivera, 1977). This example is hardly likely to be an exceptional one nor one limited to important political decisions. In considering alternative resorts for a vacation, one would probably try to imagine some typical situations one would experience at each of the resorts. The emotional feelings accompanying these images, such as joy, relaxation, irritation, and so on, would probably be taken into account, along with monetary expenses, in determining the total worth of each resort. Thus anticipatory emotions could well play a critical role in a person's nonemotional cognitive decision system.

Does this imply that emotions are the ultimate source of all personal values? Some emotion theorists appear, in effect, to believe so when they identify emotion with motivation. Tomkins (1970), for example, assumes that a person is maximizing positive affect and minimizing negative affect. James (1902) suggests that his reader imagine a person who is entirely devoid of emotion — no joy, no fear, no greed, no ambition, no anger, nothing. Is there anything left of the person that is worth making a decision about? So there is a possibility that the supposition holds. Nevertheless, one should not make a rash identification of positive and negative emotional feelings with personal values. One may have anticipatory fears about some bad consequence; this, however, does not necessarily mean that the consequence is bad *because* it arouses the expectation of fear. If an emotional feeling itself is a direct value indicator, no one would be able to *enjoy* a *horror* movie. So for the moment it seems a much sounder position to suppose, along with Ortega y Gasset (1957), that emotions reveal values and that we do evaluate, very often, the utility of a state by the emotions it may arouse. This supposition opens up a very interesting possibility; instead of simply accepting a person's value system as something sacrosanct, as is customarily done in decision theory, we may now question its rationality. A considerable advancement will be obtained only by revealing how emotions influence the development of personal value systems.

The issue of the rationality of a personal value system acquires further significance when it is considered in the context of corporate decision making, where the decisionmaker has great power and his decision may influence the welfare of many people, as in the example of President Truman described earlier. Such a decisionmaker is assumed to operate under the value system of the corporate body, but Truman, as we have seen, allowed his decision to be guided by his personal values. Few people, however, would blame Truman for having done this. Indeed, decision theory claims that an individual makes decisions exclusively on the basis of his own utilities, or his personal values, and corporate decisionmakers should be no exception. Many social planners, including decision analysts, must have suffered the frustrating experience of having their "flawless" plan rejected by the decisionmaker to whom the plan was submitted — rejection based on no reason at all, an irrelevant reason, a twisted rationalization, or even an honest reason. We can consider the example of the legislator who admits a plan is good but rejects it because it will cause him to lose votes. (Incidentally, while this constituency feedback mechanism is important in making politicians fulfill their roles properly, it is far from sufficient since it involves patent biases such as favoring "popular" policies too much and too often.) Even without this mechanism, human societies, democratic or not, are generally equipped with socially accepted and socially enforced rules that function to make corporate decisionmakers identify their personal values with those of the public. If a corporate decisionmaker does a good job, he will be praised, honored, get promoted, become famous, and so on. On the other hand, if he does his job poorly or if he pursues private values that are in disagreement with those of the public, he will be blamed, punished, humiliated, and lose his job (look what happened to President Nixon). Note that a substantial portion of these social rules are non-material, emotional ones, and at the critical moment they often play far more important roles than do material rewards and punishments.

Thus emotions fill important social functions, as will be emphasized again later. But, of course, this is not the whole story of the role of emotions in society; the effectiveness of emotions can backfire and cause great damage, too. Since a corporate decisionmaker is also an individual, he is under the sway of his own emotions, and when he is, his cognitive field, or decision scope, tends to center around the target of his emotion and thus obliterate important long-range considerations. Rash actions and hasty decisions under the influence of a strong emotion are easy to check, however. Far greater damage is done by those decisions whose emotion-based character passes unnoticed even by the decisionmaker himself because he rationalizes.

In our contemporary society, everyone has learned to rationalize his or her emotional actions since society survives, in part, on the basis of its members' suppression of asocial emotions. If everyone tried to physically hurt anyone who aroused his or her anger, our cooperative society would immediately collapse. So, if one succumbs to an impulse, one needs to provide a plausible reason to extricate oneself not only from external punishment and blame but also from internal guilt for falling below one's own standard. The fact that Sjöberg and Johnson (1978) found that people made twisted rationalizations when they broke their pledge to give up smoking may be evidence in point. Perhaps this habit of rationalization is the reason we tend to believe ourselves to be less emotional and more rational than we really are.

There is essentially nothing wrong with the fact that our values are largely determined by emotions such as love, joy, pride, and so on, as long as we are aware that they also are determined by greed, hate, fear, and the like. By becoming aware of this, our cognitive system may finally be able to come up with a solution for how to live harmoniously with emotions. For the moment, however, the situation is not that way. Interestingly enough, our ignorance about emotions is guarded by the emotions themselves. In any culture there are objects (material objects or beliefs or symbolic objects or whatever) that social mores and institutions insist should be valued highly, often for no rational reason. It becomes quite touchy to talk about these things because we are often deeply indoctrinated to respond to them with emotion. Let me mention one such example. History reveals beyond doubt that countless intercommunity or international bloody strifes have occurred because of some dispute over border territory, and in many cases the disputed areas were nothing but narrow strips of barren land that were useful to nobody. Nevertheless such a piece of land has often been the cause of all kinds of belligerent emotions experienced by the members of the two communities or nations. Countless rationalizations are made to account for the importance of claiming sovereignty over the disputed piece of land, and a person who proposes a rational solution to resolve the dispute finds all ears closed.

There are numerous cases of this sort, enough to make one ostracized ten times over if one voiced doubts about the high values assigned to all of them. This, however, is a fool's errand. The important thing is to help people understand how much we humans are under the control of emotions, and how often we use what Osgood (1978) calls "Neanderthal thinking," though I am sure that Neanderthals lived in far more harmony with their emotions than we do today.

EMOTION AND RATIONALITY

Perhaps I have overemphasized the irrational aspects of emotions in the foregoing section. Now, to restore a balanced view, let me turn to the rational side of emotions. Here, however, I will not be discussing anticipatory emotions or emotions as values, but rather will be referring to emotion in the more proper sense of the word — the emotion implied when we say someone is emotional, the emotion that generates its own characteristic decision process. Consider the spinach-hating boy again. Assume that he has suddenly remembered, before eating the spinach, an incident that happened the previous evening when he was *unjustly* scolded by his mother for a mischief he did not commit. This memory revives his anger and results in the following sequence: He feels defiant, forgets the spinach completely, is spanked, runs out of the house in a rage, and thus completely spoils his Sunday.

I am not going to attempt to demonstrate the rationality of this anger-driven chain of behavior. Individual cases are irrelevant to the issue of rationality. Even the most deliberate, well thought-out decision may result in disaster. In my opinion, "rational" is an adjective meaningfully applicable only to the *principles or rules* under which a purposive system operates. A principle or rule is rational if and only if it makes the system function (almost) optimally for a given context and under given constraints. The reason I am particularly concerned about demonstrating rationality in the system of emotions, which many may think is the most improbable place to find it, is because of the great deductive merit the assumption of rationality provides. Assume that emotions provide some animal with principles for making decisions rationally. What is the *purpose* of the system called "some animal?" Survival as a species. Constraints? Limited information-processing capacity. Context? A rather primitive, but stable, wild environment. "OK," says the computer, and it will hesitate only a fraction of a second before it spews out a list of necessary characteristics that the rational emotions should have. How nice. But perhaps I must go a little more slowly to convince anyone besides myself.

Take normative decision theory, for example. It is obviously a rationality-oriented approach characterized by a maximization procedure, and the major methodology underlying its rationality belongs to the class of *analysis-synthesis*. In the analysis phase a decision tree is decomposed into component elements (states and transitions) so that their numerical characteristics (utilities and subjective probabilities) can be evaluated *independently* of each other. In the synthesis phase these independent evaluations are then combined according to certan formula (usually expected utility) to produce the overall worth of each alternative. Let us call this type of rationality *decompositional* or *analytical* rationality; it is, no doubt, the most typical paradigm among all possible types of rationality.

The decompositional rationality of normative decision theory has been handed down to contemporary descriptive decision theory, which has recently become more cognitively oriented. In taking a more cognitively oriented view, one must pay strong attention to the fact that human cognitive operations are limited. An information-processing system with a finite capacity cannot base its rationality on fineness of its analyses alone, but must be based on efficient allocation of its analytical resources. The rational allocation principle should be stated as: Analyze finely where there is information, but combine elements together as a *chunk* where there is redundancy (Miller, 1956). Therefore, under limiting conditions of any kind, one should consider *compositional* rationality as well as decompositional rationality.

The need for compositional rationality is not restricted to the domain of information processing, since a decision-making system engages in more than just information processing. The operations of a cognitive decision system begin with detecting a decision problem — that is, a situation calling for an action. The system then gathers information relevant to solving the problem, generates alternative plans of action, conducts analysis-synthesis, within an appropriate decision scope for each of the alternatives, chooses the best alternative, and then executes it (Toda, 1976). (Of course, this description is no more than a schematic tabulation of the basic features of the decision process.)

Now, applying the principle of compositional rationality, when there is redundancy some of the phases of this decision process could be condensed or skipped entirely. When it is sufficiently understood that decision problems of a certain class always lead to the same course of action after going through deliberate information processing, the deliberate information-processing part might be dispensed with since one's decison-making capability is limited by either cost, time, or ability. This is, however, an extreme case. Most often this redundancy-skipping procedure will result in a routinized, simplified decision process. Whenever the decision problem is identified as belonging to a certain familiar class, it will be followed by routinized information processing and the activation of stereotypical alternatives to be evaluated in a more or less small, fixed decision scope. So we form habits through learning; a certain class of cognition automatically elicits a certain class of response. Let me call any such simplified, habitual way of making decisions a *decision routine*. We cope with most of our familiar decision problems, those we encounter in routine business transactions or in household chores, by resorting to decision routines that we have learned through experience. Whether it is the decision routine or the cognitive chunking, its compositional rationality is an exact parallel to Shannon's coding theorems (Shannon and Weaver, 1949). This implies the existence of an indispensable assumption for any type of compositional rationality to hold — that is, the environment of the system utilizing compositional rationality must remain stationary so that the redundancy stays where it has been in the past.

Now let us turn to emotion. First, let me demonstrate that each emotion is a decision routine. Consider "anger," for example. The emotion of anger is aroused when a certain type of cognitive appraisal of a given situation is made. Though the nature of anger-arousing cognitions will not be discussed until the end of the next section, it is doubtlessly the type of cognition that creates a decision problem — that is, it calls for an action with or without an emotion. Once an anger emotion is aroused, the individual feels an urge to engage in aggressive behavior directed toward the object arousing the anger. Note, however, that the emotion itself does not necessarily specify the particular form of aggressive behavior to be taken. So we may say that anger generates a specific *class* of alternative actions called aggressive behaviors. Unless one of the actions is impulsively executed, the choice of an action often requires intensive cognitive operations — that is, evaluating the pros and cons (subjective probabilities and utilities) of each alternative aggressive action, including, of course, no action at all, and then choosing an action. One of the well-known characteristics of such information processing under emotions is that it operates within a relatively narrow scope, centering primarily around the immediate situation. The stronger the emotion, the more difficult it becomes to consider the long-range consequences of actions and anything else that is not directly related to the immediate situation. As described earlier, the preselection of alternative actions, the stereotyped way of information processing, and the narrowness of the decision scope are all characteristics of a decision routine. Thus emotions can be considered as decision routines.

While nonemotional decision routines are learned through experience, emotional decision routines are not. The essential structure of emotions undoubtedly lies in genetically inherited programs that are modifiable only in specific details. Tracing back along the phylogenetic evolution tree for the origin of emotions, we will find that we can go quite far, at least with the basic emotions, and recent developments in ethology have discovered more and more counterparts of human emotions in other primates (see, for example, Eibl-Eibesfeldt, 1970). Thus we can think of emotions as decision routines learned on the gene level through the evolutionary process. Even though such "learning" probably takes a tremendous amount of time, time is not a crucial factor when it is the species rather than the individual who learns.

No matter at what level learning takes place, when a system learns, it should, on the whole, improve its performance and thus, by definition, increase its level of rationality. However, when improvement depends a great deal on an increase in compositional rationality, such improvement may fall apart with the occurrence of environmental nonstationarity. Note how drastically human civilization has caused our environment to change within such a short time, a time too short to allow any significant species-learning to take place for readaption. Thus we are left with a well-developed emotion system preserved almost intact with its wild-life rationality being greatly impaired by nonstationarity, but not yet completely lost. Who says our society is no longer wild?

As a result, we find ourselves in a dilemma today. It is our large brain with its accompanying capacity for elaborate information processing that has created the powerful new methodology of analytical rationality, an element that is entirely foreign to species-learning, which apparently depended only on compositional rationality. I should also point out here that the basic process of evolution has resulted, at a level more fundamental than that of species-learning, in the acquisition of greater decompositional rationality as organisms' internal and motor organs evolved in the direction of finer separation of the functions they performed and created new functions as well. But here I encounter a definitional problem. Since this process takes place not on the species level, what is the "system" that acquired a greater rationality by this? The mysterious "life" may be the only candidate. What, then, is the "purpose" of life in view of how we think about rationality? These are, of course, old questions that continue to be asked almost rhetorically. But perhaps, there is some profit in repeating the same questions with a slightly different terminology each time.

This analytical rationality that human beings have acquired has come to cause, among other things, the emergence of nonemotional, analytical decision making, which unfortunately often finds itself in conflict with emotional decision making. At the same time, the emergence of sciences and technologies as other products of the analytical mind have degraded the rationality of emotions by introducing drastic changes in our environment. In my opinion, all the grave social problems we observe in our contemporary world appear to have roots in this dilemma. It is easy to simply blame emotions as the cause of problems and insist that we control our emotions through willpower. I regard this attitude as our emotional reaction to the problems of emotions. The only rational alternative to this attitude is to respond to the problems of emotions analytically, and it seems to me that the best strategy for doing so is to analyze the system of emotions in the right context — that is, in a wild, primitive environment where the system's rationality can be high.

AROUSAL, EXPRESSION, AND
OTHER ATTRIBUTES OF EMOTION

At this point I would like to consider a few additional important attributes of emotion. However, I will do it in a rather special way; I will try to interpret each attribute of emotion in terms of the hypothesis that was put forward at the end of the last section — namely, that emotion is a rational system for animals, including genus Homo, living in a wild environment. I am afraid that I might sometimes overdo it with insufficient evidence, but my purpose for the moment is to see if the above hypothesis can act as a useful heuristic for providing more concrete hypotheses.

The relationship between emotion and motivation has long been debated among the investigators of emotions. (See Strongman, 1978, for a review of the history of the investigation of emotion.) Consider, for example, the usually nonemotional motivational state called hunger. Once an animal finds itself in a state of hunger, it will start one of the class of behaviors characterized as food-seeking. In this respect, hunger operates in a fashion similar to anger, the latter leading to an aggressive behavior. Furthermore, the emergence of a hunger state hardly appears to be a strictly physiological event. As Tomkins (1970) argues strongly for and Schachter (1967), based on his experiments with obese subjects, testifies, to feel hunger is very likely a cognitive event caused jointly by appropriate internal and external signals. Thus, all told, hunger appears to operate exactly as a decision routine. If so, this hunger routine is obviously one of the oldest outcomes of evolutionary learning (I believe that a creature that always eats whatever food is available will not feel hunger because it does not need such a routine). The question, then, is why do we regard hunger as nonemotional and anger as emotional?

I think the major distinction between these two categories corresponds to the absence and the presence of marked physiological arousal. By this, however, I do not mean that hunger creates no arousal. All the so-called basic drives like hunger have the attribute of *strength* like any emotion, and the stronger the drive, the more its operational mode resembles that of emotions. For example, a very hungry individual may hardly be able to think of anything but hunger and food, and I believe this concentration of cognitive operations on the immediate issues is caused by a mechanism very similar to that used by emotion-based central arousal on information processing. Therefore these so-called basic drives, or need-states, do not appear to be essentially different from emotions, albeit they play more fundamental roles than do most emotions in the overall survival program of animals and as a result are more resistant to degradation of their rationality by environmental instability (i.e., they are more robust programs). The fact that some of them show little apparent somatic arousal, at least when their intensities are relatively low, may be simply because such arousal is not needed. Hunting for food may be a routine business requiring no special discharge of bodily energy, or this energy may be needed only when prey is discovered.

Arguing in this manner, I would now be expected to explain why emotions require arousal. I think this is not too difficult a task to accomplish. Consider the role of the "suddenness" of an event in determining the initial strength of the emotional arousal it creates. Suppose that you are walking down a dimly lit street at night and you sense danger. Suddenly, without warning, a hand touches your shoulder from behind. You are *startled!* You are not sure whether the person touching you is a mugger or a friend. This situation is an emergency. There is not much time to contemplate upon the best action to take in case the hand belongs to a mugger. Fear, along with the adrenalin discharge in your blood stream caused by arousal, will make the choice for you. As soon as you identify the person as a stranger, or even before that, you will run with a speed so fast that even you are surprised.

Note that danger is ubiquitous in a wild environment, but if it is an expected danger, one will have had time to prepare to meet it or avoid it. When the emergence of danger is sudden, however, life and death depend on whether or not one can take appropriate action with the shortest delay and maximum efficiency, and nothing but a well-established decision routine will do the job properly. In fact, the repertoire of alternative actions that the emotion of fear provides one with is rather rich, and a minimal amount of information processing will be needed to decide among the actions. Fleeing is the appropriate action when there is hope of outdistancing the enemy. Screaming at the top of one's voice may be appropriate if help is near by. One may put up a desperate fight if fleeing is impossible, since there is a chance, however slight, that one will win the fight or scare the enemy away. One also may adopt submissive behavior and put oneself at the mercy of the enemy by displaying an expression of abject terror, which hopefully may create an emotion of pity in the mind of the powerful opponent. This last action can be effective only if the opponent is a member of one's own group or at least of one's own species. I will discuss this social aspect of emotional interplays in the next section.

The appropriateness of all these courses of action when one confronts a fear-arousing imminent danger in a wild environment is obvious. But there is one more alternative action, and it poses a puzzle. A fear-stricken individual sometimes becomes immobile, frozen stiff. Is this just the response to hopelessness or is it something akin to sham death, which may, though it actually seldom does, divert the attention of the predator whose brain is so simple that it is attracted only by objects that move? Note that "playing possum" is often the best strategy when the potential victim has discovered the enemy but not vice versa. The mystery is that this course of action is taken so often when the victim is face to face with the source of danger.

So the decision routine of fear provides, on the whole, a good collection of actions effective in the wild. But even the best decision routines used in the wild can bring about disasters when used in an artificial environment. Note that panic represents an extreme fear response. There is no need to tell the reader how panic multiplies the magnitude of a disaster, for example, when fire breaks out in a building that is teeming with people. Nothing similar to a building on fire happens in the wild, yet animals may panic to survive (unless there are also human hunters who deliberately make them panic, which is, however, an artificial situation).

Thus the role of arousal is quite clear in the case of fear. It is the preparation for immediate execution of whatever action is chosen. Without a doubt, this interpretation can be generalized to anger, to anxiety, and to several other emotions. But all of these aforementioned emotions belong to the class of negative emotions. Let us now consider a positive emotion, "joy" for example. Joy certainly causes arousal — but why, since joy, unlike fear, does not seem to have a typical repertoire of actions to be executed immediately?

In the case of joy, the lack of characteristic behavior patterns is not too surprising. Since joy is the result of a significant improvement in one's state, it is a decision problem only in the sense that any significant change in one's state calls for changes in one's plans, although such changes need not be carried out immediately. Notice that the strength of joy is positively correlated with the unexpectedness of the positive event. Consider, for example, which situation will give an individual greater joy: receiving a desired but expected promotion or receiving a desired unexpected promotion? The answer is obvious. Now let us return to the prehistoric wilderness. A hungry savage is wandering across a barren terrain quickly losing all hope of finding food. He suddenly comes across a chunk of fresh meat left, perhaps, by some predator. Such luck will, of course, give him great joy. But this savage is also in an emergency situation. He must protect himself and the food while he consumes it; in order to do so, he must stay alert and be prepared to fight off any other hungry animals that may appear.

I am not ready to claim that this *is* the cause of arousal in joy. However, as long as suddenness or unexpectedness play a critical role in arousing emotions, I think it is reasonable to assume that the physiological arousal accompanying emotion is a preparatory reaction to cope with emergencies, since any sudden event in the wild may be a potential emergency. Note also that central emotional arousal results in concentration of information processing on only the immediate issues. This is adaptive in a wild environment because no organism, when it is fleeing or fighting, should be distracted by something not immediately relevant. Such concentration of information processing becomes maladaptive in modern society, in which important (and thus emotion-arousing) issues tend to have long-range consequences and in which immediate actions become less important than deliberate cognitive information processing.

As a prelude to the subject of the social significance of emotions, which will be introduced in the next section, I would like to turn my attention to the important emotion of anger. The origin of anger can be seen in the instinctual defensive aggression of lower animals, a type of behavior perhaps as old in the evolutionary process as the instinctual withdrawal or escape behavior that is seen as the origin of fear. Imagine stimulating a lobster. It will either draw back into a safe hiding place or take the *pose* of attacking with distended claws. No one can be sure if this lobster's posture is intended to display threat, but if one considers species more advanced than the lobster, the threatening aspect of pre-attack postures becomes more obvious. One of the characteristic features of these threatening postures is that they make the threatening individual look bigger. Note the obvious rationale underlying such behavior. In defensive or provoked aggression, fighting may not be the intention of the provoked organism; if possible, it should be avoided in order to prevent the organism from being harmed in the act of fighting. Obviously, the best way to prevent fighting is to make oneself look powerful, since estimation of the *power* of a potential fighting opponent is the indispensable cognitive faculty of a surviving organism, whether it survives in the wild or in modern society. And the "size" of an opponent is apparently one of the major information sources for this estimation. If this estimation turns out to imply greater power on the part of the provoked organism than of the provoker, it will act as a releaser of fear in the provoker and, in turn, will urge the provoker to flee or at least give up trying to initiate a fight. Even though all this may look obvious, it unequivocally tells us about the role that emotional *expression* plays in interorganismic interactions. Emotional expression as a powerful form of communication may sometimes have greater survival merit than the emotional action itself, even though this power of expression comes primarily from what it appears to indicate about forthcoming actions. This leads to another obvious point. The behaviors of any animal species advanced enough to possess emotions are regulated in an anticipatory fashion, whether or not the underlying mechanism (which, by definition, is a simulator) involves a conscious operation.

Since the distinction between expression and action can sometimes become tenuous, let me employ the following definitions. An *action* is a behavior whose major effect lies in the specific result that that behavior has, while an *expression* is a display whose major effect lies in communication. Even with this definition, the distinction is not always easy when applied to human beings. A verbal accusation, for example, may work both as a threat (an expression of anger) and as an actual attack intended to hurt the opponent (an action of anger). Moreover, humans are good actors; an experienced "emotion manipulator" can easily dissemble an emotion or nonemotion. But such a ramification is only of secondary importance and is not of immediate concern.

Let us now consider the broader *class* of anger-arousing cognitions, since such cognitions need not be restricted solely to anticipated direct physical attacks. In the animal kingdom a well-known instigator of threat and aggression consists of infringement of an animal's *territory*, particularly by a conspecific. The territory of an animal may best be described as the *sphere of control* the animal has. The survival merit for a species to have such a system of individualized territories is easy to see, since it is one of the simplest means of avoiding interference between the various activities of conspecifics. Such an intraspecies regulation system works, of course, only when the rules of the system are respected; the display of threat by the holder of a territory is a challenge to a trespasser that forces the latter to choose between obeying the rule by withdrawing or not obeying the rule and fighting.

The notion of sphere of control is particularly useful when one considers anger-arousing conditions for humans. Consider, for example, possession of an object. When we say that a person owns an object, it usually means that the person has *exclusive right* of control over the object. Thus, when the person finds that someone else has tampered with, damaged, or stolen the object, his or her right is infringed upon, and the person may become angry. The rationale underlying such anger is exactly the same as that underlying territorial encroachment. In the wild, or anywhere else, one's rights may go to someone else if one does not protect them, although human groups (including modern society) usually have ways of protecting some important rights of their members collectively. The interplay of these group functions and emotions will be discussed in the next section.

One's sphere of control is not restricted to material objects; it may cover one's fellow group members as well. Suppose that someone throws an apple in between two Japanese monkeys. Usually it will be observed that the higher-ranking monkey will take the apple without receiving any protest from the lower-ranking one. Occasionally, however, particularly if the apple lands near the foot of the lower-ranking monkey, the lower-ranking monkey will show signs of picking the apple up and in doing so will invite the rage of the other monkey. Perceiving this rage, the lower-ranking monkey will cringe and usually take the submissive posture of presentation. The higher-ranking monkey will usually be appeased by this show of submission and will consummate the ritual by taking the pose of mounting and leaving peacefully with the apple. A similar exchange is also common in human society, with differences lying only in the variety and sophistication of culture-dependent human rituals. The lack of display of appropriate courtesies by a lower-status person to a higher-status one is regarded in many cultures as a severe breach of social code, giving the offended the right to punish.

Now let us consider the implications of the above statements. First note that the sphere of control, or, if one prefers, the *system of perceived rights* in the case of human beings, does not mean an absolute territory or domain in the objective world. The monkey who took the apple had rights over the apple only because he happened to be of higher rank than the other monkey present. Thus among human beings and higher primates, at least, many rights are determined *on the spot* by applying certain *rules* to the issues at hand. The effectiveness of such rules can be maintained only when they are shared by all members of the groups within which the interactions will take place. The chances are high that the underlying principles of such rules as hierarchical rank-order or status systems are genetically based. The fact that subsequent to Schjelderup-Ebbe's discovery of the pecking order in chickens, many more species have been added to the list of animals that spontaneously develop a rank-order system when a new group is formed (Eibl-Eibesfeldt, 1970) supports this notion. The actual content of these rules, such as who assumes which rank, is determined on a local basis; it usually depends on the individual's physical strength, intelligence, coalition membership (discussed in the next section), and the outcomes of contest fighting. Therefore, any specific rank order is modifiable by new events. It seems appropriate, however, particularly in the case of human beings, that each group member be characterized not only by a rank but also by a more sensitive "status" variable, a variable that may change even when the member remains in the same rank.

Obviously status is one of the most delicate issues in human and animal social behavior, and no short argument, such as that which follows, will do justice to its importance. However, since it appears to be one of the most critical determiners of human emotions, let me just summarize some hypotheses I consider relevant. Each person is characterized by a variable that may be called the person's *power*. This power is somehow represented by the "size" of the person's sphere of control, which may or may not include control over the person's own group members. The person's status is the *socially recognized* power of the person. Therefore, there is usually a time lag between the change in one's power and a corresponding change in one's status. Note that various more or less institutionalized hierarchical systems usually exist in human societal structures. Since many of the social rules operating in our societies apply directly to the positions and ranks people assume in these institutionalized systems, these positions and ranks are often important determiners of one's power and therefore determiners of one's status as well. Nevertheless, they should not be identified either as one's power or as one's status since it might very well happen that a person in a low position (or of no position at all) could have high power or high status. Remember also that these variables should be considered as multi-dimensional. A person's power and status may be high in one aspect but low in another; they are context dependent, even though there is a definite tendency for generalization across contexts. For the sake of simplicity, however, power and status will be dealt with in the following section as if they are unidimensional variables.

In the next section I will attempt to elucidate the importance of the status variable on the basis of very simple assumptions concerning the rationality of groups. I will then discuss how the characteristics of various emotions can be meaningfully linked to these assumptions via the notions of power and status.

GROUPS AND COALITIONS

When von Neumann and Morgenstern (1944) introduced the notion of *coalitions*, where a coalition is a subgroup of players who cooperate as a team, in their discussion of *n*-person games, they considered the following two conditions concerning the rationality of a coalition. Let x_i be the final gain of the *i*-th coalition member. Also let $v(i)$ be the maximum gain that i can obtain alone without being a coalition member, and $v(C)$ the maximum gain the coalition C can obtain. Then, the two conditions are: (1) $x_i \geq v(i)$ and (2) $\Sigma_i x_i = v(C)$. The meaning of the first condition, the condition of *individual rationality*, is obvious: If this condition is not met, it would make no sense for the player i to stay in the coalition. The second condition, *group rationality*, is equivalent to the Pareto optimality conditions and simply means that the total gain of a coalition should be as much as potentially possible.

In however a weak sense of the word, any group may be regarded as a coalition as long as membership is voluntary, since the voluntariness of membership implies that the condition of individual rationality is satisfied. Few real groups would satisfy the condition of group rationality in the strict sense. However, we may at least generally assume that the higher the group's rationality, the greater the group's chances for survival. And, with greater total gain, the easier it becomes to satisfy individual rationality. So viable groups tend to be those that strive to increase their level of group rationality, which is tantamount to increasing the level of cooperation among group members, primarily by reducing internal conflicts. Obviously, the most common type of internal conflict arises from the problem of how to divide group gain into individual shares without violating individual rationality. This implies, particularly when the group gain is not very high, that members with high power — that is, high values of $v(i)$ — should get more than those with low power because they are, in general, better off individually than others in the group.

Still, the gain allocation cannot be left to an unrestricted display of raw power since it may lead to unlimited extortion of the weaker members by the stronger and result in violation of the weaker members' individual rationality. Since weak members will also be contributing to group gain, a viable group should have social rules *that protect its weak members whenever necessary*.

Note that group rationality also implies inhibition of direct display of powers, since there is nothing more effective in degrading group rationality than a constant internal struggle to demonstrate each member's relative superiority in power. Such problems, however, could be solved simply by assigning each group member a value representing the member's *estimated* power. The estimation process should be open (i.e., done either through direct observation by other members of the group or through open communication), and every piece of evidence that can potentially demonstrate an increase or decrease in a member's power must be considered within this socialized information-processing channel. This socially sanctioned estimate of a group member's power is his or her status, and the problem is to develop social rules that allocate group gain relative to each member's status. If such rules are adequate, they should assure high group rationality by resolving most, though probably not all, internal conflicts by peaceful means.

While in reality human societies must operate with far more complex mechanisms than those just described, let us return to a rather primitive group culture equipped with little more than the above principles and see what kind of motivations one would develop in such a group and how various emotions could incorporate these motivations. First note that as long as higher status implies a higher share, one would seek to increase one's status, and the most natural way to do so would be to increase one's own power. Though the term *power* may sound a little too grandiose in this context, remember that increasing one's power means nothing more than expanding one's sphere of control, which can be accomplished by various means — for example, by acquiring a new object, by obtaining a new skill, or by joining a coalition. Joining a coalition means formation of an intragroup coalition, and one will gain extra power by joining one since one of the benefits will be support from coalition partners in case of conflict.

Now let me emphasize the following point: An increase in power does not automatically produce an increase in status, so the person must advertise the increase to the group members in order to make it reflect on his or her status. Suppose that a person has obtained a desired object and thus increased his or her power. This is an obvious cause for joy. As previously mentioned, joy appears to have no characteristic pattern of action (aiming at some direct effect), since a joyful situation does not require it. Instead, joy is characterized by a rather rich variety of expressions intended for communication of the joyful state. For example, the person who has acquired a desired object will most likely invite friends over to show it off. Children invariably do a boasting act when they are given a valuable gift. Certainly it is most natural to interpret these communicative acts as the necessary social recognition procedures that turn acquired power into status. Granting that this may be the most crucial function of the expression of joy, it appears that expressing joy has an additional function. Note that a joyful person often feels an urge toward conviviality, to gather friends and relatives (namely, the person's coalition partners), to treat them, to share with them a pleasant mood of joy, and to distribute gifts among them. Obviously this is a coalition event; a coalition member has a duty to share with his partners whatever gain he has obtained. By shirking this duty, one may risk not only reducing one's power by losing the support of one's partners but also may invite these partners' envy. Envy is a dangerous emotion to ignite. It is a subclass of anger and is caused by the cognition that someone else has gained in status. Note that status is a relative measure. If someone's status goes up, someone else's status will go down *unless both persons are coalition partners whose status levels are linked*. A typical form of aggression by an envious person is to put a verbal label of "shame" on the target person in order to impair the status of the latter. Of interest here is the fact that Bushmen are so afraid of inviting envy that whenever one of them obtains a valuable object (for example, a sharp knife), not only will that person part with it very quickly, but the object also will be passed around within the tribe until it loses its value (Service, 1966).

Since it is impossible to discuss all of the emotions in this way, let me finish this paper by giving an annotated list of emotions that appear to be relevant under those aspects of group functions discussed above.

Protection of Weak Members. (1) Parental love — see Love, which is discussed below. (2) Pity — caused by recognition of the helplessness of a weak member. It will urge a strong person to give away a part of his or her power. (3) Sorrow, grief — caused by a loss in power or status that usually is not attributable to the fault of another. For example, a child (a legitimate weak member) may cry, which is an obvious distress call invoking the protect-the-weak rule. An adult, on the other hand, particularly a male, cannot cry without admitting that he is weak and thereby degrading his status. (4) Submission — this typical expression of fear is listed here because it displays a person's weakness, which, in turn, may restore a proper status difference between the person and his offended opponent and may make the latter feel pity and reduce his anger.

Conversion of Power into Status. (1) Pride — hiding a loss of power to preserve status, especially when the loss is believed to be not readily observable by the public. It often produces a haughty demeanor in an attempt to signal high status or foolhardy bravery to compensate for loss in power. (2) Shame — caused by a publicly observable loss in power and therefore a loss in status. It usually occurs as a result of one's own blunder, which leads to impairment of other group members' powers. It therefore creates an urge to make oneself inconspicuous. (3) Honor — though not an emotion, it is mentioned here because it implies a social procedure for rewarding a person who has contributed to the group by directly elevating the status of this person (sometimes without an accompanying material power increase). The person's power will be increased because his or her elevated status will attract potential coalition partners (supporters). Note that shaming is often employed as a social procedure for the opposite purpose.

Coalitions. (1) Love — no one can discuss love in a few words. The essential role played by love in forming and maintaining closely knit coalitions is undeniable. Note that love leads to devotion and expects reciprocity. These are assurances against the worst enemy of coalitions (i.e., defection). (2) Jealousy — defection of one's coalition partner is often fatal because the greatest benefit of joining a coalition arises from the mutual trust among coalition partners. Closely knit coalitions are further guarded by jealousy against potential defection. Jealousy operates by first arousing suspicion when the evidence for defection is not decisive. When the defection becomes clear, anger is evoked and aggressive behavior will be directed toward either the defector, or the person who tempted the defector, or both.

CONCLUSION

The short descriptions given above neither cover all of the important emotions nor are sufficiently elaborate to give justice to those that are listed. However, they may suffice, for the moment, to convey to the reader a notion of the approach I am taking. I would like to conclude by summarizing the major points I have attempted to make in this paper. Emotions are decision-making programs developed through evolution; they seem to have been particularly elaborated in human beings. They may have first emerged for the purpose of survival of the species, but those that particularly enrich human experience seem to be directed toward increasing the level of rationality of human groups. Human beings, however, have greatly enlarged their information-processing capacity, which has given rise to an analytical, nonemotional way of making decisions. Because of the interference of emotional processes in the latter, emotions are often blamed for being the source of senseless irrationality. This blame has some truth to it, even more truth than we customarily believe there is because we are often misled by rationalizations. However, emotions still play a vital role in our everyday thoughts and behaviors, and in our analytical decision making as well, because they typically influence value cognitions. Emotion-based problems cannot be solved only by blaming emotions. Their characteristics should be understood analytically, and there appear to be ways of doing this.

REFERENCES

Eibl-Eibesfeldt, I. 1970. Ethology — the biology of behavior. New York: Holt,

Farmer, P. J. 1978. The fabulous riverboat. London: Granada (Panther Books).

James, W. 1902. The varieties of religious experience. New York: Longmans Green.

Miller, G. A. 1956. The magical number seven, plus or minus two. *Psychological Review* 63:81–97.

Neumann, J. von, and O. Morgenstern. 1944. Theory of games and economic behavior. Princeton, N.J.: Princeton University Press.

Ortega y Gassett, J. 1957. On love. Cleveland: World.

Osgood, C. E. 1978. Psycho-social dynamics and the prospects for mankind. Invited address to the UNTAR/Planetary Citizen colloquium.

Rivera, J. de. 1977. A structural theory of the emotions. New York: International University Press.

Schachter, S. 1967. Cognitive effect on bodily functioning: studies of obesity and eating. In Neurophysiology and emotion. D. C. Glass, ed. New York: Rockefeller University Press.

Service, E. P. 1966. The hunter. Englewood Cliffs, N.J.: Prentice-Hall.

Shannon, C. E., and W. Weaver. 1949. The mathematical theory of communication. Urbana: University of Illinois Press.

Sjöberg, L., and T. Johnson. 1978. Trying to give up smoking: a study of volitional breakdowns. *Addictive Behaviors* 3:149–64.

Strongman, K. T. 1978. The psychology of emotion. Second ed. New York: Wiley.

Tomkins, S. S. 1970. Affect as the primary motivational system. In Feelings and emotions: the Loyola symposium. M. B. Arnold, ed. New York: Academic Press.

Toda, M. 1976. The decision process: a perspective. *International Journal of General Systems* 3:79–88.

———. 1981. What happens at the moment of decision? meta-decisions, emotions, and volitions. In Human decision making. L. Sjöberg, T. Tyszka, and J. A. Wise, eds. Lund: Doxa (in press).

12 CAUSALITY, CONDITIONAL PROBABILITY, AND CONTROL

Sometimes we observe clear inconsistencies between what scientists argue in their theoretical treatises and the way their more secular minds function, as their daily conversations show. To give a few examples, physicists dealing with reversible physical time, devoid of past, present, and future, sometimes deplore the irreversibility of their personal time. Behaviorists, who expelled the notion of mind from their theory as unscientific, can behave just like other people, chatting about their own minds. Another example pertinent to our topic is the confusion between causal relation and covariation frequently observed in the arguments of behavioral scientists. As is now widely acknowledged, what we can directly obtain in the form of empirical data are only covariations (or correlations),[1] and while some authors are wary of making causal statements when they draw conclusions strictly from their data, others are much bolder. In any case, when it comes to arguing their problems in an offhand way, they almost invariably fall back on "causal" language.

This paper appeared in *New Developments in the Applications of Bayesian Methods*, A. Aykaç and C. Brumat, eds. (Amsterdam: North-Holland, 1977), pp. 109–24. Copyright © 1977 by North-Holland Publishing Company; used by permission. I am indebted to John Michon for his helpful suggestions.

223

Whenever such a discrepancy between official and personal statements is observed, we have good reason to suspect that something important is left out by the official theory that the authors endorsed, sacrificed perhaps to the need to compactly close one's theoretical system. In these three examples, the entities left out all involve tremendously complicated issues. Because of the obvious importance of the entities themselves, however, we cannot keep neglecting them too long. As demonstrated clearly in the case of the reinstated "mind" in cognitive psychology, there are ways and means of gradually unraveling the apparently formidable complication of the issues involved. A more general theory will be achieved by gradually exorcising myths originally attached to the entities, even though we may never reach the stage of complete clarification of these "singularly primitive" notions upon which intuitive understanding of the built-in human information processing system seems to be based.

At any rate, causality is undoubtedly one of those important and content-rich notions that require our attention. Of course, I am not suggesting that the issue of causality has not been attended; it is an issue eons old. Nevertheless, the confusion between the notion of causality and that of covariation does not appear to have been effectively removed, in spite of quite a few excellent, though often controversial, recent studies, such as those of Simon (1954), Blalock (1961), Suppes (1970), and others. To discuss each of these works is beyond the scope of this brief paper, however, and I am content if, by presenting my own view on the issue of causality within a rather limited context, some further clarification is obtained.

FORWARD AND BACKWARD PROBABILITIES

Let me first make my basic standpoint explicit. It starts with the basic fact that a really amazing proportion of our daily conversation is spent in giving some causally sounding reasons for what we have observed. So, undoubtedly, knowing causes is important and essential in our daily information processing. One of my questions will then be related to the issue of why it is so important.

On the other hand, it is also true that what we can *directly observe* as the relation between two variables is only their covariation. A high covariation does not, however, necessarily imply the existence of an underlying causal process, as perhaps most beautifully presented in Simon's paper, "Spurious Correlation." To understand spurious correlation, a very simple example will suffice.

Suppose that you ask someone what time it is. Then ask another the same question. Repeat the procedure on and off for enough number of times to compute the correlation between the two answers. Of course, the correlation must be very high, but it is spurious because we know that the time told by the first person can hardly cause the time told by the second person.

So, even though the causal relations we so often discuss in our arguments must have somehow been inferred from our direct observations, the rules of inference cannot be straightforward. Thus my second question concerns how causality can be discovered.

In order to shed even a dim light on these basic questions, I am forced to delimit the extremely complicated environment within which our mind is normally functioning into a transparent, compact formal context. For this purpose, I choose probability theory as a clean, noncausal background and see what will come out if I try to express causal relations against this background. The noncausal nature of probability theory is quite obvious. Note that the temporal relation between two events such that an event that happened later cannot exert a causal influence upon another that happened earlier is undoubtedly one of the most basic ingredients of the notion of causality. On the other hand, the temporal relation between two events, x and y, is irrelevant to the definition of conditional probability, $P(x|y)$.[2]

So, as the first step, let me introduce temporal relations between the events we consider, calling $P(y|x)$ a *forward probability* if $t_y > t_x$ and a *backward probability* if $t_y < t_x$, where t_x and t_y are the respective time coordinates of the events x and y.[3] To distinguish between these two types of conditional probabilities, we shall write $F(y|x) = P(y|x)$ if $P(y|x)$ is a forward probability, $B(y|x) = P(y|x)$ if it is a backward probability, and retain the symbol P for the general case, particularly when a probability is neither strictly forward nor backward. The reader will immediately note that Bayes' theorem gives an expression of a backward probability in terms of forward probabilities and unconditional probabilities:

$$B(h|d) = \frac{F(d|h)\,P(h)}{\Sigma_i\,F(d|h_i)\,P(h_i)}, \tag{12.1}$$

where the common interpretation of h and d are that h_i is an alternative value of the variable called the true hypothesis, h being one of them, and d the observed data, whereby $t_d > t_h$ is assumed. We shall explore the implication of (12.1) in detail later, but for the moment, notice the following two points: First, the B and F interpretation of (12.1) is just one of many interpretations of the trivial equality in the time-neutral probability theory:

$$P(y|x) = \frac{P(x|y)\,P(y)}{P(x)} \tag{12.2}$$

and, therefore, one can obtain another theorem by interchanging B and F in (12.1), which we shall do later. The second point concerns the nature of unconditional probability — that is, $P(h)$ in (12.1). Note that the general probability symbol P is attached to the unconditional probability $P(h)$ not because unconditional probabilities are, by right, atemporal. Suppose that a probability measure P is assigned to a sample space consisting of two variables X and Y, $t_x > t_y$. The two unconditional probabilities $P(x)$ and $P(y)$ are

$$P(x) = \Sigma_i F(x|y_i) P(y_i)$$
$$P(y) = \Sigma_j B(y|x_j) P(x_j).$$ (12.3)

We shall revisit the issue of unconditional probability later.

CAUSALITY

Now let me consider the relationship between causality and forward probability. Two variables X and Y are *probabilistically dependent* if for some values of Y, y and y',

$$F(x/y) \neq F(x/y')$$ (12.4)

holds for some value x of X ($t_x > t_y$ is assumed though not necessary here).

A causal relation must be something more than dependence, because dependence may be spurious. In my understanding, causality is a relation between *systems* rather than *variables*, where by system I mean a material system that can be specified without referring to its environment, while a variable is the state of a system when it is put in a certain environment.

Now let me put a necessary condition for the existence of a causal relation between two systems **X** and **Y**. There must be some variable X of **X** and some Y of **Y** that are dependent if **X** and **Y** are causally related. Concerning the choice of the two variables, there are two factors involved, temporal and environmental. According to the theory of physics, the effect of a state-change of one system can reach another only with a certain time lag. Therefore, the temporal relation between the two variables must be correctly set corresponding to this time lag, if they are to represent the causal relation between the systems; otherwise, the dependence shown by the variables will become spurious. Let me call this procedure of adjusting the temporal relation between two variables the *temporal tuning*. A troublesome aspect of this temporal tuning is that, when the relation between two systems is not strictly physical, the time lag may not be constant. An experimental subject may respond to the given stimulus with differential "latency," and the experimeter must be flexibly tuned up so as to pick up

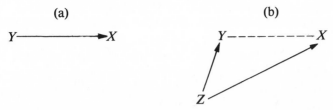

Figure 12.1. X, Y, and Z are properly tuned variables. Temporal order is from left to right. The arrow signifies a causal relation, and the broken line its absence. These diagrams do not preclude the existence of other arrows and broken lines connecting X, Y, and Z with other variables in the environment.

the correct response. Of course, we can usually do this flexible tuning with ease only because we already know the form of the possible causal relations and know what to expect. In fact, as I shall discuss later, we cannot conduct experiments, the means by which most new causal relations are found, without already knowing some causal relations. At any rate, we shall not go any further into the topic of temporal tuning in this paper, even though it involves a host of problems; we will assume instead that a proper tuning can be done among any set of systems.

Concerning the environmental factor, let me put forward the following postulate: *If a properly tuned pair of variables* show a probabilistic dependency, then either there is a causal *relation between them or there exists a third system in the environment as a common cause to both of the variables.* Namely, an observed dependency suggests that either of the two possibilities depicted in Figure 12.1 is true. I shall not argue for the defense of this proposition, except mentioning that we certainly seem to believe that a dependency (covariation) cannot occur without some cause creating it.

Put this way, it seems easy to find out whether (a) or (b) in Figure 12.1 is the case when a dependency is observed between X and Y: Create an environment within which no such common cause as Z in (b) exists, and see if a dependency (which may be in a different form) persists. Consider an example. Suppose that Z is a radio station, Y is your radio, and X is your neighbor's radio (which must exist on the opposite side of Y in relation to Z to keep the temporal relation right). This is, ordinarily, a typical case of (b). The high correlation between the sounds produced by X and Y is spurious, created by the common cause Z. But suppose now that you have a suspicion; the owner of X, a notorious prankster, may be bugging your house and broadcasting loudly whatever his bug, hidden somewhere in your house, is picking up. This is the case (a). To decide which of (a) and (b) is

Figure 12.2. Case (b) pattern created inadvertently by an insufficient control of the situation by E. N is the neighbor of E.

true, you can simply turn off your radio; by cutting off the causal influence of Z upon Y, Z ceases to be the common cause. Then if X also stops producing sounds at the same time, (a) is proven.

Really? Note that the neighbor is a notorious prankster; he might have been watching you through a telescope and, by guessing your intention, might have turned off his radio synchronously. If this is the case, what you need to do is to increase the *control* of your *experiment*, for example, by closing the window.

Now, how can this situation be depicted as a diagram? Note that control is an act that positively utilizes causal relations. An experimenter must control independent variables — independent of everything except the experimenter. This cannot be done, however, without knowing how these variables are causally regulated. So the experimenter, E, must explicitly appear within the diagram. In the above example, the control act of E not only influenced the state of Y but also affected X through the intervention of the neighbor N. So we obtain Figure 12.2, which clearly shows that the E, yourself, inadvertently served as a common cause to both X and Y to create a spurious correlation. So in order to ensure the discovery of a causal relation by an experiment, the experiment's control act over the independent variables must be exclusive, in the sense that E should never control (influence) X, the dependent variables, except through Y, the independent variables, and Y should be controlled exclusively by E.

EXPERIMENT

The specification given above is not really enough even for an idealized experiment. Note that in order to detect a dependency in the form of (12.4), forward probabilities must be estimated, and in order to estimate probabilities, probabilities must exist in the first place. A probability distribution must be assigned over a sample space consisting of a system of variables (abbreviated as SOV from now on). But, obviously, no empirically meaningful probabilities can be assigned to an entirely open SOV, where unpredictable causal influences from outside of SOV are expected. On the other hand, requiring a complete closure of SOV, open only to the experimenter, is unrealistic. In most cases, what we can expect, as the maximal standard, is that the states of all external potential causes are controlled to be fixed during the experiment. Let us designate collectively the external potential causes as C, and c as its fixed state. Then a conditional (forward) probability distribution given c can be assigned over the SOV. Although this c is usually omitted from probability notations because of the obvious notational redundancy, it does not change the fact that all the probabilities estimated in empirical research are conditional probabilities, and unconditional probability in a genuine sense is almost an artifact.[4]

Note that even if we create a SOV that is conditionally closed, it does not mean we can find out the *form* of causal dependence between the two target variables, since the SOV may still involve other variables (collectively denoted as O) that are not under the experimenter's control, while they possibly influence the values of dependent variables.

A remedy for this problem is to measure the values of O, as measuring them may be easier than controlling them. Once measured, we can legitimately expel O outside of SOV to let it join c and estimate probabilities conditional on c and o, even though this means partitioning of the data for each value of o.

In fact, the direct motivation that led me to this topic of causality is the common negligence of O created by an imperfect control, and in reality any control is imperfect. The most common situation, which will create the worst O, may be obtained when the experimenter is not really controlling the independent variables but just sampling them. For example, suppose that an investigator was interested in finding out the existence or absence of a causal relation between the habit of smoking and lung cancer. Since, obviously, he could not control people's smoking habits, he collected a very large sample of long-time smokers and non-smokers, examined each of them to determine whether he or she had ever developed a symptom of lung cancer, and obtained the frequency distribution shown in Figure 12.3 (obviously artificial). The investigator would no doubt have been very much pleased by the result which undoubtedly shows a strong, significant dependence between the two variables.

	Cancer	No cancer	
Smoking	6,800	3,200	10,000
Nonsmoking	3,200	6,800	10,000
	10,000	10,000	20,000

Figure 12.3. Artificial survey data concerning the relationship between smoking habit and lung cancer.

Male			Female		
6,400	1,600	8,000	400	1,600	2,000
1,600	400	2,000	1,600	6,400	8,000
8,000	2,000	10,000	2,000	8,000	10,000

Figure 12.4. A possible partition of Figure 12.3 data, showing independence between smoking and cancer.

However, this hypothetical investigator was conscientious and wanted to know more than this distribution told; he was not tempted to immediately draw the obvious causal conclusion from the observed dependence. So he partitioned his data for male and female samples and obtained the conditional frequency distributions shown in Figure 12.4. The implication of these distributions is obvious; it says that sex is a potential common cause influencing both smoking habit and developing lung cancer, and smoking and lung cancer are quite independent. So if you are a male (in this hypothetical place where this hypothetical survey was conducted), you are almost doomed to have lung cancer, but stopping smoking will not help you to improve your outlook. Or the partitioned data might even look like Figure 12.5, in which case smoking even helps avoid cancer. Of course, cases showing the opposite tendencies are also possible.

The reason I just said stopping smoking "will not" help you rather than "does not" is that the independence shown in Figure 12.5 may still be spurious. There are other factors, such as age, heredity, and nutrition. When the investigator further partitions his data according to one or more of these other factors, it is quite possible that an entirely different picture emerges.

I have deliberately used an artificial example here to demonstrate the freedom of choice in creating different types of partitioned data and to show how little the type of dependence obtained in one level bounds the type of dependence in a deeper conditional level. The joint probability in one level, $P(x, y|z)$, *is* an *average of* those in a deeper level, in such a way as

$$P(x, y|z) = \sum_{z'} P(x, y|z, z') P(z'), \qquad (12.5)$$

Male			Female		
6,800	1,600	8,400	0	1,600	1,600
1,600	0	1,600	1,600	6,800	8,400
8,400	1,600	10,000	1,600	8,400	10,000

Figure 12.5. Another possible partition of Figure 12.3 data, indicating the role of smoking in preventing cancer.

and the averaging can play quite a few tricks. So only when one has parceled out all the other variables involved in the given conditionally closed SOV can one conclude with confidence about the causal relation between the specified two variables. In reality, however, particularly in the area of social sciences, where the experimenter's control of the situation is bound to be relatively lax, this ideal situation will never be reached. There are customarily far more variables involved than the investigator officially attends to, or is aware of, and one will easily lose the effective size of data if one continues partitioning for all of the variables involved in O.

How can one overcome this difficulty? The answer is easy. Control the variables as much as possible. In order to control variables, however, one must know causal relations. And in order to know causal relations — well, every beginning is a beginning from scratch and one can only hope for an exponential growth of our causal knowledge. An exponential growth, however, sadly implies that the initial buildup will be tremendously slow, as typically represented by the current status of the social sciences.

The situation may be considerably improved if we can avoid making false causal statements, which could have been made with Figure 12.3-type data had the investigator not been careful or sample size not large enough to admit partition. So the important things are to let people realize the danger of spurious covariation and to encourage them to conduct large-scale experiments, which allow them to dig deep into the hidden structure of the data.

As a digression, let me vindicate spurious covariation, which is not necessarily evil once its spuriousness is known. Note that causal independence is easy to create, even though finding a new cause in the real world is sometimes very difficult. For example, let two subjects give responses under the identical environment, each without knowing the other's response. Then any covariation showing up between their responses is necessarily spurious, but can serve as a good indicator for the influence of various environmental factors on human behavior. This consideration has led me to my method of covariation analysis (Toda, 1974), which will not be elaborated here.

CAUSALITY AND CONTROL

It is time to answer the question raised in the beginning — why it is so important to know causes — and the task is very easy now. Without knowing causes, one cannot control. And if one cannot control, one cannot acquire dependable information. Evidently, however, acquiring knowledge is not the sole purpose of control. Control of environment — for example, growing food — is essential for survival. Of course, some would deplore, quite plausibly, that human control activity has gone too far; the rapid growth of the power of human material control, growing exponentially due to the mutual facilitation between information and control, now goes, paradoxically, out of our control. This again may be ascribed to our lack of knowledge; we know so little about social processes that our control power over them is proportionally poor.

Perhaps it is unfair not to mention that even a spurious covariation is important because it has a predictive power. It is only less valuable, generally speaking, compared to causal relation. For example, subduing a disaster directly is very desirable, but often difficult after the disaster has already been created. Knowing the cause of the disaster is sometimes even more desirable, because then the cause may be controlled and a future disaster may be prevented. Knowing a variable that has a high (though spurious) covariation with the coming disaster is also desirable, though comparatively less so, because it will allow one to prepare for the disaster and mitigate its impact, even if the disaster itself cannot be prevented. We must add to this that the predictive power of a causal covariation is also stronger than the comparable spurious one because of the general robustness of the former.

I am afraid that some readers may have resented my way of discussing causality so far; I have done it as if the existence of causal relations is a fact. No one can really *prove* the existence of causality, as, strictly speaking, the number of potentially causally related variables is infinite, and no control can be perfect. However, this existence has been unproven in almost the same sense as no one has ever *really* proved the existence of atoms. Human beings apparently have constantly been on the alert to discover causal relations, and, for reasons unknown, tentative causal relations begin to shape themselves up into a consistent system of natural laws. Even though natural laws tend to take a static form when perfected, as in the general theory of relativity, I am not sure if all temporally expressed causal relations should eventually be resolved into atemporal form (or more correctly, a form within which time has no direction). Such time-reversible laws are obtained only when causal relations are deterministic, as discussed by Watanabe (1969); in fact, in quantum mechanics, where probabilistic notions are essential, laws are still expressed in dynamic forms.

INFORMATION AND CONTROL

As discussed in the previous section, the existence of a close connection between information and control is quite apparent, and a duality shows up very often between them. For example, consider the well-known equality in information theory representing the amount of transmitted information:

$$T(X:Y) = H(Y) - H(Y|X)$$
$$= H(X) - H(X|Y), \qquad (12.6)$$

where H is the uncertainty measure defined as:

$$H(X) = -\sum_x P(x) \log P(x)$$

$$H(X|Y) = -\sum_y P(y) \sum_x P(x|y) \log P(x|y),$$

and so on. Now suppose that $t_x > t_y$. Then the information is transmitted from Y to X, and the first part of (12.6) properly represents the amount of information received from Y by X, measured in terms of X's uncertainty reduction about the state of Y. The last part of (12.6), however, should more properly be considered as the amount of control over X by Y, measured in terms of the reduction in uncertainty concerning the state of X when the control act y is taken by Y.

It is quite obvious that the process represented by so-called information transmission can be viewed in two ways. From the point of view of the receiver, it is a receiving of information, but from the point of view of the transmitter, it is an exertion of an influence over the state of the receiver (i.e., he is transmitting control). Therefore, the equality (12.6) can be interpreted as the equality between the amount of information and the amount of control, both measured in bits.

Note also that the amount of information is defined in terms of backward probability and the amount of control in terms of forward probability. The existence of such duality is not surprising, considering the fact that all the theorems in probability theory are time neutral. So if one can give a forward probability interpretation to some probability theorem, one must be able to give a dual, backward probability interpretation to the same theorem, and vice versa.

Now let me turn around Bayes' theorem (12.1), as promised in the second section. Note first that (12.1) allows us, in general, a certainty inference about h if we can add at will causally independent pieces of effects d_i obtained under the same cause h, where causal independence implies

$$F(d_i|h, d_j) = F(d_i|h) \qquad (12.7)$$

for any i and j, $i \neq j$. Then (12.1) is rewritten as

$$B(h|d_1, d_2,..., d_n) = \frac{(\Pi F(d_j|h)) P(h)}{\sum_i \Pi_j F(d_j|h_i) P(h_i)}. \qquad (12.8)$$

Now by turning the temporal relations in (12.8) around, we have

$$F(d \mid h_1, h_2, \ldots, h_n) = \frac{\prod\limits_{j} B(h_j \mid d) P(d)}{\sum\limits_{i} (\prod\limits_{j} B(h_j \mid d_i)) P(d_i)} \qquad (12.9)$$

if

$$B(h_i \mid d, h_j) = B(h_i \mid d) \qquad (12.10)$$

holds for any i and j, $i \neq j$. Now what kind of independence relation is this? Corresponding to causal independence, this may be called the effect-wise independence. At any rate, I originally thought that (12.9) implied the possibility of certainty prediction's corresponding to the certainty backward inference implied by (12.8) and that this was a paradox, as probability theory could not possibly lead us to the deterministic view of the world.

In fact, it was no paradox. I had forgotten to temporally turn around the structure of the situation as well. Note that Bayes' theorem (12.8) is supported by the causal structure represented by Figure 12.6a, and by turning around this structure we obtain the structure represented by Figure 12.6b, meaning that the state d of the effect system is controlled by many causes. So what is really meant by (12.9) is the possibility of a perfect control, which can be realized if we can add as many effect-wise independent causes as we wish.

Since this result strongly indicates that there is a great possibility of developing a fundamental theory of control as a dual theory to the theory of information, it is certainly fascinating to imagine creating an elaborate theory of control almost for nothing, just by temporally reversing information theory and Bayesian statistics. The duality, however, seems to have an

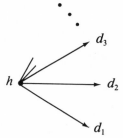

Figure 12.6a. The structure of SOV, allowing Bayesian certainty inference.

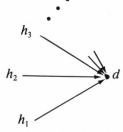

Figure 12.6b. The structure of SOV, allowing perfect control.

obvious limit. How do you temporally turn around all the arguments I gave concerning "experiment," where only forward probabilities seem to have had definite roles? To be exact, this last statement is wrong. As long as the experimenter is describing events that are not his direct perceptions, he is making backward inferences from his perception to some remote, past events. Nevertheless, the roles played in experiment by forward and backward probabilities are quite unbalanced. And the attempt to clarify what the "dual experiment" actually means is, at least, interesting. In general, we should certainly benefit greatly by further inquiring into problems concerning the nature of backward probability and the interplay between backward and forward probabilities.

NOTES

1. Hume, the probable originator of the idea, used the term *constant conjunction*, a term I should modify to *frequent conjunction* if I were to use it in this paper, since that is what we can really observe in most cases.

2. Suppes's approach (Suppes, 1970) may be viewed in the same spirit. He attempts to build a theory of causality by imposing *only* the temporal relations upon probabilities. I shouldn't say that this is impossible. But, then, my argument given at the beginning of this paper will recur.

3. As we shall see later where temporal tuning is discussed, the simple temporal order of events may not be strictly adequate for defining forward and backward probabilities. In this paper, however, I shall leave it at that. The notions of forward and backward probabilities correspond to Watanabe's predictive and retrodictive probabilities (Watanabe, 1969).

4. An unconditional probability in the genuine sense, not in the sense of the average probabilities defined in (12.3), is obtained only if

$$P(x|y) = K(x) \text{ for every } x \text{ and } y.$$

Then $P(x) = K(x)$.

REFERENCES

Blalock, H. M., Jr. 1961. Causal inferences in non-experimental research. Chapel Hill: University of North Carolina Press.

Simon, H. A. 1954. Spurious correlation: a causal interpretation. *Journal of American Statistical Association* 49:469–92.

Suppes, P. 1970. A probabilistic theory of causality. Amsterdam: North-Holland.

Toda, M. 1970. Covariation analysis: a method of additive data structure analysis for frequency tables. *Behaviometrika* 1:25–37.

Watanabe, S. 1969. Knowing and guessing. New York: Wiley.